ENCOUNTERS IN THE DARK

SEMEIA STUDIES

Steed V. Davidson, General Editor

Editorial Board:
Eric D. Barreto
Jin Young Choi
L. Juliana M. Claassens
Gregory Cuéllar
Katie B. Edwards
Jacqueline Hidalgo
Shively T. J. Smith

Number 96

ENCOUNTERS IN THE DARK

Identity Formation in the Jacob Story

Noel Forlini Burt

SBL PRESS

Atlanta

Copyright © 2020 by Noel Forlini Burt

All rights reserved. No part of this work may be reproduced or transmitted in any form or by any means, electronic or mechanical, including photocopying and recording, or by means of any information storage or retrieval system, except as may be expressly permitted by the 1976 Copyright Act or in writing from the publisher. Requests for permission should be addressed in writing to the Rights and Permissions Office, SBL Press, 825 Houston Mill Road, Atlanta, GA 30329 USA.

Library of Congress Cataloging-in-Publication Data

Names: Forlini Burt, Noel, author.
Title: Encounters in the dark : identity formation in the Jacob story / by Noel Forlini Burt.
Description: Atlanta : SBL Press, 2020. | Series: Semeia studies; 96 | Includes bibliographical references and index.
Identifiers: LCCN 2020012831 (print) | LCCN 2020012832 (ebook) | ISBN 9781628372847 (paperback) | ISBN 9780884144595 (hardback) | ISBN 9780884144601 (ebook)
Subjects: LCSH: Jacob (Biblical patriarch)—Biblical teaching. | Light and darkness in the Bible.
Classification: LCC BS580.J3 F67 2020 (print) | LCC BS580.J3 (ebook) | DDC 222/.11092—dc23
LC record available at https://lccn.loc.gov/2020012831
LC ebook record available at https://lccn.loc.gov/2020012832

Contents

Abbreviations vii

Introduction 1
    Interpretive Issues   1
    Methodology   2
    Journeying through the Jabbok   7

1. The Name 11
    Giving and Receiving Names   13
    Changing Names   22
    Saving Names   29

2. The Face 41
    Pre-facing Peniel   41
    Putting a Face on God   42
    Facial Intertexts   45
    Faces on the Other Side of the River   50
    Facing Peniel/Penuel, the Face of God   60
    The Face of All Faces   67

3. The Wound 73
    Jacob's Wound   75
    The Wound   86
    Wounded Storytellers   91

4. The Dark 103
    Dark Spaces and Dark Faces in the Jacob Cycle   104
    Waiting in the Shadows   107
    Sleeping and Waking in the (Side) Shadows   110
    Side Shadows at the Jabbok   117

	The Trope of the Blank	129
5.	The Crossing	131
	Constructing Esau and the Edomites	133
	Crossing Laban and the Aramaeans	147
	Crossing God and Humans	151
	Excursus: Crossing the Divine	155
	Coming Home	157
6.	Facing the Dark	163
Bibliography		169
Scripture Index		177
Modern Authors Index		185

Abbreviations

AB	Anchor Bible
ABS	Archaeology and Biblical Studies
Amph.	Plautus, *Amphitruo*
ANES	*Ancient Near Eastern Studies*
ASV	American Standard Version
BDB	Brown, Francis, S. R. Driver, and Charles A. Briggs. *A Hebrew and English Lexicon of the Old Testament.* Oxford: Clarendon, 1907.
CBQ	*Catholic Biblical Quarterly*
CC	Continental Commentaries
DDD	Toorn van der, Karel, Bob Becking, and Pieter W. van der Horst. *Dictionary of Deities and Demons in the Bible.* Leiden: Brill, 1995.
HALOT	Koehler, Ludwig, Walter Baumgartner, and Johann J. Stamm. *The Hebrew and Aramaic Lexicon of the Old Testament.* 3rd ed. Leiden: Brill, 1995, 2004.
IJTS	*International Journal of Transpersonal Studies*
JANESCU	*Journal of the Ancient Near Eastern Society of Columbia University*
JBL	*Journal of Biblical Literature*
JES	*Journal of Ecumenical Studies*
JESWTR	*Journal of the European Society of Women in Theological Research*
JRFM	*Journal for Religion, Film and Media*
JSOT	*Journal for the Study of the Old Testament*
JSOTSup	Journal for the Study of the Old Testament Supplement Series
KJV	King James Version
LW	Luther's Works
LXX	Septuagint

MT	Masoretic Text
NEB	New English Bible
NICOT	New International Commentary on the Old Testament
NIV	New International Version
NJB	New Jerusalem Bible
NJPS	*Tanakh: The Holy Scriptures: The New JPS Translation according to the Traditional Hebrew Text*
NRSV	New Revised Standard Version
OBS	Oxford Bible Series
OTL	Old Testament Library
OTM	Old Testament Message
ResQ	*Restoration Quarterly*
RSV	Revised Standard Version
SCJ	*Stone-Campbell Journal*
Sir	Sirach
TLOT	Jenni, Ernst, with assistance from Claus Westermann. *Theological Lexicon of the Old Testament*. Translated by Mark E. Biddle. 3 vols. Peabody, MA: Hendrickson, 1997.
VT	*Vetus Testamentum*
WBC	Word Biblical Commentary

Introduction

Interpretive Issues

The Jabbok encounter (Gen 32:22–32) is set within a narrative that is richly complex, not least because of the relational interplay of the protagonist and his god. The faces of the protagonist, Jacob, and antagonist, Elohim/Ish (God/Man), are both revealed and concealed in their darkened encounters with each other. Their identities are, like the scene in which the story is situated, obscure. This obscurity leads Samuel Tongue (2014, 3) to express a sentiment similar to my own: "I have been attracted to this story as an exemplary text that raises dust, obscuring the scene, provoking many commentators to try and interpret what is going on before the dust settles again." The obscurity of the story—demonstrated through the images/metaphors of name, face, wound, darkness, and crossing—drew me to it in the first place. Those images draw me still and compel me to make the central claim of this study: that the poetics and rhetoric of the narrative around name, face, wound, darkness, and crossing constitute a fruitful way of understanding embodied and contested individual and collective identity in the exilic/postexilic period. The driving theme is one of identity—the identities of the characters, of the community that produced the text, and of contemporary readers who engage the text. These multiple identities correlate to the multiplicity of meaning within the text itself and the rhetorical reasons for that multiplicity.

The Jabbok text is one that asks, like Elohim, "Why do you ask my name?" Why ask for one meaning, for one name, for one face, when many possibilities have opened themselves? In its unwillingness to surrender to and to be the target of a singular interpretation, the story continues to unfold and to multiply meaning (Derrida 1995b, 85).[1] Therefore, I also

---

1. Derrida's assessment of apophatic literature rings true for the Jabbok story: "This literature forever elliptical, taciturn, cryptic, obstinately withdrawing, however,

explore the link between *how* the text multiplies meaning and *why* the text multiplies meaning. This is a text that asks about names, reassigns names, and is a discursive space for a community to reconsider identity, especially in the postexilic period.

Methodology

My method of approaching the text is decidedly interdisciplinary and eclectic. Grounding my approach in biblical narrative criticism, I use the poststructuralist insights of Jacques Derrida and Jacques Lacan. I also draw on collective memory studies, feminist analysis, and ethical analysis through Emmanuel Levinas and others, as well as theology. I am a confessional, orthodox Christian scholar. I wrestle seriously with these texts precisely *because they are my texts*. These texts are, in one way or another, texts I uphold as sacred, inspired, true, and meaningful in my own life. The methodologies I work with in this study both converge and diverge from traditional, orthodox Jewish and Christian belief. In particular, convergence occurs around the nature of God: God has desire, God feels things deeply, God is ineffable, beyond us, to name a few. These methodologies are helpful tools, both to affirm faith commitments and to wrestle deeply with those faith commitments. For me, wrestling with the faith is at the heart of genuine relationship to God. Christians at all times and in all places have wrestled with God. Jacob's story captures this. Allowing God to hold on to us even as we wrestle with God is at the heart of Judeo-Christian faith. The God available for wrestling is at the heart of this book, too. Ultimately, *Encounters in the Dark* is a book about God, and it is a book both for the academy and for the church.

As already mentioned, biblical narrative criticism is the grounding methodology for this book. In order to encounter the dark, I acknowledge that faces must be put on the characters in the story. Indeed, the language of character and story is the language I use throughout, so I refer even to God as a character in the story. I take this approach because I am seeking the kind of truth about which Madeleine L'Engle (2002, 86–87) speaks:

---

from all literature, inaccessible there even where it seems to go, the exasperation of a jealousy that passion carries beyond itself.... It holds desire in suspense, and always saying too much or too little, each time it leaves you without ever going away from you." Apophatic literature, Derrida claims, is literature meant for exile.

> Truth is demanding. It won't let us sit comfortably. It knocks out our cozy smugness and casual condemnation. It makes us move.... There is no way that you can read the entire Bible seriously and take every word literally.... And that is all right. The Bible is still true. People have always told stories as they searched for truth.

In speaking about Jacob, God, and the others in the Jacob cycle (Gen 25–50) as characters in a story, I look for the deep meaning that the author(s) is attempting to convey. Rather than a threat to our theology or our sense of the veracity of the Bible's claims, narrative criticism is a tool to illumine meaning. Narrative criticism is concerned with the world of the story in its search for truth, which means that it is a tool that naturally raises questions. I foreground my interpretation using this tool because raising questions in the search for the truth is my interest, too. Here, L'Engle (1996, 23) also expresses my own sentiments well: "The minute we begin to think we know all the answers, we forget the questions, and we become smug like the Pharisee who listed all his considerable virtues and thanked God that he was not like other men." I am interested in reengaging the questions this story raises, *as story*. Part of what narrative criticism provides, then, is a sense of who these characters are, spotlighting Jacob's many failures as a moral agent in relation to everyone else in the story world. More importantly, in this case, narrative criticism exposes just how arduous it is to draw a face on Jacob's antagonist. The anonymous nature of Jacob's opponent dovetails into the theological implications of a divine character who pursues and wounds in the dark.

My approach is ethically nuanced, giving attention to the various faces that are put in jeopardy by Jacob in the story world or that are depicted negatively for rhetorical ends. This study is also sociopolitically aware, considering not only the story's poetics but also its rhetoric. The nature of my approach necessitates multiple tools for analysis. Therefore, I use an array of lenses, including deconstruction, psychoanalytic theory, feminist analysis, Levinasian ethics, narratology, and socionarratology. The variety of methods employed in this study correlates to the images/metaphors in the text that I explore—name, face, wound, dark, and crossing. These images/metaphors function as icons, windows that open up the world of the story.

Consequently, a discussion of how images/metaphors function in narrative is critical for grounding my methodology. I, therefore, draw on the work of David Gunn and Danna Fewell, who have noted that the multivalence of language creates a "thick" texture, where words can participate simultaneously in more than one pattern. In their words, "Language lures us—allures us—from one word to another, from one meaning of a word to another, from the literal to the metaphorical, from one part of a text into another, from one text to another. The text lures us, and we cast the lure as readers" (Gunn and Fewell 1993, 147). As a result, the connection between text and reader is central. The interface between the face of the reader and the textual face allows for the reification of meaning—and, more importantly, a plurality of meanings. No word or sign is ever in a completely fixed relationship with meaning, what is signified. Meaning is difference, and the meaning of words is in constant deferral (155). This leads naturally to a discussion of the ways in which words are used metaphorically. Drawing on Derrida's first essay to Edmond Jabés, Francis Landy affirms that metaphor is an agent of *différance*, a nonsignifying difference that marks the origin of poetic speech. Metaphor, infinitely equivocal, is the origin of language (Landy 2001, 263). Language is this infinite equivocality that allows a metaphor to exist in a particular time, but also to transcend that time. The images/metaphors in the Jabbok story are rooted in their multiple literary histories (e.g., the retelling by the prophet Hosea; see Hos 12:2–6)—and within the sociopolitical contexts undergirding them, even as they transcend those contexts. Moreover, words—metaphors—make "worlds," as Ellen van Wolde (1994) says. Indeed, Gunn and Fewell (1993, 157) assert, "Whole stories can become metaphors that point to particular ideas or experiences. The telling of a story, the writing of a text, is often an attempt to control—to influence an attitude, to reinforce a worldview, to reconfigure a critical experience."

Within the Hebrew Bible, the Babylonian exile and its aftermath is *the* critical experience. This experience is, in one way or another, the central trauma undergirding every major story in the Hebrew Bible. The Jacob cycle generally and the Jabbok text specifically is also a whole story that attempts to remember Israel's tenuous and tumultuous relationship with God, with itself as a nation, and with proximate others. This happens in part through the use of metaphor.

The metaphor of the name, for example, demonstrates a self-awareness on the part of the community producing the text around the character of Jacob. Within the Jacob cycle, he is an ambiguous figure who appears destined from the beginning to supplant his brother (Gen 25:23). His actions are nevertheless censured, to an extent, by Esau, whose tirade centers on the aptness of Jacob's name (Gen 27:36). Some prophetic traditions even use Jacob's name to excoriate the people (e.g., Mic 2:7; Isa 48:1). The name therefore becomes a kind of spoken admonition—do not act like *Jacob*. Elsewhere Jacob's name suggests a close relationship to God, where iniquity will be forgiven and fortunes will be restored (e.g., Isa 27:9; Jer 30:18; see Pss 20:1; 24:6; 46:7; 75:9). Likewise, the metaphor of the name also symbolizes other realities—the inscrutability of God, who refuses to reveal his name (Gen 32:29)—and the reality of the nation's self-understanding as one who struggles both with Elohim and 'anāšîm (God and humans; Gen 32:28).

The metaphor of face underscores the anxiety surrounding looking on the divine and living (Exod 33:20), but also the reality that such encounters might nevertheless take place (Gen 16:13; see Deut 34:10). Philologically speaking, the duality/multiplicity of *face* in Hebrew correlates to the many faces that linger at the Jabbok. These include the many iterations of the divine face Jacob encounters throughout the story, which may or may not be the same face he encounters at the Jabbok. Also included in the multiplicity of face are the faces of those who have deceived, have been deceived, or have been discarded throughout the story—Esau, Isaac, Rebecca, Rachel, Leah, Bilhah, Zilpah, and the children. At the Jabbok, and in the face of his opponent, Jacob must face these faces too. The metaphor of the wound symbolizes the central trauma of the Hebrew people—the Babylonian exile—which was believed to be orchestrated by the hand of God (e.g., Hab 1:1–11; Isa 10:5). The wounds in the story, like the names and the faces, are multiple: the psychical wounds sustained by Jacob before arriving at the Jabbok; the invisible wound received by Jacob at the hand of an invisible assailant at the Jabbok; the wounds of Jacob's antagonist, which propel him to pursue, wound, and bless Jacob in the first place; and the wounds of the community telling the story. Closely aligned to the wound is the metaphor of the dark, which functions spatially and temporally to represent the darkness of exile. Jacob's journey is based on a dispersion, an expulsion (Gen 28:10), where he is, more times than not, encountering and bartering with God in the dark (28:20–22; 32:10–13, 22–32) or, likewise, deceiving or being deceived, with darkness as his temporal companion (25:29–34; 27:1–29; 29:21–30). Darkness is embodied in the multiple time spaces of Rebecca's womb and the nocturnal spaces of Bethel and the Jabbok. Finally, the metaphor of the crossing symbolizes all that has taken place to exile Jacob and the nation of Israel from home—and all that must take place to return. Crossing is predicated on expulsion and the deferment of promises made to another patriarch, Abraham (15:12–16). Jacob's crossings are also multiple—he must cross the Jabbok itself, he must reconcile with Esau, and he must cross past a divine or divine-human opponent. The metaphors of the name, the face, the wound, the dark, and the crossing function in multiple ways. Metaphor becomes the primary way in which this particular story multiplies meaning.

Each of these metaphors, then, is useful for the interdisciplinary work of this project. They demonstrate not only *how* the text multiplies meaning—but also *why* the text multiples meaning. The metaphors help to underscore the work that the text is doing, namely, the Jabbok encounter is a whole story that represents the ambiguity felt by the Israelite community around its origins, around its relationship to God, and to the experience of exile and return. As Gunn and Fewell (1993, 156) affirm, moving beyond the surface meanings of words into the realm of metaphor allows for multiple meanings, which present the reader with ambiguity. In the Jabbok encounter, ambiguity is a central feature to the story. This is demonstrated by the uncertainty of the identities of the characters and their interrelationship(s). Ambiguity is also demonstrated through the undecidability of the text itself (e.g., who is acting and being acted on), variously described by Roland Barthes (1988, 247) as unmaking, explosion, and dissemination. Nevertheless, this allows for what Gerhard von Rad (1973, 324) calls "inner spaciousness." This inner spaciousness allows not only for a multiplicity of meaning but also for a multiplicity of tellings.

As Derrida and Landy (2001, 265) both state, metaphor is a form of memory, and it is metaphor that "transfers," creating the "possibility of continuity." In this way, the metaphors in the story work to create a past for ancient Yehud, making the present—which is painful and liminal—a habitable space. The Jabbok story is, to borrow a phrase from socionarratologist Arthur Frank (2010, 20), a story for Israel to grow up on. Nevertheless, the story is also adaptable to contemporary readers who see in its metaphors something useful to describe their own lives. Tongue's "multiple canonicities" extends traditional biblical authority (such as poetic, historical, moral, and philological/critical) into the ways in which these canons of authority enact the paradox of both limit and permission in poetic retellings. Contemporary poems such as those by Alden Nowlan, Yehuda Amichai, and Jamie Wasserman all point to an intertextuality that is both affective and culturally adaptable (Tongue 2014, 167; see Nowlan 2013; Amichai 1986; Wasserman 2010). While analysis of these contemporary poems is beyond the scope of this study, these (re) tellings do demonstrate the portability of this particular story. The dark encounter between God and Jacob slips textual boundaries and represents fears and desires centering on relational reconciliation. The Jabbok story displaces safe or comfortable pictures of God for pictures that are at best confusing and at worst distressing. The resulting *effect* is *affect*: this is a story that disturbs because it withholds something of God's quiddity[2]— God is the presence of an absence, or an "elusive presence," as Samuel Terrien (2000) says. The elusiveness or ambiguity of this story, its characters, and its meaning(s) will form the basis of an analysis that is both exegetical and meditative.

Journeying through the Jabbok

This study opens with a discussion of the two metaphors that speak to Jacob and Elohim/Ish's identities—name and face. In order to encounter the dark, I discuss the names and faces of the characters who find themselves in that darkness. In the chapter titled "The Name," I use the tools of biblical narrative criticism, specifically borrowing from the insights of poststructuralists such as Derrida (1995b) to explore the names of Jacob, Israel, and Jacob's wrestling partner. The encounter at the Jabbok invites an exploration of the idea of giving, receiving, and saving names. When interpellation occurs around names (personal, political, divine, or geographical), subjects and places are linked in ways that reveal but do not exhaust individual or collective identity (Althusser 2001, 116–18).[3] In particular, in refusing to be named, Jacob's opponent transcends the notion that a name can act as a container for identity. I link Derrida's (1995b) poststructuralist analysis to an interpretation of "The Name" that borders on the *via negativa*. In dealing with Exod 3:1–17 as a critical intertext, I explore the challenges associated with naming God, demonstrating the possibility for escaping a presumed finality to giving/receiving names.

---

2. By suggesting that in the Jabbok story the character of God may share the same spectrum of good inclinations and evil inclinations as does Jacob, the narrative deconstructs the notion that God's inclinations must always be good.

3. Althusser defines interpellation as a "hailing" that takes place when a subject is cast into a specific mold by the ideological world she inhabits. A subject is thus fixed, locked into the contours of time, space, and characterization that the hailing subject has created. Althusser's concept of interpellation is dealt with in greater detail in chapter 1.

Chapter 2, "The Face," explores the claim that Jacob sees Elohim face to face and lives (Gen 32:31). Like "The Name," this chapter is also an exploration of the identities of the story's central characters. I draw critically from the feminist analysis of Serge Frolov (2000) to foreground the faces of the women and children in the story. His reading, when coupled with the ethical works of Levinas (1985), exposes Jacob's failures as a moral agent. I engage the many other faces who are sent on ahead of Jacob, potentially into harm's way, but whose presence nevertheless linger at the Jabbok. Here, again I draw on Gen 16:1–21, and its doublet, 21:9–21, as crucial intertexts, to highlight the Janus-faced nature of the divine character, who at once appears both compassionate, elevating the oppressed to agency and subjectivity, and to sanction the well-being of the men he chooses to the detriment of others in the story. God appears behind it all, bringing about his designed plan or purpose, as in the story of Jacob. In particular, the (s)election of Jacob indicates the (dis)election of Esau, as well as the narrative expendability of the women and children. I also show how, at the Jabbok, Jacob is presented with the ethical imperative to answer for all the faces he has put in jeopardy.

In chapter 3, "The Wound," I transition from the identities of the characters to the identities of those telling the story. I argue that the Jabbok encounter is composed by a community of wounded storytellers who discover in Jacob's wound (Gen 32:25–26) a source for their own trauma. As a community who experienced a fracturing of all that was known—family, land, and ritual—Jacob's wound is an invisible symbol of communal pain. Drawing on the socionarratological insights of Frank (1997) and the poststructuralist work of Lacan (1977), I trace the contours of Jacob's wound narratively and sociologically. Narratively, I assert that the Jacob cycle opens with lack—with a desperate man pleading to Yahweh on behalf of his barren wife (Gen 25:21). Lack is central to the events that unfold and for understanding what motivates the characters to act in the ways that they do. I demonstrate that Jacob and Esau are mirrors for all the other lacks. Jacob is wounded, or cut, in the words of Lacan, the moment he discovers himself to be trapped in the discourse of the Other. His alienation, however, ironically leads him toward subjectivity. I also contend that at the Jabbok, both Jacob and his wrestling partner experience a mutual vulnerability. Moreover, whatever else may be said about Jacob's opponent, at the Jabbok he demonstrates a profound relationality. His desire renders him vulnerable to Jacob, whom he pursues, wounds, and blesses. Finally, I suggest that Jacob's wound and limp are the excess or trace of trauma that never goes away. The excess of Jacob's wound indicates that Israel's story is both about the chaos of communal disintegration and about the quest to wrestle honestly and to make meaning out of suffering. Their grasp on life, on the land, on God, is tenuous, and always already wounded and wounding. The wound is already there before the story is (re)told—a story with an invisible assailant and an invisible wound. The story remains, like Jacob's wound, half-open.

Chapter 4, "The Dark," moves beyond questions of identity and identity politics to a discussion of temporality and space. I trace the many images of darkness in the Jacob cycle and in the Jabbok text. The darkness of Rebekah's womb is a space where Jacob and Esau's bodies and stories are kept, as well as a temporal period of gestation (Gen 25:19–26). The dark of the night, at both Bethel (28:10–22) and the Jabbok (32:22–32), is where Jacob encounters a divine being or beings. Finally, the darkness covers Isaac's aged eyes, blurring his vision and enabling Jacob and Rebekah's deception (27:1–29). In this chapter, I draw on the theopoetic writings of Catherine Keller (2003) to destabilize a wholly negative interpretation of darkness and to situate it theologically. I also utilize Mikhail Bakhtin's (1990) concept of the chronotope to argue that the dark authors and is authored by those who inhabit it, traverse it, and sojourn in it. In so doing, human and divine agency function alongside the dark in order to form identity. What follows is a discussion of the darkness in the divine figure that Jacob encounters, drawing on Derrida's (1995a) concept of trembling and the *kryptō*. This metaphor of the dark, like all the others, is not merely about the story world of the Jabbok scene but is also an expression of the darkness of the Babylonian exile.

In my final chapter, "The Crossing," I argue that the crossing of the Jabbok River functions on three levels: the spatial, the human, and the divine (Gen 32:23–24). Rebekah's womb functions as the threshold that must first be crossed. The oracle at the boys' birth attests that the struggle between Jacob and Esau will extend to their ancestors (25:21–26). I explore multiple citations within the Hebrew Bible (Num 20:14–21; Ps 137; Lam 4:21–22; Mal 1:2–3a, 4a; Obadiah) that demonstrate the complex and protracted relationship between the Israelites and the Edomites. This literature attests to the reification of boundaries crossed by Jacob and Esau. Jacob's interactions with Esau—and also with Laban—reveal a text that delights in trickster antics amid the real struggle for resources and power. I bring collective-memory studies into conversation with the socionarratological insights of Heather McKay (1987), arguing that the Jabbok encounter is in part a story about a displaced person transitioning from home and back again. Here, too, the story represents the fears and needs of the postexilic community of Yehud.

In conclusion, this study has implications for the Jacob cycle as well as for the ancient community of Yehud. The Jabbok encounter remembers a past that is, at every literary moment, punctuated with a question mark. From the end of Deuteronomy, where the people stand on a precipice and wonder whether they will take hold of the promises made to them so long ago, to the end of Israel's primary history, where monarchy fails and land is lost, the children of Israel's (hi)story represent the partial fulfillment of deferred promises. The story is about exile, about wandering in wilderness and in darkness and asking, "How long?" The Jabbok encounter is about a melancholy search for home for a community grappling with its identity, with its relationship to God, and to the land. The Jabbok encounter encapsulates each of these fears and anxieties. The encounter demonstrates that blessing may not turn out the way they envision it and that blessing is frequently ambiguous and complex. Beyond Yehud, the Jabbok encounter testifies to the power of stories not only to represent worlds but to continue to create them. To tell and to read stories is to engage in a decidedly human endeavor, one with implications for how individuals live and move and have their being in the world. The characters of Jacob and God are, like those of us who read and write about them, complex and surprising. Their names, their faces, their wounds—the darkness they inhabit and the spaces they cross over—are always already ambiguous and multiple. The multiplicity of meaning, the multiple spaces they occupy, make their story compelling and allow us to find our place in it. The story's inner spaciousness creates space for us, too.

1
THE NAME

> You have a name you did not ask for. All your life, this name will prey on you. But at which moment do you become aware of it?
> —Edmond Jabès, *The Book of Questions*

Within the Hebrew Bible, the giving of a name is intertwined with a character's identity and destiny. Biblical characters are named by someone other than themselves—by parent(s), narrator, even the divine (e.g., Gen 21:3; Exod 2:10; Ruth 4:16–17; Isa 8:3–4, to name a few). In one notable instance, even the divine character is named by someone else (Gen 16:13). In her study of anonymous characterization in the Hebrew Bible, Adele Reinhartz (1998, 6–8) says that proper names "define" biblical characters. Following Reinhartz, a proper name must refer to a character's essence. Reinhartz's comments on the function of a proper name are an indispensable introduction to the subject but nevertheless fail to consider the emotive and ethical dimension of naming—namely, that if a name is given, then a name is also received, whether one wants to receive it or not. If a name limns a character—defines the character, as Reinhartz says—then a name also limits a character. Like an oracle that foreordains a character's destiny (Gen 25:23), a name may suggest that a character's identity is closed—consonant, vowel, consonant, nothing further to be said.

But such is not the case in the Jabbok story, where character and plot are foregrounded in equal measure. Indeed, the encounters at the Jabbok hinge on the saying and the withholding of names—Jacob, Israel, and God, the Name that refuses to be named.[1] Both Jacob and the Name are faced

---

1. In this chapter, *the Name* refers to Jacob's wrestling partner, who is named by the narrator as איש ("man") and by Jacob as אלהים ("God"). The character himself, however, resists such signification, choosing instead to keep his name a secret.

with the choice to say their name(s) and thus to reveal their identity(ies) or to withhold them and save their identity(ies).

The choice on the part of the Name to leave his own name a mystery but to (re)name Jacob provides an important reminder about characterization—characters are like people in real life. They may not act consistently; we may think we know them, and then they make choices that surprise us. People change over time through circumstances and their relationships with other people. We are not flat characters in our own story. We are round characters. Likewise, biblical characters are capable of changing subject positions.[2] When Jacob says his name, it is both an expression of suppressed identity and also a confession of guilt.[3] Only then can his subject position change. When he transcends his name for a moment in the dark, he is hailed in a different way, (re)named Israel. When such an interpellation occurs around names (personal, political, divine, or geographical), characters and places are linked in ways that reveal but do not exhaust individual or collective identity.

Characters, like people, also maintain multiple concurrent identities, relating differently in their different roles. I relate differently to my husband than I do to a student or a friend. I am still the same person, but in my relationships, I reveal different facets of myself, and I am called by different names: wife, daughter, friend, or teacher. Sometimes, I purposefully withhold parts of myself; other times, that withholding is not purposeful but is a matter of circumstance. Therefore, no one person can know me fully, and neither can I know myself fully. Instead, I see through a mirror darkly (1 Cor 13:12). Biblical characters function similarly. They may exhibit polynomialism—excess, a plurality of names. They may be

---

2. A flat character is known for his predictability and one-dimensionality. He may possess only one or two defining character traits. A round character, by contrast, may possess many different qualities or traits, and those traits may be contradictory, conveying a more realistic picture of personhood. A round character may change her mind or develop in other ways over the course of the narrative. For a helpful discussion of flat and round characters, see Gunn and Fewell 1993, 75–76. Their work builds on the seminal work of E. M. Forster, Robert Alter, and others.

3. Implicit in Jacob's name is the idea of crookedness, deception, manipulation; he is one who grabs at the heel. In one key moment in the narrative, rather than saying his name, Jacob obfuscates—he claims to be Esau instead (Gen 27:18–25). When Jacob is face to face with Elohim/Ish at the Jabbok, he is forced to say his name, "Jacob," and, implicitly, it is a confession of all that he is and has been—one who has deceived, has followed Esau heel to toe throughout the narrative, and has run from his family.

multiple signifiers crowing around a proper name. By contrast, they may not say their names at all, instead leaving only traces, pronouns—*he*, *she*, *it*. Jacob's opponent is such a character. Jacob's opponent refuses to reveal his name, further confusing his identity and complicating the encounter. When we read the Jacob story, we see that names are given and received, names are changed, and names are withheld and therefore saved (Gen 25:24–26; 29:31–35; 30:1–24; 32:27, 29).

Giving and Receiving Names

> So he said to him, "What is your name?" And he said, "Jacob."
> —Genesis 32:27

At the beginning of the Jacob cycle (Gen 25–50), Esau receives a name that aptly describes him: "The first came out red, all his body like a hairy mantle; so *they* named him Esau" (Gen 25:25).[4] Whoever did the actual naming, the plurality of the naming indicates a communal desire to name him and to welcome him appropriately into the arms of the barren woman and the husband who prayed for his birth. By contrast, Jacob is "behind" (אחרי) and "grasping tight" (אחזת), vividly described by Avivah Zornberg (1995, 165): "his perspective filled with his brother's legs." The duality of coming from behind and grasping onto someone else is no mere birth report; it is a reality that illuminates Jacob's character as the narrative unfolds. The narrator describes Jacob only in relation to Esau and forestalls the telling of his name as long as possible. He is אחיו ("his brother"), who grasps his hand בעקב ("on the heel") (Gen 25:26). When Jacob is named, he is named only in relation to Esau. Zornberg (1995, 165) notes that Jacob is described "only in not being clearly characterized at all. There is a neutral quality to him; he defines himself as Esau's shadow." The twins are (mirror) opposites of one another, with Jacob appearing second. Still, Jacob is no mere afterthought of the womb; this birth sequence, which is linked to name giving, is part of what connects Esau and Jacob. The naming of these brothers is just one instance in over one hundred in the Hebrew Bible where a name is conferred on a person or place (Key 1964, 55). The sheer volume of these occurrences raises questions about the significance and meaning of giving and receiving names, particularly as it relates to Jacob and Esau.

---

4. Unless otherwise stated, all biblical translations follow the NRSV.

The widely held belief among scholars echoes the early sentiment of von Rad (1973, 83): "Name-giving in the ancient Orient was primarily an exercise of sovereignty, of command." Similarly, Johannes Fichtner (1956, 372, emphasis original) avers: "The name is not only an indicator of the distinction of different entities but also the *determination* of the essence of the named entity—be it person, place, or object." George Ramsey (1989, 30) notes Rabbi Abba's view: "A name is regarded as possessing an inherent power which exercises a constraint upon its bearer: he must conform to his essential nature as expressed in his name."

Ramsey argues that this understanding of naming should be reexamined. While his comments are aimed primarily at offering a minor corrective to Phyllis Trible's examination of the naming of Eve, Ramsey's general statements about the giving of names are pertinent to the naming of Jacob and Esau. Ramsey outlines three primary ways in which names are given and received in the Hebrew Bible.

First, Ramsey concedes, there are certain texts in the Hebrew Bible that seem to indicate that the giving of a name is intended to exemplify control or authority over the person being named. Ramsey cites several instances where kings bestow a new name on individuals (e.g., Gen 41:45; 2 Kgs 23:34; 24:17). In this category Ramsey (1989, 32) also includes warriors who conquer a territory and name it after themselves (e.g., Num 32:31–42; Josh 19:47; 2 Sam 5:6–9). Second, Ramsey categorizes instances of naming that commemorate something that had already happened at the time of naming (and not necessarily to the recipient of the one named; e.g., Gen 26:20–21; 29:33; 30:6; Josh 5:9; 1 Sam 4:21). Third, Ramsey provides several counterexamples that challenge the idea of naming as an act of subordination or control. Ramsey cites the episode where Hagar names God after experiencing him by the spring in the wilderness on the road to Shur (Gen 16:13). Ramsey (1989, 33–34) states, "It is difficult to imagine that the narrator intended us to understand that this woman who marvels at her encounter with the divine is exercising some sort of control over God." Ramsey concludes, "Taken all together, the evidence indicates that, instead of thinking of name-giving as a determiner of an entity's essence, the Hebrews regarded naming as commonly determined by circumstances. The naming results from events which have occurred" (34). In the case of Jacob and Esau, Ramsey views their names as related to characteristics the bearer has already exhibited: "As a person is, so he is named" (33). Ramsey's general statements about naming are useful in challenging traditional assumptions about naming in the Hebrew Bible. Nevertheless, his comments, like Reinhartz's, fail to capture adequately the complexity of giving, receiving, and saving names in the Jacob cycle.

Namely, what does it mean to *receive a name*? In the Jacob cycle, receiving a name first means understanding that it is a passive act; instead of writing his own script, a character is written into a script. As Frank has indicated, receiving a name means being cast into a script written by someone else. Not only is an individual's agency at stake—his self-knowledge is also limited. When Jacob receives his name, the community scripts a truth about him that he will recognize only later at the Jabbok, perhaps at the time when he is old enough to recognize the script and to make a decision about it for himself. His naming functions as a kind of communal, narrative whisper, a secret script—"We know a truth about you that you yourself have not yet recognized. We name you Jacob, because we have recognized something *Jacobish* about you." Indeed, Frank (2010, 30) says that stories are about characters resisting or embracing (or perhaps failing to recognize) the character into which they have been cast, usually as the result of some trouble. This recognition, whether a character welcomes the mold into which she has been cast or eschews it, occurs when subject meets subject. Louis Althusser notes that all persons are hailed as subjects by other subjects. When a person is hailed on the street—"Hey, you there!"—the moment she turns to address the one speaking, she is already a subject. For Althusser, hailing, or what he has labeled the "interpellation" of individuals, is an ideology that casts characters into a specific mold. By responding, "Yes; it really is me!" a subject obtains the recognition that she occupies a specific place in the world, a "fixed residence" (Althusser 2001, 116–18). Thus a subject is fixed, locked, into the contours of time, space, and characterization that the hailing subject has created. Only after acknowledging that she has been interpellated—by narrative ideology, the expectations of others, or even God—can a character change her subject position.[5]

Of course, the question for biblical characters is the same one we face in life: Do we want our lives to remain as they are, or do we need and want to change? Is our life satisfying, or is change necessary? Will we disappoint those around us if we make major changes, or will our change benefit our community? What are the implications of our sub-

---

5. Frank 2010 defines subject position as the character's more or less reflective awareness of who the type of narrative requires him to be and what being that character requires him to do.

ject position changing and of our subject position remaining the same? As Frank (2010, 51) trenchantly states, "The subject ... feels a tension between hitching a ride on the immanent volition of the story and being carried where a story usually goes, versus the *possibility* that this time things could turn out differently: either the story might have changed, or the protagonist might this time, through some act of will, rewrite the story by acting differently from what the old story required" (italics added). Surely in the case of the naming of the child, the intention is not to subordinate or totalize, as Ramsey (1989, 32–33) notes. Nevertheless, receiving a name—from parent(s), or, in the case of Obed (Ruth 4:17), from a community—does suggest that a script, a reality, has been composed that a subject must first recognize and then choose to accept or reject. Will a subject remain an *Obed*—a servant—to a community, or will he rewrite the story, change the name? A subject must in fact *receive a name*—recognize it, take stock of it, and determine whether to uphold or undermine it. For much of the story, Jacob does in fact hitch a ride on the narrative already written for him. At the Jabbok, the possibility for revision is extended to both Jacob and the Name. Still, a question remains as to whether the community's giving of the name Jacob is intended as a derogatory riposte, a label to be eschewed, or one to be celebrated. Jacob's name, like his relationship with both father and mother, is one fraught with ambiguity.

The narrator explains that Isaac loves Esau because of the game in his mouth (Gen 25:28a). Rebekah loves Jacob, but no reason is given for her love. Moreover, the text is taciturn regarding Isaac's love for his second son; his feelings are not named. Instead, it is Rebekah who holds the story in her womb, a place dark and undefinable; it is a place that Isaac will symbolically experience when he must pronounce his blessing as a blind person (27:1). Indeed, the boys' relationships to both father and mother are central to their characterizations and to the narrative itself. These interrelationships also betray a second aspect of receiving a name: that such an act is not merely about the one named but rather occurs in conjunction with a host of (inter)relationships that are brought to bear on the one who is named. I did not come into the world as a fully blank slate; like every child, I came into the world in the embrace of parents who have likewise been cast in various roles and whose genes and life experiences affect me. Therefore, naming is not only about one script; it is about multiple, concurrent scripts—mothers, fathers, and the scripts into which *they* have been cast. Receiving a name involves the recognition that the script is not only about the character receiving the name but also about the one(s) conferring that name.

Esau, for example, becomes a man connected to his father. Esau is a man ידע, "knowing" game, a man of the field. He is associated with a specific skill, a specific station or calling in life, one that gets him out of doors and entangles him in the world outside the family tents. Esau's life involves risk, and it is one that focuses on the immediate; his is a life outside. His is also a life seemingly outside tradition—he takes wives outside his clan (Gen 26:34–35; 36:1–5) and cedes the rights of primogeniture willingly (25:32–34). He is a man sure of who he is and of what he wants.

In contrast to Esau, Jacob is described not as one who knows, a man of knowledge, but rather as one who sits, who continues to remain where he is. The text describes him as ישב אהלים ("dwelling in tents") and איש תם (a "sound" or "wholesome man"), a "plain man"; when focalized through the eyes of his mother, he is practically "perfect" in every way (Fewell and Gunn 1993, 74). While Esau knows about life outside, Jacob's knowledge is limited to what is inside. He dwells in tents, where he is close to home and safe. If there is truth to be told from the outside, Jacob does not name it, because it is not in his purview. He cannot name something he does not know. Jacob is תם—"simple," "innocent," "childlike," unstained by the world outside his mother's tents. His immobile life is, perhaps, marked by the "Fear of Isaac," by Isaac's fear.[6] While the narrative depicts him this way, however, his name and the events that unfold belie this description. Indeed, Jacob's self-description does not include the word תם ("complete, innocent, perfect, simple"). Instead, he describes himself as חלק ("smooth") (Gen 27:11). The connotation of this adjective is physical—Jacob's body is smooth when juxtaposed with Esau's hairy body. When Rebekah persuades him to masquerade as Esau,

---

6. The phrase "Fear of Isaac" occurs in Gen 31:42, פחד יצחק, appearing alongside the "God of my father, the God of Abraham" in Jacob's altercation with Laban. Jacob uses the phrase again in 31:53, in the context of making an oath with Laban. Scholars are divided about whether the phrase refers to an epithet for God. See Wenham 1994, 278; Westermann 1985, 497. Conversely, the phrase may refer to some fear Isaac may have felt before God or to some other fear demonstrated in the larger narrative, e.g., the Akedah. The interpretive payoff of this ambiguity in relation to Jacob is that it demonstrates that Jacob, as Isaac's son, would have surely been raised under the faith of Isaac, even if he may not have claimed it as his own (e.g., Gen 27:20b); moreover, as Isaac's son, psychologically speaking, he would have also known the things Isaac "feared" and may have even appropriated them subconsciously as his own.

Jacob protests that Isaac will know the difference between the two sons based on the smoothness of Jacob's skin. However, the deeper connotation of the root is one who is smooth of speech—to be smooth or slippery, to fabricate. When Jacob says that he is smooth, he reveals a deep reality about his character. While the narrator describes him as innocent, this man of his mother's tents is smooth enough to dupe his brother not once but twice (27:36). Ironically, it is his smoothness, rather than the hair his mother covers his body with, that enables him to convince his father that his name is Esau (27:26–29).

Despite the prevarication that dominates the scene, a quiet poignancy settles there too. The patriarch is old, wrinkled about the skin, the Akedah never far from narrative memory. His eyes have grown dim, dark around the edges. It is the twilight of his life, and what he appears to desire is intimacy with his son; three times he calls for him to גשה־נא ("come closer") (Gen 27:21, 25, 26).[7] In the preceding scene, Jacob's desire is unnamed. The idea is Rebekah's—Jacob merely acquiesces. His protestations are not on the moral ground of forgery of identity or theft of blessing. Rather, his response to Rebekah is enigmatic: "Perhaps my father will feel me and I become in his eyes like one who mocks" (Gen 27:12, translation mine). The word Jacob uses—כמתעתע—is from the root תעע, meaning "mocker, a person who mocks" (BDB 1073), here the rare *pilpel* participle. The word is not a *homologoumena*, but it is rare in the Hebrew Bible, occurring only here and in 2 Chr 36:16; Jer 10:15; and 51:18. Zornberg (1995, 149) includes Ramban's suggestion that part of this mockery may have included Jacob changing his voice. If such was the case, however, Isaac still discerns the difference: "The voice is Jacob's voice" (Gen 27:22b). Zornberg's (1995, 150) analysis of כמתעתע cuts to the heart of Jacob's self-identity and relationship to God and others:

> To jest with this ... is to disrupt one's access to God-in-the-world. It is to be guilty of a kind of frivolity that disassociates one from others, from continuities and larger purposes. To abandon one's individuated selfhood, to trifle with the voices of others, is ultimately to undermine not only the differences, but the connections, between people.

---

7. The volitional mood of the phrase גשה־נא ("come closer") demonstrates the desire, wish, or command of the speaker. Here, a superior, a father, is speaking to an inferior, a son, and therefore the phrase is an imperative. The threefold repetition of Isaac's request captures the intensity of his desire.

If the first reason Jacob gives is enigmatic and obscure—that he may appear as a mocker or trickster, one unserious in his relationship to his father—the second reason he gives is clear and pragmatic, that he may receive a curse rather than a blessing (Gen 27:12). Rather than receiving what is intended, he fears he may receive the opposite.

Indeed, throughout the narrative, Jacob's actions are prompted by fear—his own or someone else's. Fear, rather than desire, motivates his decisions.[8] Jacob does not name what he wants, only what he fears. Desire—or the absence of it—is masked by fear. In the scene with his mother, he vocalizes his fear and is then muted, silent while Rebekah dresses him in Esau's clothing. For Shmuel Klitsner, Jacob's actions are not only immoral; they are a telling demonstration of his dissociation from the self. Klitsner (2009, 70) states,

> The scene begins with Jacob subsuming his own identity into that of his mother and concludes with his assuming the identity of his brother.... No wonder this simple dweller of tents is capable of responding, "I am Esau your firstborn" (Gen. 27:19). He is, in his mind, a marionette uttering the words of a ventriloquist, as he is operating in complete disassociation from self.

Yair Zakovitch notes that, while Jacob is referred to as Rebekah's "young son," he is in fact forty years old (Gen 26:34). Zakovitch (2012, 30–31) states, "The image of a forty-year-old man standing, arms outstretched, waiting for his mother to dress him invites ridicule and wonder. Submissive obedience may be a tolerated excuse for a young boy who carries

---

8. In the scene following Jacob's deception of Isaac, he is told to flee because of his mother's fear (Gen 27:42–45); upon his dream/vision at Bethel, Jacob is described as "shaken" (28:17) and asks for a "safe" return to his father's house (28:20–22). In his dealings with Laban, he notes Laban's face was not to him as it had been previously (31:1–9), prompting him to flee after the angel of God, the God of Bethel, appears to him in a dream (31:10–13). Just prior to the scene at the Jabbok, Jacob is described as "exceedingly afraid" over the thought of meeting his brother again (Gen 32:8). In his prayer, Jacob describes what he fears may happen to him (32:10–13). His subsequent actions toward Esau—sending his family ahead, sending gifts, referring to himself as Esau's servant—are all demonstrations of his fear (32:14–22). Even after their reconciliation, Jacob's delay/deferral/deception about traveling behind Esau to Seir but going to Shechem instead (33:12–18) may be an indication that he still does not trust Esau's intentions.

out his mother's morally questionable directions, but certainly not for a grown man."

On the level of character, it is true that Rebekah pulls the puppet strings, with her son as a silent marionette. However, an examination of the narrative itself reveals a subtler ventriloquism—the trickster oracle (Gen 25:23–26) has already hailed Jacob to move and to speak *Jacob(ly)*. He is, to borrow a phrase from Frank (2010, 50), an "inveterate doer" of all things *Jacob* because he has been dressed for the role of trickster. The ideology of the story has hailed him to act the way that he does. Long before arriving at the Jabbok, Jacob has been dressed in trickster clothes and given a trickster name he did not ask for.

When Jacob arrives at the Jabbok, he carries with him more than the family and the wealth he has acquired along the way—he also carries all the expectations the narrative has placed on him as *Jacob*. For the author(s) crafting the story and for the audience receiving the story, the etymology of Jacob's name would have been a narrative cue that his story will involve trickery. Therefore, it would have come as no surprise that Jacob's actions throughout the story involve, on a generous reading, a skillful way of moving through the narrative world—and, on a less generous reading, a manipulative spirit that God will wrestle with at the Jabbok.

But Jacob is not the only name he carries with him. The names Esau, Isaac, and Rebekah, brother, father, and mother, cannot be far from his consciousness either. The names—Jacob, Esau, Isaac—are the only things Jacob cannot send across the river. Everything and everyone else, he can disencumber, but these names must remain. And once again, Jacob is אחרי—"behind." Again he delays. Again he defers. Zornberg notes that it is Jacob's perpetual lateness, his perpetual delaying, that characterizes his name. She states, "What is at issue is indicated in the expletive effect of Jacob's name, as Esau so derisively uttered it: 'Was he not then named Jacob that he might outwit me these two times?' (Gen 27:36) (translation mine).... What maddens Esau is Jacob's reluctance to confront, his distrust of the face of the other. He will wait offstage, preparing his lines until they are word perfect" (Zornberg 1995, 232). What is to be, Zornberg says, is to be as fully preconceived in the mind as possible. Jacob "choreographs" sheep and goats, sending messages of "endless stimulation" while Jacob himself continues to bide his time, leading from behind (Zornberg 1995, 233). Surely the psychological baggage he carries with him is also part of his delay.

Klitsner points to the previous scenes of deception, particularly with Isaac, as the psychological baggage Jacob carries with him. He states,

> How many times must Jacob's unconscious have played over the repeated question of Isaac? "Who are you, my son?" Yes, but really, who are you? How many times must Jacob have returned to the numerous points at which he could have retreated, to the opportunities Isaac gave him for withdrawal? How many times over the ensuing decades of exile from his parents did he hear the echo of his own twice repeated responses, "I am Esau, your firstborn.... It is I"? Are we to assume that the rhythmic insistence of the terms *his father, my son* (*your brother*—at the end) that so sting the reader, fall on the seemingly deaf ears of Jacob without lasting impression? (Klitsner 2009, 76–77)

When Jacob finally speaks his own name, then, it is both an acknowledgment of the truth and a confession of guilt. Gordon Wenham (1994, 296) concurs that in divulging his name, Jacob also discloses his character, as Jer 9:4b states: "Do not trust because every brother surely *Jacobs* and every companion walks slanderously" (translation mine). In the words of Archie Phinney, "You inveterate doer of this kind of thing!" (Frank 2010, 50). As an inveterate doer, Jacob's mechanism for handling conflict has involved evasion and escape, as Klitsner notes. The truth of his actions, however, and the truth of his name are one and the same—*Jacob*. Both the name and the action(s) are crooked. He has acted *Jacobly* because he is Jacob. Before arriving at the Jabbok, the truth of his name has been suppressed by saying someone else's name and reserving his own; his movement in the world has involved a kind of *not telling*.

Klitsner notes the importance of the key word (נגד, "to tell"), which occurs as a volitional in 27:29 with the particle נא and once as a noun, גיד, in verse 32, denoting the thigh/sinew. In Jacob's conflict with Laban in Gen 31, the Hebrew root also occurs in verses 21, 22, and 27, where the narrator emphasizes Jacob's *not telling*. At the Jabbok, Jacob is confronted with his own *not telling*, and he is, for the first time, forced *to tell*. He must tell (*hagîd*) the repressed trickery of the goat (*gədî*) that posed as venison and whose skin impersonated Esau's hirsute arms. The injury of the sinew (*gîd*) compensates for the *gədî*. Above all, Klitsner (2009, 139) says, the goat of deception finds rehabilitation in the form of the sinew, the telling. The sinew is to be associated with the telling:

> What is the evasion of falsehood that has been repressed (*nashe*) and now needs to be spoken (*hagid*)? Of course, it concerns Jacob's name (*shem-ekha*). Jacob had "dislocated" his true identity when he assumed the false identity of "I am Esau." By telling his real name ("I am Jacob") in order

to receive the blessing of his adversary, Jacob has finally become blessed. And on the level of literary "triple-entendre," we have now arrived at a profound identification of *gid hanashe* as both "dislocated sinew" and as "telling of the forgotten [repressed]," with its phonetic echo—*hagida na shemekha*, "pray tell me your name." (Klitsner 2009, 141)

While Klitsner views the Jabbok scene as Jacob's realization of a suppressed identity, literary critic Erich Auerbach (1953, 18) claims that Jacob's struggles (here, his struggle at the Jabbok) reveal individuality: "It is only in the course of an eventful life that men are differentiated into full individuality. Such individuality is palpably consummated in the Jacob story from womb to grave, perhaps for the first time in Western literature." While it is true that Jacob is a round character and more developed than Abraham and Isaac, his identity is nevertheless constructed by an oracle and its god, mandating his movement in the narrative. But when Jacob finally says his name at the Jabbok, he takes ownership of his suppressed identity. Only after doing so can his subject position change. Jacob's (re)naming can only take place after he has said his name. Receiving a name means a character must understand the meaning and implications behind his name before deciding to uphold or undermine it. Jacob's becoming Israel hinges on his recognition that he is Jacob, on truly *receiving the name that he has been given*. At the Jabbok, Jacob faces both the Name and his own name—understanding all the implications of being named *Jacob*.

Changing Names

Your name will no longer be Jacob, but Israel.

—Genesis 32:28a

Part of the promissory blessing made to each of the patriarchs includes a "great name," an indicator of geopolitical dominance. The various iterations of the blessing indicate its unilateral nature. God alone makes the promises, requiring only the faith of those blessed.[9] Thus the giving of the name, including the giving of the name Israel, occurs not through Jacob's work or duplicity but rather is provided as gift (Gen 12:2; 17:5;

---

9. The third iteration to Abraham is the only possible exception, where circumcision is required as a condition for covenant (Gen 17:9–14).

28:13–15). Still, like the man who bears it, this name is fraught with ambiguity throughout the nation's history. On the one hand, Israel serves as a moniker for communal identity, defined and maintained through a shared myth of origins, histories, and cultures and by a sense of solidarity with a specific territory (Mullen 1993). On the other hand, the name is difficult to assign to a particular historical moment; indeed, the name seems both to unite and to divide those who claimed it. The particular people who associate themselves with this name are also bound to a particular god, Yahweh. While there are complications surrounding Israel, the great name promised to the patriarchs, the name is significant both for the patriarch narratively and psychologically and also politically for the nation he represents.

Etymologically speaking, ישראל ("Israel") relates to the verb שרה ("to struggle, to fight, to persist, to exert oneself, persevere"). Wenham (1994, 296) notes that ישראל means "El (God) fights," which is not exactly the same as "you have struggled with God." He cautions that popular etymologies in the Bible often play on the name rather than provide precise historical etymology. The LXX and the Vulgate relate ישראל to the verb שרר ("to rule, be strong"), possibly because the idea of God fighting proved incompatible with one strand of Israelite theology. ישראל ("Israel") has also been linked with the adjective ישר ("just, straight, right"), related to the ancient poetic name Jeshurun (Num 23:10; Deut 32:15; 33:5, 26).[10] Instead of the connection to Yeshurun, William Albright suggests it correlated to Ethiopic and Arabic stems meaning "to heal," hence, "God heals" (Wenham 1994, 296). Finally, Robert Coote relates it to the noun משרה ("government"), "El judges," which is similar to Martin Noth's early suggestion, "May God rule" (Wenham 1994, 297).

A survey of the above references in Deuteronomy, as well as one in Deutero-Isaiah (Isa 44:2), suggests an attempt to clear Jacob's bad name by disassociating the man and the nation from deceit and cheating.

Zakovitch (2012, 109) contends that Deutero-Isaiah may have alluded to the story of the patriarch's birth. In choosing to portray Jacob as ישרון

---

10. The theology cited by Wenham represents just one strand of thought in the Israelite mindset regarding Yahweh. Just as the children of Israel desire a king, in part to fight their battles for them (see 1 Sam 8), so too Yahweh is depicted as a warrior god. In particular, prophets such as Isaiah use terminology such as "Yahweh of Armies," indicating a god of warfare (Isa 1:9; 3:1; 6:3; see also Zech 1:14–17; 8:1–23; Mic 4:4; Nah 2:14; 3:5, among many others).

("honest, upright") already in his mother's womb, the prophet demonstrates Jacob did not win his status through deceit. If Deutero-Isaiah's intention is to clear Jacob's name, the prophet Micah intends to drag it through the mud again. Micah contrasts the names Yeshurun and Jacob in order to censure the Israelites:

> Should this be said, O house of Jacob?
> Is the LORD's patience exhausted?
> Are these his doings?
> Do not my words do good
> to one who walks uprightly? (Mic 2:7)

Micah disagrees with the name change in Gen 32:29, arguing that the people are cheaters who are undeserving of the name Israel (Zakovitch 2012). Similarly, Isa 48:1 addresses the nation with the name "House of Jacob" rather than Israel, because their swearing and deceitful behavior renders Jacob a more suitable name than Israel (Zakovitch 2012). However the etymology of Israel is understood, the name is significant not only for the man but also for the nation.

Stephen Geller (1996, 19) notes that most patriarchal narratives have a national dimension of significance, recognized by the rabbinic dictum *ma'ase 'abot siman lebanim* (מעשה אבות סימן לבנים), "the actions recounted of the patriarchs are indicative of what would later happen to their descendants." Geller's interpretation of the name change is worth quoting in full:

> The relationship is typological, almost magical. The building of altars, the acquisition of parcels of land, the journeys through the length and breadth of Canaan, all these foreshadow, even effect Israel's later occupation. There is surely no other place in Genesis where the reader is more attuned to a resonance of past and future than Genesis 32. The situation is extreme: the eponymous ancestor of the nation is about to receive the national name—no casual matter. Edom may receive its name trivially from a pot of soup (Gen. 25:30); it is a trivial people. Israel is God's firstborn (Ex. 4:22), the first nation of the earth (1 Sam. 7:23), "supreme among the nations" (Deut. 26:19; 28:1). Its naming is almost a cosmic event. (Geller 1996, 19)

The event as Geller describes it is celebratory. Israel is the nation chosen by God to be his special people; under God's wing they will take refuge. The relationship is one of protection and blessing. Nevertheless, from the perspective of social-science theory, scholars such as Rainer Kessler (2008) note how vague (and certainly not fixed) the term Israel is throughout biblical history.

In the narrative of the exodus event, Israel represents the whole people from the time of their sojourn in Egypt, marking the transition from Genesis to Exodus. While this portrayal applies the name Israel from the beginning to all the tribes including Judah, the usage becomes more differentiated as the royal period begins. During this period, when the text speaks of political enemies, it distinguishes between Judah as the Southern Kingdom and Israel as the Northern Kingdom. This differentiation begins with David—he is anointed first by "the men of Judah" to be "king over the house of Judah" (2 Sam 2:4), and later he is anointed by "all the elders of Israel" to be "king over Israel" (2 Sam 5:3). Yet at the same time and in the same textual context Israel can also refer to the whole people, including Judah. When the elders of the northern tribes remind David of God's promise that he will shepherd "my people Israel" (2 Sam 5:2), this surely refers to the whole nation. This dual meaning of Israel—at times representing the Northern Kingdom, at other times representing both Israel and Judah—is typical for writers during the royal period of Israel's history.

New questions arise, however, at the end of the eighth century as a result of the Assyrian exile. Some Israelites were exiled out of the land; others were allowed to stay in the land; Israelites in both groups have ultimately—or will ultimately—reside alongside people from other nations. These realities raise discernible tension in determining who is and who is not Israel, as well as raise questions about what it means to be Israelite. Does the population of the former Northern Kingdom, where the Assyrians settled other peoples alongside those who did not pass into exile, belong to Israel? Do those who remained in the former Southern Kingdom belong to Israel? Or is the concept to be restricted to the later members of the Babylonian diaspora? Does it become detached from the land itself if those who remained in Babylon, but not all those who live in the territory of the earlier kingdoms, are Israel? (Kessler 2008).

Kessler notes that there are three components to consider when referring to Israel. First, the consciousness of ethnic solidarity was expressed primarily in the construction of a common genealogy. Second, the relationship to the land was integral and retained even by those in the diaspora. Third, it is impossible to speak of Israel apart from its relationship to Yahweh (Kessler 2008). For Kessler, the question concerns when a social history of Israel begins. The biblical narrative depicts Israel's beginnings at the Jabbok scene, with the prehistory of the ancestral families. Historically speaking, however, should Israel's beginnings be traced to the Davidic-Solomonic kingdom, or even to the middle of the royal period? The distinction between Israel's prehistory and history underlies this discussion, but for Kessler the name Israel on the Merneptah stela indicates that a group identified as Israel emerged on the international scene in the thirteenth century. For Kessler, then, Israel's social history must begin in the transition from the Late Bronze Age (1550–1200 BCE) to the Iron Age (1200–1000 BCE). Nevertheless, tension remains between the biblical text, which uses the folkloristic Jabbok scene to establish its origins, and the historical realities established by social-science methods and evidence from material culture.

Narratively speaking, the Jabbok text also represents tension in the relationship between the nation and its god. While briefly acknowledging the multivalent nature of Israel's association with a "nemesis of the night," Walter Brueggemann views the Name primarily as a "promise-keeper of the day," viewing the Name as beneficent, and his relationship with the nation positively. Brueggemann (2010, 268) claims, "Something happens in this transaction that is irreversible. Israel is something new in the world. Power has shifted between God and humankind. Israel is the one who has faced God, been touched by God, prevailed, gained a blessing, and been renamed." For Brueggemann, the renaming event is a marker of hope—it demonstrates a Name who wants good things for the nation. David Carr's treatment of the Jacob cycle is less theological and more political than Brueggemann's but nevertheless views the tradition(s) behind it positively. In reading the "fractures" in Genesis, Carr highlights the political theology in the Jacob cycle. Carr's reading functions on two levels. First, so-called precursor materials celebrated the "trickster traditions" of Jacob and his family, finding a home among those resistant to Davidic-Solomonic power structures in the royal period. Jacob's visits to the named cultic sites at Bethel, Mahanaim, Penuel, Sukkoth, Shechem, and Ephrath, later forbidden by Yahweh and his prophets in the royal period as sites other than Jerusalem, allow Jacob's ancestors to envision resistance to these policies. This allows Jacob to function as both national hero and national ancestor, with the Jabbok episode linking Israel to a new ethnopolitical unity (Carr 1996, 298). Carr's political reading also transports an ancient set of texts about early ancestors' struggles with landlessness, namelessness, and vulnerability to the present concerns of those in Babylonian diaspora. This reading represents a "crucial loosening of the tie of Israel's pre-land traditions to a specific sociocultural present" of the readers. Those who perceived themselves as landless, nameless, cursed, and vulnerable could find in the proto-Genesis composition hope for their present situation (308). The readings of both Brueggemann and Carr focalize different aspects of the Jacob cycle, yet both read the Jabbok text as essentially positive and celebratory.

On the level of story, the Jabbok encounter raises familiar questions about the fate of the patriarch and his ancestors. The story is first and foremost about the (re)naming of a man, Jacob, under dark and dangerous circumstances. If the promise of Israel's god is to bestow on it a great name, thus securing its place as a great nation on the international scene, that promise is threatened if the eponymous ancestor does not make it through the night. Still, the patriarchal narratives are rife with circumstances that place the promise in jeopardy. How can Abram and Sarai inherit land when others inhabit it? How can there be ancestors when the ancestress is barren? How can the ancestors inherit the land if they live in slavery in Egypt and then die in the wilderness? Here, David Clines's reminder about the theme of the Pentateuch is apt. If the theme of the Pentateuch is about the partial fulfillment of land, blessing, and promise, then it also implies the partial nonfulfillment of the promise or blessing of the patriarchs (Clines 1997). Therefore, the promise that Israel will actually become Israel or, once it has become Israel, will remain as such, is always already punctuated with a question mark.[11] The Israelites are always, in one way or another, searching for the promised land. While these are important realities to consider, first and foremost, in the Jabbok narrative, Israel is about a particular man hailed in a particular narrative.

Scholars who have examined the name change from the perspective of the man rather than the nation have done so in a moralizing way. Jacob is a crooked character, and the name change is romanticized by exegetes as representing a moral change in his character. Jan Fokkelman even likens

---

11. Indeed, at the end of the Pentateuch, its hero looks out over the land, surveying it just before he dies (Deut 32:48–52; 34). Once the people enter the land, the books of Joshua and Judges represent threats both external and internal to the achievement of their goal (e.g., Josh 13:1; Judg 1). At the end of the Deuteronomistic History, when land and name have been destroyed, the final king of Judah, Jehoiachin, sits at the table of the Babylonian ruler, Evil-merodach (2 Kgs 25:29). Even as a ray of hope is predicted in the postexilic period, the weeping writer of Lamentations depicts a different scene, one where rape, brutality, and hunger affect every man, woman, and child (Lam 1–5).

the name change to baptism, calling it "the most important baptism of the Old Testament." He claims that "the evil and long-awkward name of Jacob is thrown away and exchanged for a beautiful, theophorous name" (Fokkelman 1975, 215–16). Viewing the name Jacob pejoratively, he maintains that the change to ישראל ("Israel") was necessary to curb the pride and deceit of Jacob. Fokkelman avers,

> That obstinate, proud, grim resistance to God is now what he displays on the banks of the Jabbok—and there it is also ... knocked down. Literally.... He adorns him with the name "Israel" on the ground of (*kī!*) his recognition of Jacob's unique nature. The name "God fights" may mean: God fights with you, because he is forced by your stubbornness and pride. (216–17)

Fokkelman's moral exegesis of Jacob's character does not stand alone in scholars' treatment of this passage. Similarly, Henry Knight (1992, 453) states: "The story suggests a change. The old Jacob—the one who was the trickster, the deceiver, the supplanter—might have stolen the chance to name the other, just like he once usurped his brother's birthright.... In this episode, however, Jacob respected the limit. Jacob was satisfied not having the name of the other." Knight maintains that the trickster Jacob was satisfied simply to wrestle with his past, his trickery, his pain, deception, and shame. However, the text clearly shows that Jacob's satisfaction in not knowing the Name was due not to his willingness to respect the limit, but rather to the Name's refusal to be named.

While it is tempting to engage in theological romanticism regarding the name change, it must be noted that even after being (re)named, Israel also remains Jacob. The patriarch is referred to by both names throughout the remainder of the narrative and is even (re)named once more in Gen 35:9–15. The presence of this doublet acknowledges either that the first name change at the Jabbok was insufficient, or that, quite simply, a different editorial tradition underlies each text. Either way, both this text and the remaining Jacob narrative indicate that the patriarch maintained this dual identity throughout his life. Indeed, that the old name is kept, saved, is significant not only psychologically but also in terms of narrative memory. Klitsner (2009, 128) connects Bethel, previously named Luz (see Judg 1:22), to Jacob's double (re)naming in Gen 35:9–15, asserting that the preservation of the prior name and identity are indispensable for further evolution of character. Even in renaming him Israel, never must his old name be forgotten. Both names will be preserved, for they describe both the man and the nation. Vestiges of both are retained in Israel's narrative memory. Both contain the truth of Israel's story. And both must be named.

Even in the (re)naming, however, it must not be forgotten that the patriarch is still interpellated. He speaks the name given to him by the story, only to be (re)interpellated once more. He has now been hailed as one who wrestles and prevails. He is unable to refuse the name given to him through an act of will or prevarication of speech. For Derrida (1995b, 84), the giving of a name can create a potentially binding contract between the one giving the name and the one named:

> One can have doubts about it from the moment when the name not only is nothing, in any case is not the "thing" that it names, not the "name-able" or the renowned, but also risks to bind, to enslave or to engage the other, to link the called, to call him/her to respond even before any decision or any deliberation, even before any freedom. An assigned passion, a prescribed alliance as much as a promise.

When the Name (re)names Jacob, the two are linked in a hierarchical relationship where the named is subordinated to the Name. Like his father, Isaac, Israel will live the rest of his life with the memory of his own Akedah, here a figurative binding. He will be bound not only by the old name but by the new name as well; and bound to the one who has named him and to his origins. The same Name who told him to return to his father's house (Gen 31:3) will also order his steps the rest of his days (e.g., 35:1–15). And even as the Name is present to him, Jacob later recalls that his days have been "few and evil" (47:9). Moreover, this binding relationship between the two did not assuage the disappointment upon (re)turning home, where interfamily strife and hardship marked his final days. Israel has been nominally and geographically interpellated by the Name—told who he is to be and where he is to go. His wrestling partner, however, escapes interpellation by refusing to be pinned down to one name and to one place.

Saving Names

> Why do you ask my name?
>
> —Genesis 32:29

When considering the Name encountered at the Jabbok, the interpretive challenges are both textual and theological. Textually speaking, the polynomial nature of the Name, called both אלהים ("a god") and איש ("a man"), as well as אל ("El") in the Peniel label, complicates making statements of any certainty about the identity of Jacob's opponent. Theologically, the narrator's construction of the character of the Name demonstrates deep ambivalence about unraveling the mystery of the divine. Something of the dangerous mystery must be kept. Something of the Name must be saved. The question, "Why do you ask my name?" (Gen 32:29) can be interpreted dismissively as a means of misdirection, or derisively as a means of stating the obvious. However we deal with the question, the Name remains enshrouded in mystery. The Name remains anonymous. The Name is a stranger to Jacob, unclear in conveying intention both at the moment of battle and of blessing. The Name is thus unnamable.

Contemporary studies of the naming of characters in fiction are helpful entryways to discussing the Name. Thomas Docherty (1983, 48) notes that one approach to characterization views the proper name as a summation of the character's essence; the name is believed to contain the entire significance or existence of a character in a self-integrated whole. This approach essentializes, seeking to pin down a character and to know him fully. Modernist and postmodernist literature, however, problematizes the totalizing nature of this approach. Another issue is the existence of the anonymous character, a character without a name. Reinhartz (1998, 9) notes that if a proper name is meant to convey the essence of a character and to construct identity, then its absence implies the converse—the "effacement, absence, veiling, or suppression of identity." In the absence of a proper name, the role a character plays is the next best marker of identity, yet Reinhartz acknowledges that role does not in of itself constitute personal identity. While the role of an anonymous character may be known, knowledge of vocational identity does not imply intimate understanding of the character. Reinhartz (1998, 12) adds: "Even the most vivid of our anonymous company are nonetheless blurred around the edges, as if the outlines of their identities were traced by dotted lines rather than encased in a solid frame." For a character who refuses both to self-identify or to confirm what Jacob may suspect, and whose face is also enshrouded in darkness, the lines drawn around him are indeed dotted.

Drawing on the writings of Samuel Beckett, Docherty raises the question of how to describe a character that cannot be pinned down to one name. Following Beckett, Docherty maintains that there are characters that are simply unnamable. These characters are those who make themselves anew at every moment, thus transcending all past or anterior selves (Docherty 1983, 68). The unnamable cannot be known. The unnamable is therefore anonymous and therefore free to be what he/she wants to be. The writings of Docherty and Reinhartz raise questions about the Name Jacob encounters at the Jabbok. Is the Name the unnamable? Is the Name a kind of apophasis, an absence best (un)known through negation, a trace of (some/no)thing? Or is the Name a kind of hyperpresence, assuming the weight of every name Jacob has encountered thus far, a kind of name above every name? (see Phil 2:9). Moreover, can it be said that the Name transcends even itself by (re)making itself, much like Beckett's unnamable character? If so, what is the purpose of this (re)making and (re)naming?

At the Jabbok specifically, the Name is polynomial. The narrator refers to Jacob's opponent as "man"(Gen 32:24), while Jacob believes he has seen "God" (32:30). The Name also tells Jacob his name has been changed because he has striven with אלהים (God) and with אנשים (men) and prevailed (32:28), though it is unclear whether the Name refers to the present moment or previously in Jacob's struggles prior to the Jabbok encounter. Prior to the Jabbok, Jacob's experiences also demonstrate the ambiguity and multiplicity inherent in divine manifestation. At Bethel, Jacob encounters a multitude of names, all of which appear to carry traces of divinity: מלאכי אלהים ("messengers of God," Gen 28:12), יהוה ("the LORD," Gen 28:13a, 16, 21), יהוה אלהי אברהם אביך ואלהי יצחק ("the LORD the God of Abraham your father and the God of Isaac," Gen 28:13b), and אלהים ("God," Gen 28:20, 21). The names at Bethel are sometimes self-referencing, at other times named either by the narrator or by Jacob. Here, it is unclear whether the biblical author is simply unsure how to reference traces of divinity, whether multiple sources and therefore different names underlay the Bethel text, or whether these distinctions are intended to represent Israel's consciousness of gradations of divinity within the heavenly realm.[12] Whatever the solution, the confusion remains. The polynomialism inherent in the Bethel text does not make clear statements about who—or what—Jacob encounters. Jacob and his family's encounters outside Bethel and Peniel also demonstrate the textual resistance inherent in assigning just one name to the divine. When opening Leah's barren womb, the Name

---

12. Evidence for this can be found in diverse places in the HB, for example in the vestiges of the first creation story, where preexilic ideas about a heavenly council nevertheless found their way into postexilic texts in the Primeval History: Gen 1:26; 3:22; 11:7. Vestiges of the heavenly council also appear in the book of Job: Job 1:6; 2:1.

is יהוה ("the Lord," Gen 29:31–35). When competing with her sister to bear more children than Rachel, Leah acknowledges the Name as אלהים ("God," Gen 30:17–24). In the conflict with Laban, Jacob receives a word from יהוה ("the Lord," Gen 31:3) yet also encounters in a dream מלאך האלהים ("the messenger of God," Gen 31:11), who later declares himself to be האל בית־אל ("the God of Bethel," Gen 31:13). And at Mahanaim, Jacob is met again by מלאכי אלהים ("messengers of God," Gen 32:1). In addition, Ronald Hendel provides a trenchant reminder that ambiguity exists within the name אלהים itself—it can be translated as "God" or "gods." For Hendel, this lack of clarity at the Jabbok may represent "cultural amnesia," which involves the forgetting of an older, non-Yahwistic deity. Hendel (2010, 44) asks, "Striven with God or with gods? For the nation of Israel to exist, the god who strives with Jacob must be compatible with the Israelite framework of memory. Hence, if not Yahweh, it must be Yahweh's angel, and not a night demon or a river god or any other non-Yahwistic deity." Indeed, in the imagination of the preexilic prophet Hosea, Jacob wrestles with the Yahwistic angel (see Hos 12:4).

Reinhartz (1998, 155) notes that "character confusion in the heavenly realm" raises questions about the boundaries among the divine beings themselves, the boundaries between the divine and human beings, and the boundaries between divine beings and God himself. She notes that divine beings—angels—can function as personal guides, agents of God, instruments of destruction, warriors, or harbingers of divine presence (Reinhartz 1998). Moreover, the boundaries between angels and God are sometimes indistinct; while an angel may act in God's name, first- and third-person forms of address are interchangeable, and God frequently appears alongside an angel or is identical to it (Reinhartz 1998). Historical critical scholars have attributed these nominal inconsistencies to source criticism, to authorship and redaction over time, as Reinhartz (1998, 162) acknowledges: "These areas of indeterminacy might be attributed to the whim—or perhaps the carelessness—of the narrator or to the vagaries of the redactional process. But a significant number of angel stories play on these confusions. Such stories frequently portray the difficulties faced by a human character in identifying correctly his or her angelic adversary or conversation partner." Historical-critical methodology is intended to unravel the mystery by explaining these inconsistencies in a diachronic way. However, von Rad's (1973, 324) early intuition that the looseness of the Jabbok text yielded an inner spaciousness may also apply to discussion of the Name. Rather than viewing the polynomial nature of the Name as a problem to be solved, allowing the Name space in which to breathe may demonstrate that his ambiguity is actually a gift. The anonymity and therefore unnamability of the Name creates space for transcendence and elusiveness, markers of divine encounter.

Outside Jacob's encounters in Genesis, the Name exhibits similar reticence to disclose too much of his identity. Judges 13:17-23 is an intertext to the Jabbok encounter where the Name is also withheld:

> Then Manoah said to the angel of the LORD, "What is your name, so that we may honor you when your words come true?" But the angel of the LORD said to him, "Why do you ask my name? It is too wonderful."
>
> So Manoah took the kid with the grain offering, and offered it on the rock to the LORD, to him who works wonders. When the flame went up toward heaven from the altar, the angel of the LORD ascended in the flame of the altar while Manoah and his wife looked on; and they fell on their faces to the ground. The angel of the LORD did not appear again to Manoah and his wife. Then Manoah realized that it was the angel of the LORD. And Manoah said to his wife, "We shall surely die, for we have seen God." But his wife said to him, "If the LORD had meant to kill us, he would not have accepted a burnt offering and a grain offering at our hands, or shown us all these things, or now announced to us such things as these." (NRSV)

The text in Judges plays on similar themes in the Jabbok encounter—the request and refusal of the Name, fear of divine aggressiveness, and seeing אלהים ("God"). Here as with Jacob's various encounters, the Name is polynomial—named אלהים ("God") by Manoah but referred to as מלאך יהוה ("messenger of the LORD") and also יהוה ("the LORD") by the narrator. Here, however, the Name offers an answer to Manoah's question—he cannot know the Name because it is הוא־פלאי ("too wonderful"). The term פליא ("wonderful") also carries the connotation of incomprehensibility, that which cannot be comprehended by the human mind or that which is outside the realm of understanding. Here the refusal of the Name involves its ineffability; Manoah and his wife simply would not have comprehended it.

Elsewhere, even when the Name *is revealed*, a measure of concealment, elusiveness, ineffability is retained, as Terrien (2000, 119) affirms: "The God of biblical faith, even in the midst of a theophany, is at once *Deus revelatus atque absconditus*. He is known as unknown." The elusive—or "too wonderful"—nature of the Name suggests a spilling over, an (absent) excess. This excess leads us, ironically, to abandon language, because language is ultimately an insufficient tool (though perhaps the only tool) to speak about God. For Derrida (1995b, 58), it is the Name of God that is the "bottomless collapse," an "endless desertification" of language itself. Jacob's encounter with the Name, like Manoah's, demonstrates the fragility of language to describe it. Only a bottomless collapse remains, a kenosis or emptying of discourse, where the Name exceeds the capabilities of language to contain it. This showcases a God who does not want to be confined to or restricted by a name imposed on him. The Jabbok text conveys the transcendence of the Name, as one unpronounceable—G-d—but that nevertheless has left his presence on the page. Independent of other signifiers, the Name is Derrida's Transcendental Signified, who has left behind traces of presence, but only traces. The presence or trace left behind is, in Terrien's words, an elusive one, one capable of naming but not of being named. It is this (absent) excess, so maddening, so elusive, that is the gift, or in the words of the text, the blessing, the Name inscribes on the page.

The story of the incomprehensibility of the Name in Judges does not stand alone. The story of Moses's encounter at the burning bush (Exod 3) is another example of divine ineffability outside the Jacob cycle. As is frequently the case in the Hebrew Bible, particularly in the Priestly tradition, concerned with holiness and categorization, theophany is accompanied by some kind of spatial limitation (see Exod 19:7–23; 20:15–18; 33:17–23; 34:29–35, to name a few).[13] At the burning bush, Yahweh limits full disclosure of personhood through a common Priestly requirement—the holy must not "mix" with the common: "Then he said, "Come no closer! Remove the sandals from your feet, for the place on which you are standing is holy ground" (Exod 3:5 NRSV).

Moreover, the revelation of the divine Name itself may also function in a limiting or self-distancing manner. At the least, its meaning is highly ambiguous. In his discussion of the interpretation of Yahweh, Karel van der Toorn notes that the name Yahweh may be read as either a promise ("I will certainly be here") or an allusion to the incomparability of Yahweh

---

13. In a more general sense, prophets, priests, and kings also act as representatives between God and the people. They are, in their bodies, the spatial limitations prescribed by a God whose holiness requires distance. Certainly, the requirements for holiness on the part of the divine are not the only reasons given within the biblical corpus for this distance. Most notably, the people's request for a king is viewed by God as a kind of divine rejection (1 Sam 8:4–8).

("I am who I am," i.e., without peer). Van der Toorn refers to the Israelite explanation as a "piece of theology rather than a reliable etymology" (*DDD*, 1711–30). Further complicating the scene: it is the messenger/angel of the Lord who appears at the burning bush (Exod 3:2); it is Yahweh who sees that Moses turns aside to look (Exod 3:4a); and it is God who calls to him out of the bush (Exod 3:4b) and who identifies himself as the God of Abraham, Isaac, and Jacob (Exod 3:6, 15, 16). Later, the deity tells Moses that he had not made himself known to the patriarchs by the name Yahweh (Exod 6:2–3), contradicting the revelation to Abram in Genesis 15:7. Scholars such as Julian Morgenstern have pointed to this complexity, offering the expected source-critical response (Parke-Taylor 1975, 46–47). Van der Toorn also provides additional historical possibilities for the etymology and meaning of the name. Yahweh may be an abbreviated name of a defied ancestor: YHWH-El ("May El be present"), linked to Mari texts: "Yahwi-Illu," or the reconstructed cult name El YHWH ("El who reveals himself"). He links YHWH to a storm god and maintains that El has a solar appearance; theophany texts present Yahweh as a solar deity. Moreover, official gods such as YHWH of Zion (Ps 99:2) and of Hebron (2 Sam 15:7) point to poly-Yahwism (*DDD* 1711–30).

Whatever the historical background for the divine name, narratively speaking, Yahweh's self-revelation is a purposeful summons linked to a specific call on Moses's life—to lead the people out of enslavement. Moses becomes not merely an intermediary; he is also an embodied reminder of the patriarchs (including Jacob), whom they had long forgotten after four hundred years in Egypt. Moses links the people back to their past, to the here and now of their current situation, and into hope of future liberation. Appropriately, Wouter Jacques van Bekkum (2006, 7) reminds us that the derivation of the divine name, from היה, is in the imperfect, which can be translated as a present, past, or future tense. In Exodus Rabbah, the tense of the verb appears linked to the atemporality of the divine. Rabbi Isaac said: "God said to Moses: Tell them that I am now what I always was and always will be; for this reason the word אהיה is written three times" (Shinan 1984, 119–21). Similarly, rabbinic explanation implies God's help and involvement during times of exile and oppression (Exod 3:7), as van Bekkum (2006, 8) affirms: "'I am,' therefore means: I am in virtue of my deeds; it is I who am with my creatures in their hour of trouble and need, it is I who am with my people in times of suffering." In surveying rabbinic interpretations of the divine name, van Bekkum (2006, 8) adds:

> This and similar expositions seem to imply that the divine name in the form of the tetragrammaton possesses some kind of a protective value for both community and individual, an aspect which ... became essential in Jewish magic and mystic lore, strengthened by the fact that the tetragrammaton in the sense of "being," either "being there/existing" or "being with," establishes the revelation of a name, or rather a title without any additional relevant information with regard to the divine essence. The divine name "as it is" asserts the transcendental and hidden nature of this deity.

The hidden nature of this deity—an ineffable Name—is a pervasive theme in rabbinic interpretation as well as kabbalistic thought. In classical kabbalah God is without name (van Bekkum 2006, 14). As the Infinite, God is understood as "He is in Himself," correlating to Abraham Abulafia's view that the actual name of God does not occur in the Pentateuch; the tetragrammaton and the expression Ehyeh ("I am," "I will be") are only allusions to or reflections of the real or true name of God (van Bekkum 2006, 14). Indeed, Yahweh's self-revelation at the burning bush may well be interpreted as occlusion rather than revelation—a kind of divine "mind your own business."

Not unlike the desire of interpreters to unravel the mystery of the Name, Jacob's question at the Jabbok is simultaneously a curious one and also perfectly reasonable. Given the severity of the fight, it seems Jacob might have been better served speaking in exclamations rather than interrogations—please do not harm me!—rather than inquiring about the Name. If the Name were in fact knowable, what would be the benefit in knowing it? Scholars have tended to respond to this question either with cynicism or romanticism. Knight and Brueggemann are paradigmatic of these responses.

For Knight (1992, 454), Jacob's question refers to the crookedness of his nature: "Perhaps Jacob, then, inquired more deeply about his own motives in the encounter: Why did he want to know the intruder's name? Did he want to control the man, which he would be able to do if he learned the outcome? Did he want to master the encounter and the one whom he encountered?" Knight's comments are not unreasonable in light of Jacob's character; moreover, knowledge of the Name might have helped Jacob to win the battle. Perhaps in knowing the Name, Jacob could have in fact killed the Name. For Derrida, to pin down the name exactly is to limit, to kill, to limit to a signifying trace. To assign a name is for the arrow to hit and not cause a limp but to kill completely. To name is, in some sense, to kill. By contrast, to withhold the name is indeed to save the Name.

On the other side of the interpretive spectrum, Brueggemann (2010, 269) suggests that Jacob's desire to know his opponent's name expresses desire for intimacy: "[Jacob] reverses roles and dares to ask the name of the stranger, even as he has been asked his name (v. 27). He wants to know God's name, the mystery of heaven and earth. Like the couple in the garden (Gen 2–3), Jacob/Israel wants to overcome all the distance." The stranger stops short of giving what Brueggemann calls the "ultimate gift"—the revelation of his name. God remains God, Brueggemann (2010, 269) says, his "hiddenness intact." Even in the garden, which Brueggemann references, יהוה אלהים ("Lord God") views the couple's knowledge of "good and evil" (Gen 3:22–23) as dangerous.[14] Distance between that which is divine and that which is human must be maintained, as numerous encounters throughout the Hebrew Bible suggest (e.g., Gen 3:22; 11:7; Exod 3:5; 19:21–25; 33:20–23). In Derridian terms, however, intimacy with the Name is achieved not through knowledge but through abandonment of knowledge, not in knowing the Name but in saving it. Derrida (1995b, 78–79) states, "It is necessary to leave all, to leave every 'something' through love of God, and no doubt to leave God himself, to abandon him, that is, at once to leave him and (but) let him (be beyond being-something). Save his name [*sauf son nom*]—which must be kept silent there where it itself goes [*il se rend lui-même*] to arrive there, that is, to arrive at its own effacement." Real intimacy, or real desire, is awakened in letting go of God, in releasing one's grip, which is what the Name implores at the Jabbok: "Let me go, for the day has broken" (Gen 32:26a; see John 20:17).[15] What is achieved is a letting go and a fleeting intimacy. For Derrida (1995b, 79), the desert is the other name, if not the proper place, of desire. In the desert, desire necessarily leads to desertification. There, desire grows in the midst of absence; desire and desiccation take place in the desert, where the Name refuses to be named. Knight's and Brueggemann's respective interpretations of Jacob's motivations notwithstanding, another possibility (impossibility really) exists for the Name's refusal to be named, namely, that Jacob already knows the answer to the question he has posed.

---

14. The Hebrew phrase "good and bad" (טוב ורע) is a merism that refers to knowledge of "everything."

15. While I am referring to the phrase philosophically, historical-critical scholars viewed the request as indicative of an ancient superstition that said night spirits/demons had to be released before dawn or risk losing their magical power. See. Gunkel 1997, 347; 1987, 84; and von Rad 1973, 318–25.

Fokkelman contends that the assailant's refusal to disclose the Name does not mask his identity but rather reveals it. Fokkelman (1975, 217) states, "The 'man' parries Jacob's question with a counter-question, 'Why do you ask my name?' He then refuses to reveal his identity straight away; but at the same time his refusal points to his secret and draws attention to it! ... But Jacob, do you not ask for the sake of asking? (Think and you will know the answer!)." The answer to Jacob's question, then, is like his assailant—hidden in plain sight. The secret is that Jacob already knows the secret. The many names that Jacob has encountered are all (un)contained in the Name (un)revealed at the Jabbok. The Name is God.

Examining the scene through the lens of narrative theory and cognitive science momentarily shifts the discussion from theological uncertainty regarding the Name. As Catherine Emmott has shown, a character's cognitive status may be linked to how much or how little of her name the narrative reveals. Characters who are at the forefront of narrative attention may be identified merely by a pronoun. Conversely, a character who is less cognitively present may require a name or some other full noun phrase to introduce her (Emmott 2003, 297). If we apply Emmott's theory of cognitive status to the Jabbok story, full disclosure of the Name is unnecessary. As a character, the Name is at the forefront of the reader's imagination. The Name is also focalized through Jacob, the other primary character in the narrative. The use of a pronoun in Gen 32:26a, 27a, and the withholding of the Name generally at the Jabbok, may suggest a character of such prominence that no further description is necessary. Although this may not always be the case, on one reading, a lack of naming may, narratively speaking, serve to reinforce the centrality of a character (Emmott 2003, 299). Theologically, Hebrew thought views the character of G-d as certainly the most central of all. The ineffability of G-d is woven throughout Jewish theology, from rabbinic traditions to kabbalah.

What matters most, then, is that the secret is not shared but kept. Or, in Derrida's (1995b, 58, emphasis original) terminology, saved:

> They name God, speak of him, speak *him*, speak *to him, let him speak in them*, let themselves be carried by him, make (themselves) a reference to just what the name supposes to name beyond itself, the nameable beyond the name, the unnamable namable. As if it was necessary both to save the name and to save everything except the name, *save the name* [*sauf le nom*], as if it was necessary to lose the name in order to save what bears the name, or that toward which one goes through the name. But

to lose the name is not to attack it, to destroy it, or found it. On the contrary, to lose the name is quite simply to respect it: as name.

What the Name calls for is a kind of *Gelassenheit*, a letting go, even a forgetting. In releasing the Name before dawn, the Name is allowed to retain its mystery, (un)make itself anew once more. For the Name, there is not nominal reciprocity at the Jabbok, a mutual revelation of the "I AM," as there is with Moses at the burning bush (Exod 3:6); though here too we could read similarities rather than contrast: "I AM who I AM" may also imply occlusion rather than revelation.

But at the Jabbok, the Name is not I AM. The Name is rather the Unname, the Unnamable, the Name that cannot be spoken, G-d, the I AM (NOT). The Name is the (un)made, constantly (un)making and elusive, never enclosed by a frame but traced, and leaving traces, like the dotted lines described by Reinhartz. The Name is the Apophatic, an absence best (un)known through negation, a trace of (no)thing, a container for every name but (un)contained by (no) name. Derrida (1995b, 68) observes, "In the most apophatic moment, when one says: 'God is not,' 'God is neither this nor that, neither that nor its contrary.' … It is a matter of holding the promise of saying the truth at any price, of testifying, of rendering oneself to the truth of the name, to the thing itself such as it must be named by the name, that is, *beyond the name*." The Name inscribes on the page as gift this elusiveness, this Unname; not a signature but a *countersignature*, a postscriptum. The Unname is a word after a word that is really no word at all. And so in the absence of the Name, in the absence of a word, Jacob must name something else, not P/person but place.

For both Bruce Vawter and Kevin Walton, Jacob's inability to know the Name results in another kind of naming. Unable to name a P/person, Jacob names a place, Peniel. Vawter (1977, 351) asserts, "Jacob is brought to the realization that the God whom he has *seen face to face* is not to be named, and so he names Peniel instead" (emphasis original). Similarly, Walton (2003, 87) maintains: "If Jacob is unable to give a name to God, he is at least able to name the place where he has experienced God." For Jacob, this results in going where he cannot see—the darkness of the Jabbok—to hear what he cannot hear—the Name, as Angelus Silesius says: "Go there where you cannot; see where you do not see; Hear where nothing rings or sounds, so are you where God speaks" (Derrida 1995b, 44). Here the proper name El is attached to a place where El's presence is felt. As Ramsey (1989, 34) notes, "If the act of naming signifies anything about the name-giver, it is the quality of discernment. When Jacob, e.g., gives the name to Bethel (Gen 28:19; 35:7; 35:15) or Peniel (Gen 32:31) or the altar of El-Elohe-Israel (Gen 33:20), he exhibits awareness of God's activity and presence." Jacob acknowledges that, at Peniel, presence can be felt and some outline of a face can be traced.

2
The Face

The written page is no mirror. Writing means confronting an unknown face.

For if we cannot see His face it is because, of all the faces we scrutinize, His is the one that cannot be shown or contemplated.
—Edmond Jábes, *The Little Book of Unexpected Subversion*

Pre-facing Peniel

When Jacob declares that he has looked upon the face of Elohim (God) and lived (Gen 32:31), he names the place Peniel, "Face of God." Upon meeting his brother the following day, Jacob declares that to see Esau's face is like seeing the face of Elohim (Gen 33:10). This climactic scene and its postface is just one in the long stretch of patriarchal narrative (Gen 25–50) where the Hebrew writer(s) subtly employs the imagery of face. The Jabbok encounter is not a stand-alone episode but is pre(face)d by Jacob's interactions with all the faces in the narrative. Throughout the Jacob cycle, faces are concealed, revealed, confused, and even fused.[1] Behind the story world also exists the cultural and theological anxiety surrounding facing God; as well as the difficulty in drawing a face on, or characterizing, the divine character, who appears not as one face but as many faces. Like the פנים (face) itself, which only appears as a dual, so too the faces of these characters are multi(face)ted. At the Jabbok, Jacob's vision of Elohim's face

---

1. Jacob's face before his father's aged eyes (Gen 27:1, 21–25); Leah's face in the marriage canopy (29:21–25); the night and the refusal of the God/man to say his name effectively conceals his identity at the Jabbok encounter itself (32:22, 24); the faces of the God/man and Esau appear to merge after the Jabbok account with the claim that seeing the face of Esau is like seeing the face of God (33:10).

compels him, in Levinasian terms, to the Face—and to the faces—who bid him not to kill.[2] Moreover, it is not until Jacob glimpses the mysterious man at the liminal, nocturnal space of the Jabbok River, itself visited by midrashic, faceless specters, that Jacob must face his own identity. He is *Jacob*—a trickster, one who has manipulated other characters in the story for his own benefit. At the Jabbok Jacob must respond to his own right to be in the face of every other face he has encountered, or in Bakhtinian terms, to recognize how others have authored him and how he has authored others (Bakhtin 1990).

What I offer here is both an exegesis of the story and an ethical engagement with its characters. I use a philosophical/ethical/psychological framework that exposes Jacob's many failures as a moral agent. The application of this framework allows questions and interpretive possibilities to emerge that move beyond the exegetical to the ethical and existential. My analysis also reveals Jacob's opponent as a character who is, like the patriarch he wrestles, a trickster. This exploration of the story's poetics naturally leads to questions of rhetoric: How does such a critical self-portrait of the patriarch and, at times, his opponent, serve a community of storytellers? Who is telling this story, and why are they telling it? The sociopolitical implications, explored later in the book, indicate that this is a community struggling with its identity, its relationship/ownership of the land, its relationship to a God who wrestles in the dirt, and its future after exile.

Putting a Face on God

Of the exegetical elements in this passage, the identity of Jacob's assailant has received the most attention by scholars who attempt to understand it. In Levinasian terms, just who is the Face that summons a response? When the Face engages in a mutuality of being and in a willingness for dialogue, encounter is possible. Nevertheless, as Fewell and Gunn (1993, 89) attest, drawing a characterization of God in the Hebrew Bible is notoriously complex:

> Coming to some understanding of the character of YHWH is one of the great challenges of the Hebrew Bible, not only of its narrative. Of course,

---

2. Here, the capitalized Face—and also the Face of all faces—refers to Jacob's wrestling partner.

we can make it simpler by treating component stories as wholly discrete so that we see not one character but many. On the other hand, as we have seen, the canonical shape of the Bible may incline us to keep looking for a single character, even if complex, mysterious, enigmatic, and quite often frustratingly elusive.

Additionally, Stuart Lasine (2012) offers several cautions when attempting to characterize the divine character.[3] While Yahweh's words to Moses appear sacrosanct—"'But,' he said, 'you cannot see my face; for no one shall see me and live'" (Exod 33:20)—the broader literature of the Hebrew Bible calls this seemingly inviolable injunction into question. Ian Wilson (2009, 107) has noted that the phrase "face to face" occurs five times in the Hebrew Bible, and each is related to a specific encounter between God and one or more humans—Jacob (Gen 32:31), Moses (Exod 33:11; Deut 34:10), Gideon (Judg 6:22), and the people of Israel (Ezek 20:35). Moreover, Hagar's vision of El (God)/the angel of the Lord—and his vision of her (Gen 16:7–13)—is also an intertext to the face-to-face encounter at the Jabbok.

Mark Wessner has uncovered four elements involved in each of these encounters. First, the *panim el panim* ("face to face") encounters are divinely initiated. Second, each encounter involves profound intimacy between God and the human. Third, these encounters are born out of intentional solitude on the part of the human. And fourth, they provide supernatural verification for the individual involved (Wessner 2000, 170). While Wilson draws on Wessner's study, he maintains that the result of such encounters is not limited to intimacy between the human and the Divine. Rather, within the corpus of the Hebrew Bible, the divine face appears to play two contrasting roles—one who blesses and one who instills fear in the seer.

---

3. Lasine offers the following cautions throughout the book: What if what narratologists call the coherence or incoherence of a character is actually due to redaction? How much universality can be claimed regarding the thoughts, attitudes, and motivations of biblical characters in relation to the (post)modern (hu)man? What, for the ancient Hebrews, constituted a self, and how much of an inner life (*homo clausus*) did these individuals possess? Should characters' speech be taken at face value, or their motivation(s) be considered? If so, how much can be claimed about motivation when few characters in the Hebrew Bible (including God) have a thought life? What should be the role of psychology in characterization? Finally, how are readers implicated in the weighing of biblical hearts? Lasine raises valid questions that must serve as a caution in the characterization process.

In the Aaronic blessing (Num 6:24–26), the divine face is portrayed as a source of blessing and life and thus associated with חן ("favor") and שלום ("peace"). After meeting Esau following the Peniel encounter, Jacob affirms that seeing his brother's face is like seeing the face of God (Gen 33:10). Here Jacob's family reunion entails the blessing of a fresh start. Thus Jacob's *panim el panim* ("face to face") encounter is about blessing and revivification (Wilson 2009, 107).[4] Mesopotamian literature parallels the positive encounters of the face to face in the Hebrew Bible (107), yet in ancient Israel, statements made by Jacob (Gen 32:31), Gideon (Judg 6:22), Manoah (Judg 13:22), and Hagar (Gen 16:13) seem to indicate that the Israelites saw in the divine face a source of death and not blessing (Wilson 2009, 109). However, in the encounter at Peniel, Jacob faces the Face of God and glimpses *both* death and blessing.

Johanna Stiebert (2016, 25–26) notes that the anthropomorphism of God—the ascribing to God body parts such as a face, hands, or feet—ultimately gives way to describing God's appearance less corporeally. The anxiety on the part of the writers, described through the experiences of Moses (Exod 3; 33), Isaiah (Isa 6), Ezekiel (Ezek 1), and others, is linked to the fear of idolatry, the worshiping of an image. For Stiebert, the typical explanation offered by source criticism is not satisfying. The typical explanation is that the J-source represents an earlier, more anthropomorphic picture of God, and by the time we arrive at the latest source, the P-source, God appears more transcendent. For Stiebert, however, "The steps of progression over time are therefore not as clearly signposted or as linear as source criticism sometimes suggests—again the result is polyphonic" (27). Over time, particularly in medieval Judaism, the tendency around pictorial depictions of God was to allegorize—a hand, foot, or face symbolized God's presence (29). Despite the anxiety around divine corporeality in various stages of Jewish history, the voice of God appears less controversial (31). Indeed, the night surely obscured the Face at the Jabbok, and the Name remained unspoken, but the encounter *does* allow for a voice. While a full treatment of the history of divine corporeality is beyond the scope of

---

4. Royal inscriptions of the Old Babylonian king Samsuiluna (1749–1712 BCE) state that the gods Zababa and Ishtar raised their "faces of life" toward the king, empowering him to build the wall of Kish. Later inscriptions of Neo-Assyrian king Assurbanipal (668–627 BCE) and Neo-Babylonian king Nebuchadnezzar II (604–562 BCE) also speak of shining, empowering divine faces.

2. The Face

this book, what is clear is this—the face of God in the Hebrew Bible and in the Jabbok encounter is a complex issue.

Here, however, I am concerned not only with God's face; I am concerned with all the faces in the narrative. Throughout the Jacob cycle, Jacob's treatment of the faces all too easily forgotten—the women and children—appears analogous. Like Elohim (God), it seems that Jacob may also choose to impart blessing or death.

Facial Intertexts

As Lee Humphreys (2001, 195) has noted, though there are many times in the story world of Genesis that God engages humans directly, the encounter at the Face of God is the first encounter where it is clearly stated in terms of seeing. Certainly, the two wrestle, so touching and holding are also involved, but here my interest is in seeing. Humphreys notes that seeing is also part of the Hagar story. Therefore, a brief engagement with Hagar—and with the one she is said to have seen—will prove illuminative for the encounter at the Face of God.

After Hagar runs away from Sarai, the narrator states that Hagar is found by an angel of the Lord (Gen 16:7), yet Hagar later exclaims that she has seen El (God; Gen 16:13). Hagar's encounter with this divine character demonstrates, once again, his multi(face)ted portrayal in the Hebrew Bible. On the one hand, the angel of the Lord is the only character who actually speaks to Hagar, recognizing her as a speaking, feeling subject.[5] To both Abram and Sarai, she is שפחה ("slave girl"; Gen 16:2, 5-6). Aside from the narrator, the angel of the Lord is also the only character who *names her*—a recognition of her social location. She is the גר—the stranger. While Hagar (and Ishmael) stands uncomfortably outside the covenantal promises made to Abram, she is also not beyond divine reach. The angel of the Lord *shows up*, a compassionate recognition that he has heard her silent cries (see Exod 2:23-25). He asks her a question that is both social and also existential: "Hagar, slave-girl of Sarai, where have you come from and where are you going?" (Gen 16:8).[6] While the question can

---

5. For a discussion on the complexities of the name "angel of the Lord" and other authorial traditions naming the divine, see pages 29–33.

6. In Job, YHWH poses a similar question to the Satan—"Where have you come from?" (Job 2:2). In the second creation story, YHWH Elohim asks the Adam, "Where are you?" (Gen 3:9).

be read geographically, it can also have multiple meanings. The question posed to Hagar appears to be less about educating the angel of the Lord about her geographical location than about *Hagar naming what her life has been about*. The angel of the Lord is not inquiring about whether she has been in Egypt or in Canaan or anywhere else. Rather, the angel of the Lord actively engages her in a discussion about her own life. The conversation is an acknowledgement of her pain, where she has been לקח ("taken") and נתן ("given") to Abram לשבת ("to remain") with him as wife (Gen 16:3).

In all of this, Hagar is passive—passed from Sarai's hand to Abram's bed—and voiceless. Abram ויבא ("entered") Hagar and she conceives, but unlike Rachel and Leah, no cry of exultation is uttered. The conception of a child is not thought to bring her closer to her husband, as with Leah. In the conception of a child, neither does she experience love (Rachel), nor is the decision to conceive about exercising her own autonomy (Leah). Rather, once Hagar discovers she has conceived, her mistress is lowered in her eyes (ותקל גברתה בעיניה, Gen 16:4). The semantic range for קלל can include viewing someone (or something) as "slight" or "trifling," but it can also refer to "cursing." The meaning of the phrase—exactly how the weight of Hagar's feelings shift toward Sarai—may depend on whether Ishmael increases Hagar's status or whether he is an additional weight to be placed on her shoulders.

In the doublet or second telling of this story, Ishmael is placed on Hagar's shoulders (Gen 21:14). He is both the literal and symbolic weight she is forced to carry from a home that is not her own to the wilderness, where the narrative will leave her. While God is with the boy (21:20), Ishmael is nevertheless a visual reminder of Hagar's "affliction" (16:6, 9, 11). Hagar has remained בידך ("in the hands of")—that is, under the power of—Sarai. Ishmael is a symbol of the power differential between the two women—the one, powerful, rich, free, incorporated into the promissory blessings of Yahweh through her husband; the other a stranger in a strange land, slave, and an outsider to the promissory blessings made to Abram. On the other hand, Hagar does something Sarai cannot do at this point in the narrative—bear a child. For a woman in the ancient Near East, conceiving a (male) child meant a cultural promotion; a woman's worth was tied to her ability to produce an heir for her husband. Hagar does what Sarai cannot, and subsequently, Sarai is lowered in Hagar's eyes. For perhaps the first time, Hagar gains a measure of value and self-worth.

In the second iteration of the story, Elohim (God) hears the cry of the child, and the angel of Elohim opens Hagar's eyes to see the well of water

2. The Face

in front of her (Gen 21:17, 19). On the surface, this is a God who sees pain and suffering and responds to it. She may be discarded, mistreated, by Abram and Sarai, but the divine character appears to display compassion where his servants lack it. Nevertheless, it must be admitted, Elohim also endorses Hagar and Ishmael's expulsion (21:12–13).

The question of what kind of divine character Hagar encounters hinges, however, not only on the divine character's acknowledgment of her pain. In the angel of the Lord, Hagar also experiences a face of God who tells her: "Return to your mistress and humble yourself under her hand" (שובי אל־גברתך ו התעני תחת ידיה; Gen 16:9). Here, the use of התעני, the *hithpael* perfect of ענה, implies that upon Hagar's return the relationship with Sarai will again involve affliction. The angel of Yahweh calls her to return to the certainty of slavery and the likelihood of abuse. Moreover, the promises made by the divine character—whether he is called the angel of the Lord (Gen 16) or Elohim (Gen 21)—are also ambiguous. Trible (1984, 16) notes that both promises are "fraught with ambivalence." The promise of numerous descendants lacks the covenantal context that is crucial to the patriarchs. Second, the promise of a birth of a child appears ambivalent as well. The child will be a "wild ass of a man." Thus the divine promise of Ishmael means life at the boundary of consolation and desolation. Two words characterize him—hand and face: his hand will be against everyone, just as Abram tells Sarai that Hagar is "in your hand" (Gen 16:6), as well as the angel of the Lord's orders to Hagar, "Return to your mistress and suffer affliction under her hand" (16:9), so too will Ishmael's face be "against the face of all his brothers" (16:12). Karolien Vermeulen (2017, 802) offers this helpful word: "As a poetic device, body parts exploit the inherent spatiality of the parts, directing readers in their understanding of the dynamics of the story." Here, as in other places in the Hebrew Bible such as Judg 4:9, the body part *hand* is a euphemism for power (804). Hagar remains under the power of Sarai, just as Ishmael will have power over others.

Christopher Heard (2001), however, notes the ambiguities involved in translating Gen 16:12. At issue is whether Ishmael's relationship with others will be combative or cooperative. The previous clause, "his hand against everyone, and everyone's hand against him" (Gen 16:12), on first glance, seems to imply an adversarial existence. Heard states, "The common decision to read the saying with an adversarial sense may be prompted, in varying degrees, by the reasonable assumption that an Israelite narrator is likely to be negatively disposed toward Ishmaelites" (70).

The word *face* builds on his mother's action, who claims, "from before the face of Sarai my mistress I am fleeing" (Gen 16:8). Trible (1984) states that in Ishmael, Hagar's story continues. Yet it is God's justice toward Hagar and Ishmael—or the supposed lack of it—that has proven most troubling for some interpreters.

Fewell's (2003) beautiful, midrashic, Levinasian reading of the text addresses questions of theodicy, or the Face of God in the midst of suffering. In her retelling of the Hagar story, she applies a hermeneutic of suspicion to the character of the angel of Yahweh, particularly in Hagar's question to the angel: "How could you possibly be the god of Abram and the god of the slave woman too?" (44). Contra Fewell, Hemchand Gossai (2010, 15) exonerates the angel of Yahweh by noting that the water is provided, even without Hagar calling (contrast Moses in the wilderness). Even as one voiceless, she is provided for. Gossai notes that for all oppressed people this story provides a basis for hope and life—that Yahweh hears the silent cries of all people, whether the silent cry of Hannah (1 Sam 1–2) or the cry of millions around the world. Hagar demonstrates that deliverance does not presuppose a certain religious orientation. Abram and Sarai are not reprimanded by God, but neither is Hagar abandoned; the hostile environment of Sarai's household is countered by the hospitable setting of the wilderness. This wilderness experience signals a new beginning for Hagar, where Yahweh does what Abram and Sarai fail to do—namely, to enter into conversation with Hagar.

For Fewell (2003, 52), seeing and being seen mean that these two have seen each other's faces and must now live up to each other's expectations. Hagar will do what he has asked, and he must do what he has promised; encountering the face of the Other is ethically obligating. In his discussion of the face-to-face encounter between Jacob and Esau, Gerd Theissen (1990) frames ethical obligation around hoped-for reconciliation. This reconciliation, whether between individuals or, perhaps here, between Hagar and Yahweh, or ultimately between Ishmaelites and Israelites, goes beyond appeasement and quid pro quo. For Theissen, it is reconciliation that is at the heart of face-to-face encounters such as the one between Jacob and Esau, Hagar and Yahweh, or Ishmael and others. Theissen notes plaintively that we do not actually see God's face, but that when people reconcile, the face of God shines. For Theissen, however, the face of God is, to put it in Pauline terms, glimpsed through a mirror darkly; in the here and now, reconciliation is only partial. Total reconciliation is, for Theissen, "a longing that asks too much of us" (17). The avoidance of violence and sorrow in conflicts casts the narrative fate of Ishmael in an intriguing light, due to the interpretive ambiguity of Yahweh's promise to Hagar about the fate of her son.

The promise that her son will be a wild ass of a man may indicate freedom. Ishmael's hand will be against everyone, but he will not be under anyone else's hand. Hand, a euphemism for power, retrieves and counters the theme of power and oppression symbolized by Sarai's hand. Despite a seemingly violent existence, Ishmael will not have to endure the humiliation "under a hand" that Hagar has endured (Fewell 2003, 44–66). Upon Hagar's return to affliction, the narrator says nothing but merely provides the formulaic report of birth (Gen 16:15–16). The narrator's ending, Trible notes, continues to undermine Hagar, restoring her name but silencing her voice, stressing not her motherhood but Abram's fatherhood. Patriarchy, Trible says, is well in control (Trible 1984, 19; see also Gossai 2010, 20). The conclusion to a scene otherwise focused on women resumes Abram's story. Ultimately, Fewell's (2003) reading, which combines the story in Gen 16 with its doublet in Gen 21, requires the human to work alongside the divine. The "God of seeing" has betrayed Hagar and does not insist on the "right thing" being done for her and her son. Rather, Fewell notes, the ending of Gen 21 is double edged. On the one hand, God is present and protects, yet, on the other hand, the notion of divine presence and protection permits the reader (as well as Abraham) not to worry about their welfare. Abraham provides nothing for his foreign wife and mixed child, thus sanctioning his (and God's) lack of generosity with the implicit response, "Don't worry. Leave it to God. The Hagars and Ishmaels of the world will be alright" (Fewell 2003, 52).

Ultimately, for Fewell (2003, 52), this text, which I view as a facial intertext with the Jabbok story, demonstrates the two-faced nature of the divine character as one who hears and is compassionate, elevating the oppressed to agency and subjectivity, but also as one who ultimately appears to sanction the well-being of the men (patriarchs) he chooses. Moreover, this intertext suggests a kind of complementary causation. In spite of the morally questionable things (in this case) the patriarch(s) does, God is behind it all, bringing about his desired plan or purpose. The actions of God appear to communicate that the ends justify the means. Human agency and divine will commingle, as in the story of Jacob. The alternate readings of the divine character by Fewell and Gossai demonstrate the various lenses through which the divine character may be read—this is a character who is protecting the interests of some over others, or this is a divine character who finds a way to bless each character if we look hard enough. Both readings are compelling for different reasons.

However we read the divine character in the Hagar story or in the Jabbok story, what is essential to note is this: the world of the story highlights the values of the culture. The Jabbok story highlights the narrative expendability of the women and the children. In other words, some faces are just more important than others, both to the narrator and to Jacob. This is demonstrated most clearly in Jacob's willingness to jeopardize the safety of his wives and children.

Faces on the Other Side of the River

In his examination of the Jabbok encounter, Frolov (2000, 56) critiques historical-critical, structuralist, and sociopolitical models that have neglected to mention the faces of women and children in Jabbok encounter. Scholars have long noted that the placement of the wives and their children reflect Jacob's preference for Rachel and Joseph. Frolov's reading highlights Jacob's actions as immoral and fear based, alleging that when he crosses his family over the Jabbok, he uses them as a "human shield." According to Frolov, the subsequent struggle at the Jabbok demonstrates a kind of narrative punishment for Jacob's mistreatment of his family. Frolov claims two things demonstrate the punitive nature of the encounter. First, the stories about the ancestors of Israel (Gen 12–35) tie together the promise of progeny and land; the attack, then, functions as the divine response to the patriarch's reluctance to defend his household. Second, Jacob's symbolic demotion in status is the immediate outcome of the encounter; he comes last of all in the caravan, demonstrating that because he neglected his duty, he is the most expendable member of the group (Frolov 2000, 57–58). Ultimately, Frolov asserts: "Viewed in a non-patriarchal perspective, the story of Jacob's return to Canaan becomes anti-patriarchal. Tacitly expressing the ancestor's cowardice, treachery and lack of faith, it graphically demonstrates that gender-based distribution of roles—that is, of power and expendability—not only degrades females but also corrupts males" (58). In the end, Jacob fails the test of patriarchy.

Frolov purports to examine the other side of the river, yet his reading merely gestures to the faces of the women and children involved. The patriarch—and patriarchy—remains his focus. Jacob's family is a tool used by Frolov to show that the narrator and/or God have censured patriarchy by wounding it at its procreative core. Rather than characterizing the faces "on the opposite side of the river," their faces are literally disfigured in Frolov's analysis. They remain in what Martin Buber and Levinas (1989b, 63) have both called "the sphere of the It." By remaining in the third person, the sphere of the It, they can be "disposed of" in the story world by Jacob. They can also be disposed of by the narrator, who in particular excludes the face of Dinah. Finally, they have been disposed of by interpreters who have not only ignored the ethical dimension of Jacob's actions with respect to his family but have, like the patriarch himself, considered these women and children to be narratively expendable. By focalizing the faces of these female characters and their children, I demonstrate that at the Jabbok, the faces of Jacob and his opponent are not the only ones that should be considered. Indeed, rather than attempting to determine the identity of only one face—the face of Jacob's opponent—imaginative space should be made to consider the multiplicity, the multiple faces involved, in the פנים ("face").

Given Rebekah's disdain for Esau's wives (Gen 26:34–35; 27:46–28:6), it is imperative that Jacob select a wife from among his kin (Vawter 1977, 297).[7] In the Hebrew Bible, foreign women are frequently a source of contention for the "good Israelite men" who marry them because these women shift loyalty from Yahweh to foreign deities (see Deut 7:1–6; 1 Kgs 11:1–8; Ezra 9:1–2; Neh 13:23–27). Ultimately, prophets such as Jeremiah, Ezekiel, and Hosea (e.g., Jer 3; Ezek 16; Hos 1–3) all blame destruction and exile on Israel and Judah's propensity for idol adultery. During the period of the reconstruction, the expulsion of foreign women and their children prevents the "holy seed" from being polluted.[8] Narratively, then, Rebekah's annoyance with Esau's foreign wives is not the angst of a mother-in-law; instead, her ire reflects xenophobia of all the Hagars, all the strange women, in the midst of the בני־ישראל (sons of Israel). Thus Jacob's (s)election of an Israelite wife is crucial to solve Rebekah's angst; at a deeper level, however, the eponymous ancestor of Israel must be remembered as one whose choice of wife was consonant with the ideology—the fears, anxiet-

---

7. Vawter notes that the Horites (and Hivites) are simply one of the names for the Canaanites in Genesis. While the Israelites became acquainted with the Hurrians at the time of their conquest of Canaan, it is fairly certain there were none in patriarchal times. Therefore, the wives of Esau, called Hittites, are most likely the Philistines of Gen 26, popular anachronisms with respect to the indigenous population.

8. The prophetic imagination depicts disagreement concerning who exactly was the "holy seed," the returnees or the remainees (see Jer 24:1–10; Isa 6:13).

ies, and convictions—of Yehud.[9] Fewell and Gunn maintain that Rebekah manipulates the ill-sighted Isaac's irritation with Esau's wives; they become the impetus for Jacob's send-off. Fewell and Gunn (1993, 75–76) state, "Of course, Rebekah has hit a sore spot with Isaac.... He hardly longs to have more Hittite women join his household. Rebekah's lament is a threat to his own peace.... Isaac may have the authority, but Rebekah has orchestrated the events. Jacob leaves, twice blessed, because of his mother's foresight and initiative." He escapes Esau's anger (Gen 27:41) because Rebekah convinces the passive Isaac that Jacob's leaving is in the family's best interests (27:46). As Fewell and Gunn point out, it is in Rebekah's best interests that God's plans come to fruition. As a man who represents the future, Jacob's safety—and later his safe return—are paramount to the continuance of Jacob's line (Fewell and Gunn 1993, 74).

Upon his arrival in the land of the "sons of the East" (Gen 29:1), Jacob approaches a well, a narrative signal that a betrothal is imminent. At first glance, Jacob and Rachel's meeting appears to be nothing more than a type scene (Gen 24:1–67; Exod 2:15–22). However, it is striking for the level of emotion it portrays— Jacob kisses Rachel and וישא את־קלו ויבך ("lifted up his voice and wept"). The narrator describes Rachel vividly: ורחל היתה יפת־תאר ויפת מראה ("and Rachel was beautiful of form and beautiful of appearance"). Moreover, Jacob is said to love Rachel, a rare expression in the Hebrew Bible, and it is this love for her that makes the seven years agreed on—a narrative signal for completion or perfection—seem בעיניו כימים אחדים ("in his eyes like a few days"). Even after being duped by Laban, Jacob agrees to work another seven years for Rachel. The narrator notes that Jacob loved Rachel more than Leah (Gen 29:30), and Yahweh saw that Leah was שנואה ("hated"). Fewell and Gunn (1993, 78) focalize the family dynamics through the eyes of the women:

> Rachel has beauty of form and *face*. By implication Leah is not so stunning. Leah, on the other hand, has "tender" eyes, affective, responsive eyes. In contrast, there seems to be nothing noteworthy about Rachel's eyes. Leah looks; Rachel is looked at. One woman, on account of the way men look at her, inspires love, but the other woman, on account of the way she looks at others, may actually be more capable of returning love.

---

9. Such a reading of course depends on a postexilic date for the redaction of Genesis.

However, Leah is never said to receive this love in return, even though she is, as Fewell and Gunn (1993, 78) note, "fertile to a fault." While Rebekah was also barren, Yahweh allowed her to conceive because Isaac prayed on her behalf; Yahweh is not said to take note of her condition prior to Isaac's intercession. Here, however, no one prays on behalf of Leah. In each naming of her son, she gives voice to the bereft nature of her existence. Overall, however, she is a silent participant in her own life. Perhaps, her quiet passivity compels Yahweh to hear not an outward cry (e.g., God in Exod 2:23–24) but a pain that dare not whisper its name. The result is an active response by Yahweh— he does not merely allow her to conceive, as he does with Rebekah. Here, Yahweh ויפתח ("opens") her womb. While the narrator describes Leah as having "weak eyes" (Gen 29:17) and as unloved by Jacob, her face is not invisible to Yahweh; he וירא ("sees/ notices") her pain.

Following the birth of her first son, Leah describes her life as one of עני ("affliction" or "poverty") and expresses a previously unvoiced hope—for the love of her husband. While Leah describes her life as one of affliction, she also recognizes that it is the Lord who looks on her affliction and responds (Gen 29:31–32). In the book of Job, Job's affliction is also noted. In Job, however, the tone around affliction is decidedly different, less about rejoicing about the Lord's removal of affliction and more about others who offer moralizing statements about why that affliction has taken place. In Job, it is Elihu who offers sermonizing statements about the nature of affliction and its intersection with God's deliverance and human iniquity. Elihu tells Job that God "delivers the afflicted by their affliction" (Job 36:15). Moreover, he also warns Job not to turn toward iniquity in the midst of his affliction; God is a teacher like no other (Job 36:21–22). Robert Martin-Achard states that עני (affliction) is a general expression for suffering in various forms: affliction, suffering, debasement, or oppression. The term may indicate individual suffering, such as Job's, Leah's, or Hagar's; it may also indicate the suffering of the children of Israel and the city of Jerusalem after the catastrophe of 587 BCE. Martin-Archard notes that in the majority of cases, the suffering of the people or the believer is depicted in relation to Yahweh: God cares about the suffering of his people and frees them from it (*TLOT* 2:934). Leah, with her tender eyes, is indeed seen by Yahweh, yet if freedom from her affliction means freedom from a family where she will always be unloved, she is never truly free.

When she conceives Simeon, her second son, she expresses similar gratitude to Yahweh—and for the first time, it is disclosed that Jacob's lack of love for her is noted not only by the narrator. She knows that she is שנואה (hated). The lack of Jacob's love is part of her self-description—she is the unloved one, or the hated one. The naming of her third son, Levi, demonstrates an augmentation of Leah's hope—that bearing three sons for Jacob will ילוה ("attach") him to her. The hope for this change in relationship, and the bearing of a fourth son, Judah, leads her to praise Yahweh, who has, in her estimation, allowed this to unfold. No description is given of Jacob's feelings about the birth of his sons, nor does the narrator comment about any change of feeling for Leah. Fewell and Gunn (1993, 78) affirm, "But instead of finding a place as wife and lover, her role as mother is reinscribed: she conceives and bears more sons." Leah is never attached to her husband; she is instead perpetually afflicted, impoverished, humbled, and humiliated by her status as the unloved wife. As Zornberg (1995, 211) notes: "Her tears generate her many children. For a formidable energy builds up in her, in her deprivation; she takes Rachel's place under the marriage canopy; and in the darkness, in which forms and structures become fluid.... Leah *becomes* Rachel." Just as Jacob masquerades as Esau, so too in the fluidity of the night, where faces fuse, Leah gives Jacob what Rachel cannot. Fed on countless caresses and countless hungers, Leah nevertheless tastes the bread of affliction (Deut 16:3).

As the etiological narrative of the twelve tribes of Israel continues to unfold, the naming of each son conveys the hopes, aspirations, and anxieties of both Rachel and Leah.[10] A familiar commingling of human agency and divine intervention allows both women to conceive multiple times, even in the wake of infertility and Jacob's passivity (Gen 30:2). While both Rachel and Leah take the initiative to give their slaves to Jacob, they nevertheless attribute their success to Elohim (God; Gen 30:6, 17–24). Throughout successive nights of competitive conceptions,

---

10. For Leah, Reuben exemplifies Yahweh's compassion for her affliction and the hope that her husband will love her; Simeon further demonstrates that Yahweh has heard that she is unloved; Levi, the hope that Jacob will attach himself to her; Judah, her praise to Yahweh for her success in conception; Gad represents the luck Leah feels in competition with Rachel; Asher's birth garners her communal respect; Issachar, her reward for giving her maid to Jacob; and Zebulun, a choice gift that will lead, she hopes, to her husband's exaltation of her. Rachel's children represent a spectrum of hopes and dreams as well: Dan represents Rachel's vindication over Leah; Naphtali is also named for the contest she waged with her sister; and Joseph, a final son who is added to her. Benjamin, whom Rachel calls Ben-Oni ("the son of my affliction"), is the last child born to Rachel before her death (Gen 35:16–20).

Jacob is voiceless, save for his exasperated statement that God is the one Rachel should blame for her inability to conceive (Gen 30:2). These scenes feature Jacob as a silent marionette controlled by his wives and by the reproductive whims of Elohim. Fewell and Gunn (1993, 78) note that it is Laban's trick toward Jacob that entraps the women in a system that forever pits them as enemies:

> Bound together in their marriage to Jacob, the women are like two prisoners chained together. Neither is able to escape the other. Used by their father to procure Jacob's labor, they are allowed no right to speak, no right to choose their mate or their future. They both live, wedded to Jacob, and therefore to each other, in "unwholly" matrimony.

While the wives' desire for children is voiced, Jacob remains largely silent about how he feels about his burgeoning family.

After Joseph is born, however, Jacob decides to journey home with his family en masse, as family tensions run high (Gen 31:1-3). Laban's face was not to him as it had been before (31:5). In her study of sight and insight in Genesis, Talia Sutskover (2013) notes that in the Jacob narrative, the phrase ראה פנים ("saw the face") holds special import. In Gen 31:5, Jacob says ראה אנכי את־פני אביכן ("I saw the face of your father"), yet "the God of my father has been with me." Sutskover notes, "This propinquity between Jacob's sight of Laban's face and the divine command to go back to Canaan (Gen 31:2, 3) may hint at a divine intervention, that God himself influenced Laban's expression, and thereby signaled to Jacob to take steps and leave" (165).

Whether God is the unseen impetus for the change in Laban's face or not, Jacob clearly constructs the story he tells his wives around divine intervention. After telling Rachel and Leah about a complicated dream—piled high with talk of Elohim (Gen 31:11, 13)—the women side with Jacob over their father. As Humphreys notes, Jacob constructs the situation in a way that all but forces his wives and children to come with him. Jacob's story is designed for the women to take sides, essentially cutting off all ties with their father—to leave Laban and their kinfolk, and come to a land that their husband will show them. Humphreys (2001, 183) asserts, "Jacob constructs his story within the story. It is a story that sets no middle ground.... Without overtly calling for it, he leaves them no choice but to choose. And he weights the options by placing God fully on his side and thereby against Laban."

Furthermore, Humphreys (2001, 183) says, God is woven into what transpires between Jacob and Laban, justifying his riches. Rachel and Leah answer as one: "Then Rachel and Leah answered him, 'Is there any portion or inheritance left to us in our father's house? Are we not regarded by him as foreigners? For he has sold us, and he has been using up the money given for us. All the property that God has taken away from our father belongs to us and to our children; now then, do whatever God has said to you'" (Gen 31:14–16). For Rachel and Leah, home and security are no longer with Laban—they are with Jacob. On him they place their hopes for a secure and lasting future. Moreover, it is a future dependent on Jacob's self-actualization, as Fewell and Gunn (1993, 77) affirm: "Indeed at the heart of Jacob's story is his struggle to divorce himself from his flesh (red) and his bone (white), that is, his kin, and to claim his own identity." Jacob attempts to take the family with him without telling Laban (Gen 31:17–18). In what he has called an itinerary or travel narrative, Thomas Brodie (2001, 320) notes that Jacob "sets his face" towards the mountain (Gen 31:21).[11] This geographical about-face, glimpsed through the contours of Jacob's face, is unsurprising given Jacob's penchant for running away. This time, however, Jacob does not run alone. He takes a caravan of faces along with him for the dangerous journey. Nevertheless, something of their affliction may prepare them for the difficulty of the journey ahead. It is this strength born from affliction, perhaps, that enables Leah, Rachel, and the children to go away from their father's house to the land that their (husband) will show them, uncertain whether blessing or death will follow (see Gen 12:1–3).

Yet to be determined is whether the women and children are anything more than property to Jacob (Gunn and Fewell 1993, 51). Laban accusatively calls them "captives of the sword" (Gen 31:26). In the ensuing conversation, Laban refers to them as belonging to him—"Then Laban answered and said to Jacob, 'The daughters are my daughters, the children are my children, the flocks are my flocks, and all that you see is mine. But

---

11. Brodie also draws a comparison with Luke's Jesus, who is said to "set his face" toward Jerusalem (Luke 9:51). Where in Luke, Brodie notes, the narrative turn is sharp, in Genesis the setting of the face is "late and enigmatic." Following Brodie's analysis, the overarching narrative presentation of Jacob is of one who is perpetually late, who follows "from behind." His gradual movement, or setting of the face, is narratively comprehensible due to his characterization. While Jacob's movement may be late, it is certainly not enigmatic.

what can I do today about these daughters of mine, or about their children whom they have borne?'" (Gen 31:43). Cultural norms would have viewed the women, children, and flocks as property. However, Laban's desire to bid his family farewell, as well as the pact that he makes with Jacob not to תענה ("afflict") them or add other wives (31:27–28, 50; 32:1), implies fatherly affection and protection. The pact certainly recognizes the impoverished (emotional) state of at least one of Jacob's wives. Brodie (2001, 324) affirms: "Laban's brief speech manages to use images that touch a wide range of the human heart's experiences and feelings: the agony of the women who are driven as prisoners of war, the celebration of music and song, the sweet sorrow of kissing goodbye." The scene is poignant: the covenant is cut, and a multiplicity of stones represent a multiplicity of faces. Nevertheless, in the next narrative sequence, Jacob's endangerment of these faces demonstrates that Laban's anxieties were well-founded.

In the sequences prior to and immediately following the Jabbok encounter, the women and children function either as Jacob's expendables or as his excuses. The obsequious language Jacob uses ("to my lord," Gen 32:5), as well as the מנחה ("presents," 32:14) he sends, demonstrates his anxiety. Moreover, after hearing that Esau is approaching with four hundred men, Jacob is ויירא יעקב מאד ("exceedingly afraid," Gen 32:8). Jacob's fear is well-grounded, since four hundred men is the size of a militia heading for battle (1 Sam 22:2; 25:13; 30:10; Zakovitch 2012, 96). For Brodie, Jacob's fear of death is central to the two-panel scene, which outlines his relationships both with Laban and also with Esau. "Shades of fear hover over Jacob's life. Real harm does not happen, but it comes close and has to be prevented, first by dream (31:24, 29; cf. 31:7), then by covenant (31:52)" (Brodie 2001, 322). In the case of Esau, Jacob responds to his fear through pragmatic and pious actions. As a result, Jacob divides his possessions into two camps, reasoning if Esau הכהו (smites) one, the other may escape. The use of the *hiphil* form of נכה (smite) suggests a violent attack, clearly in keeping with Jacob's assumption that Esau will יבוא והכני אם על־בנים ("come in and smite me, mother and children," Gen 32:11). This phrasing occurs in only one other biblical verse, the law that forbids taking both mother and offspring from a bird's nest (Deut 22:6–7), connoting "unparalleled brutality" (Zakovitch 2012, 98). Yet it is mother and children that he ויעברם ("takes across") ahead of him (Gen 32:24). Jacob prays for his own protection (Gen 32:12) and seeks his own favor: כי־אמר אכפרה פניו במנחה ההלכת לפני ואחרי־כן אראה פניו אולי ישא פני ("He said that I may cover his face with the gift to go toward his face; and after I will appear to his face, perhaps he will uplift his face,"

Gen 32:21). Jacob's actions violate the ברית (covenant) cut between Laban and himself (31:44), of which Yahweh and Elohim are witness. The cutting of the covenant, the covenantal language, and the sharing of the meal indicates that this was intended to be a formal, binding agreement between, in this case, two parties who have every reason to distrust one another. Jacob's actions demonstrate that Laban's fear that his daughters may be mistreated was apt—they are divinely given (33:5–6) property and apparently expendable. Indeed, Fewell and Gunn (1993, 80) ask:

> Does anyone prevail in a system that pits brother against brother, sister against sister, a system blithely sanctioned alternately by God's silence and God's arbitrary participation? The God of good and evil, who both blesses and cripples Jacob, also blesses and curses these women, on the one hand granting them renown as the two women who "together built up the house of Israel" (Ruth 4:11), but on the other forever marring their hopes of life and love with fragmentation, alienation, even death.

In order for Jacob to be an "I," he must be faced with a "Thou." Yet within the patriarchal system, this man and his divine patron are not met with a "here I am" on the part of these women. The system, of which Yahweh and Jacob are a part, silences them, and their faces remain barely visible.

After the encounter at the Jabbok, Jacob tells Esau that the women and children have been given to him as a result of Elohim's favor—חנן אלהים (Gen 33:5). When Esau inquires about the reason for המחנה (the camp) he has met, Jacob again uses the language of favor: ויאמר למצא־חן בעיני אדני ("And he said, 'to find favor in the eyes of my lord,' " Gen 33:8). When Esau protests that Jacob should keep what is his (33:9), it is unclear whether he meant the series of gifts Jacob previously sent (32:14–22) or whether Jacob intended to give his entire family or a portion of them to Esau as מנחה (present). In so doing, Jacob depicts himself as abased before the face of Esau, who acts like the divine, receiving his offering. Jacob's arrangement of his family (33:1–2)—with secondary wives and their children first, the unloved Leah and her children next, and the loved Rachel and Joseph last—does suggest an anxiety deep enough to consider such a plan, but also a hope that such a plan will prove unnecessary. Even if Jacob did not intend to give them as gift, he may have expected to use them as a visual reminder of the faces to whom Esau is linked.

Whatever the reasoning, Esau initially rejects Jacob's present. Jacob continues to press him using the language of favor: ויאמר יעקב אל־נא אם־נא מצתי חן בעיניך ולקחת מידי ("And Jacob said please, I pray, if I have found favor in your eyes, then you take from my hand," Gen 33:10). To see Esau's face, Jacob says, is like seeing the face of God. Thus Jacob presses Esau again, reasoning: כי־חנני אלהים וכי יש־לי־כל ("because God has favored me and because there is to me everything," 33:11). After urging him, Esau accepts. While Elohim ultimately delivers Jacob from Esau, effectively answering Jacob's prayer prior to the Jabbok struggle (32:12), Jacob's actions demonstrate that the women and children—his possessions—are easily discarded. Regardless of his "love" for Rachel (29:18–20), she is still a face forgotten in the face of Jacob's fear and cowardice. Indeed, Levinas (1989b, 73) casts a poignant reminder: "Is dialogue possible without *Fürsorge*?"[12] As a response to the essential misery of the Other, *Fürsorge* also gives genuine access to the Other. Jacob's love for Rachel is a love of narrative emotion, effusive in its expression but devoid of care for her being. For Leah, Bilhah, and Zilpah, even a nominal description of love or concern is absent.

The women and children are objects of Jacob's use once more following the Jabbok encounter. Still uncertain of Esau's change of heart, Jacob uses them as an excuse for why the two families cannot travel together: "Then Esau said, 'Let us journey on our way, and I will go alongside you.' But Jacob said to him, 'My lord knows that the children are frail and that the flocks and herds, which are nursing, are a care to me; and if they are overdriven for one day, all the flocks will die'" (Gen 33:12–13). Jacob convinces Esau to journey ahead, while he travels at the pace of the children and the cattle (33:14). Jacob never arrives at Seir but instead travels to Succoth and ultimately שלם (safely) to Shechem. Narratively, from this moment the women and children are largely defaced, save for mention of the rape of Dinah (Gen 34:1–7), Rachel's burial notice (35:16–21), and the list of Jacob's descendants who journey with him to Egypt during famine (46:5–27). Leah's death is not recorded, except to say that she is buried alongside Isaac and Rebekah (49:31). The faces of the women and children, never major players in the narrative anyway, recede into the background. Narratively, their faces are forgotten. They are literarily disfigured by the lack of subjectivity accorded to them by the narrator. Not only in the Jacob cycle but in the ancestral narratives as a whole, the women and children are narrative adornments, largely cast in similar facial molds. No thought is given to their feelings about journeying across the river alone, and neither Jacob nor the narrative as a whole inquires.

---

12. The German term *Fürsorge* deals with care, welfare, and solicitude.

Facing Peniel/Penuel, the Face of God

After Jacob sends his wives and children across the ford of the Jabbok, two faces remain—Jacob's and his opponent's. Before even arriving at Peniel, however, it seems that his opponent's face must necessarily fade into the night. When it comes to seeing the face of God in the Hebrew Bible, the seer will typically glimpse it "through a mirror darkly."[13] The cultural and theological anxiety surrounding encounters with the divine are well attested in the Hebrew Bible (Exod 33:20, 23; Judg 13:22), and spatial limitations preventing full disclosure are often mandated by the divine figure himself (Exod 3:5–6; 19:10–13; 33:20, 23). At other times, an individual stands, at times literally, at times figuratively, between the people and God (e.g., prophets, priests, or kings in Exod 20:18–21; 34:29–35; Num 11; 14; 1 Sam 8, to name a few). Second, even when an individual is said to have experienced some manifestation of God's presence, the multi(face)ted nature of the divine character precludes making definitive assessments about the nature of this character. For instance, is the angel of the Lord intended to be a figure wholly separate from, or strikingly analogous to, El or Elohim? At the Jabbok, is the איש (man) Jacob encounters (Gen 32:24) the same figure he later identifies as אלהים (God; 32:30)? Eighth-century prophet Hosea (re)imagines that the encounter occurred between Jacob and an angel (Hos 12:4). How similar or dissimilar are these manifestations or multiple faces of the divine character? At times, the (multi)plicity of faces portray opposing characteristics. On the one hand, the divine character appears to care about those who are oppressed and who cry out to him (e.g., Gen 4:10; 15:3–5; 18:22–33; 19:18–22; 21:17–21; Exod 2:23–25); on the other hand, his aid appears provisional and (s)elective (e.g., Gen 16:9; 19:26; 21:12–13). Moreover, even among those he (s)elects, the divine character appears willing to consider violent course correction (e.g., Gen 6:11–22; 7:22–23; 11:7–9; 19:1–26; 32:24–31; Exod 4:24; Num 11; 14; 16).

In Levinasian terms, the divine figure is an other, like the human. As such, the encounter with the divine, as with any other, is "a relationship with what always slips away" (Levinas 1989d, 49). Mystery, Levinas asserts, constitutes alterity. Levinas states, "The other as other is not here an object that becomes ours or becomes us; to the contrary, it withdraws into its mystery" (49). While the narrator claims Jacob has seen Elohim face to face, spatial,

---

13. See Yahwistic texts such as Gen 2–3; 4; 18 for exceptions.

temporal, and nominal parameters keep full disclosure at a distance. This character not only is invisible to the senses but is, more importantly, unable to be imagined fully. The struggle of pushing away and pulling toward, characteristic of wrestling; the night, which effectively conceals faces; and the refusal to yield his name—all conceal the face Jacob is said to "see" (Gen 32:31). While this God may be in danger of being physically pinned down, God refuses to be metaphysically pinned down (32:29).

For Levinas (1989d, 48), alterity makes the other *Other*: "The Other as Other is not only an alter ego: the Other is what I myself am not." Moreover, it is the Other's otherness that renders the *impossibility* of the face to face *possible* and allows for a (genuine) I-Thou relationship. The genuineness of this relationship, however, is dependent on the *mutuality* of being and the willingness for dialogue by both. Levinas (1989b, 66–67) states:

> It is impossible to remain a spectator of the Thou, for the very existence of the Thou depends on the "word" it addresses to me. And, it must be added, only a being who is responsible for another being can enter into dialogue with it. Responsibility, in the etymological sense of the term, not the mere exchange of words, is what is meant by dialogue, and it is only in the former case that there is meeting.

The face-to-face encounter at Peniel is the first time in the narrative that Jacob is compelled to say, "I am Jacob." Inside of this self-disclosure may rest a painful reality. Jacob's "I am" is no mere handshake—it is also an expression of guilt: "I am Jacob, a grasper." As Levinas (1989d, 49) says, identity recoils before its affirmation; it is not guilty per se, but accused and responsible for its presence. Jacob is forced to face the essential poverty or nudity of his own face, perhaps for the first time. His opponent poses the question that elicits Jacob's response; this dialogue places the two in an I-Thou relationship. Jacob is an I who is addressed by a Thou, Elohim/Ish (God/Man).

Strikingly, however, a Levinasian reading must acknowledge that the existence *even of Jacob's opponent* depends on Jacob. Jacob's opponent is a Thou only when faced by the face of another, an I. Both Jacob and Elohim/Ish speak each other into being at Peniel. While Levinas (1989d, 49) affirms the synonymous nature of alterity and mystery, this mystery (or transcendence) is also where ethical conversation begins. The ethical begins at the point where the I becomes conscious of the Thou as beyond itself (Levinas 1989b, 72).

The Thou does, indeed, stare Jacob in the face and offer him transcendence. Elohim/Ish is an "indeclinable nominative," a name that names but refuses to be named, a Face that appears but only in darkness (Levinas 1989a, 81). Yet there appears to be something of transcendence in Jacob, too. For if focalization and position is reversed—if Jacob is the Thou and Elohim/Ish the I, then Elohim/Ish appears to admit weakness: "Let me go, for the day is breaking" (Gen 32:26). Jacob appears to possess power over his opponent, the (possible) ability to release or to kill. When their positions are inverted, it is Elohim/Ish who faces Jacob's face and implores, "Thou shalt not kill" (Levinas 1985, 89). Levinas states:

> There is first the very uprightness of the face, its upright exposure, without defense. The skin of the face is that which stays most naked, most destitute. It is the most naked, though with a decent nudity. It is the most destitute also: there is an essential poverty in the face; the proof of this is that one tries to mask this poverty by putting on poses, by taking on a countenance. The face is exposed, menaced, as if inviting us to an act of violence. At the same time, the face is what forbids us to kill. (86)

A moment of pity exists in this *Zwischen* (between the two), where Jacob is even responsible for the face of God, where even the face of God is rendered exposed, vulnerable, to Jacob's *Auffassen*. For Levinas, *Auffassen* (understanding) has always been a *Fassen* (gripping). Even in his name—יעקב—Jacob's mode of being in the world is violent. He knows through usurpation, or grasping. A prima facie reading demonstrates that Jacob's understanding or knowledge of the Face before him comes through a violent seizure, a wrestling match, in which Elohim/Ish must beg for release (Gen 32:26). However, Zornberg notes that in Hebrew, *grasping* is not an odious word. It does not necessarily connote violence but rather fascination (Moyers 1996, 286). Grasping is therefore Jacob's fascination with or "hunger" for, in Levinasian terms, he knows not what, which catalyzes his actions.

Nevertheless, it appears that Jacob's prayer is actually the catalyst for the face to face:

> And Jacob said, "O God of my father Abraham and God of my father Isaac, O Lord who said to me, 'Return to your country and to your kindred, and I will do you good,' I am not worthy of the least of all the steadfast love and all the faithfulness that you have shown to your servant, for with only my staff I crossed this Jordan; and now I have become

two companies. Deliver me, please, from the hand of my brother, from the hand of Esau, for I am afraid of him; he may come and kill us all, the mothers with the children. Yet you have said, 'I will surely do you good, and make your offspring as the sand of the sea, which cannot be counted because of their number.'" (Gen 32:9–12)

Among other things, prayer may also function as a means for understanding and therefore "gripping" the divine. There is, after all, something of wrestling involved in the posture of prayer. Jacob's prayer, here and also at Bethel (Gen 28:20–22), is an attempt, perhaps not to wrestle but to wrest a blessing out of God. It is blessing, after all, that Jacob continually seeks. For Samuel Balentine, Jacob's prayer continues the "general narrative portraiture" of Jacob, the "supplanter," the "grasper," the "exploiter." Characterizing Jacob's prayer as caricature or parody, Balentine (2000, 64) states that "Jacob's prayer represents but one of several attempts to control his own destiny through a shrewd combination of cunning and piety." Certainly, Jacob's narrative characterization of one who is manipulative is in play here. Equally important, Jacob's prayer, itself an act of gripping a face, catalyzes their meeting. Therefore, Jacob throws the first (symbolic) blow, not the Face. Even the Face is rendered vulnerable to Jacob's *Auffassen*, even as he resists (Gen 32:26) and ultimately escapes totalization, while simultaneously blessing and wounding Jacob.

What, then, *is exposed* at Peniel, the Face of God? In the words of Levinas (1985, 86), what is exposed at the Face of God is signification without context; the essential nudity or poverty of two faces, devoid of other signifiers, is exposed. For Levinas, all that is within one's passport, so to speak—profession, family relationships, accomplishments, manner of dress and speech—are null and void in the nudity of the face. Face is meaning all by itself. Face leads beyond (86–87); it is multiplicity, simultaneously containing yet uncontained by (even transcending) all that both have brought with them to the Face of God—their identities, their interactions with others in the narrative, and their interactions with one another. The Face of God transcends Peniel, the place named the Face of God. Even as the Face of God contains Peniel, it is not limited to this geographical locale. This character has left traces of himself in the echo of Isaac's prayer (Gen 25:21); in the slick darkness of Rebecca's womb (25:21–26); in the manipulative, trickster antics of Jacob toward Esau and Laban (25:30–34; 27:1–40, 30:25–43), seemingly propelled by the trickster oracle at the beginning of the Jacob cycle (25:23); and in the movable property Jacob acquires (33:11). Even as the Face of God contains the iterations the divine character(s) brought to Peniel, such as El, Elohim, the angel of the Lord, he too is not contained by them. The faces—of both Jacob and Jacob's opponent—are oneness that contains multiplicity. This complexity underscores the mystery of the faces that meet at the Jabbok.

In his monograph on beauty and the enigma, Landy notes the chthonic blurriness between mystery and death. Landy (2001, 44) states, "Mystery is beautiful when it is not terrible. Beauty is never far from death, either, for we long to humanize what we most fear." A vacillation occurs between that which is man and Elohim, that which cannot possibly be man. The Face of the Other—whose beauty can only be seen from far away, Landy contends—is also a Face that bids Jacob not to kill, even as that Face also holds the possibility of killing Jacob. That Face contains all the expressions and emotions of the faceless specters Jacob has carried with him—love, longing, and loss; fear and pain; betrayal and duplicity; piety, protection, and provision.[14] The Face is at once otherworldly and this-worldly; at once monstrous, able to kill, and plaintively beautiful, begging not to be killed. Mystery and multiplicity cohere in the Face.

Philologically speaking, פנים ("face") is itself a multiplicity. According to the *Theological Lexicon of the Old Testament*, this noun is only dual in form. The editors delineate six usages of פנים in the Hebrew Bible: "face" in the proper sense; "appearance" and so on in an expanded usage; "glance" (with the eyes); "person, someone"; "anterior, surface," in a figurative meaning; and various prepositional uses (*TLOT* 2:997). The originally biradical stem *pan* is attested in all branches of the Semitic language. As a verb, the stem occurs in the Hebrew *pnh* ("to turn"); in the Aramaic *pny* ("to turn, return"); the Akkadian *panû* ("to turn, take the lead"); in the Arabic *faniya* ("to pass away"); and in the Ethiopian *fannawa* ("to go away") (995). Philology and philosophy cohere at Peniel, the Face of God. The face, which is a synecdoche for the person's whole being (1001), is also that which is always already turning and returning, passing by, going away. At once the "mirror of the soul" (Sir 13:25) yet also producing a darkened image (1 Cor 13:12), the face is always already eluding, escaping, evading the "grasp" of the Other, even at the meeting of face to face. The פנים ("face") is like the חבל—that which is "merest breath," that which

---

14. This occurs through Jacob's defacing of the real faces in front of him: e.g., Esau, Isaac, Rachel, Leah, and Laban.

appears only to disappear again. While whole person meets whole person, the meeting does not contain the person, for according to Levinas (1989b, 66), *(hu)man is meeting*. The (per)son is that which goes *per*—through—that meeting. Yet it is for the purpose of meeting that face meets face, as Levinas (1985, 87) affirms that the face and discourse are connected. And it is discourse that occurs at Peniel; indeed, it is discourse that is the purpose of Peniel. Peniel is where Jacob must respond to his right to be. A word is spoken out into the void, rendering null and void everything save face meeting face, rendering null and void everything save the Face containing and transcending every other face, and rendering null and void everything save the address and its required response. The Face renders what is impossible—seeing the Face of God and living (Exod 33:20)—possible through the Face that begins all discourse. Jacob can respond to his right to be only in facing that Face. Brodie (2001, 332) says that the wound "contains" the greater world of blessing. Likewise, here the Face contains all the faces in Jacob's (narrative) field, even his own. Only in responding to the word spoken into the void can Jacob address the poses he has put on, remove the masks/other faces he has worn and deceived, and face the multiplicity of the פנים (face).

Even if his opponent refuses to be pinned down, Jacob is not too afraid to face him and to say what he wants—blessing and safety. In grasping both Esau's birthright (Gen 25:31-33) and his blessing (27:18-19), Jacob (and later Rebekah) demonstrates that it is familial, material, and spiritual primacy that he desires. He desires the economic/material gain that accompanied reception of the birthright (Deut 21:17), and he desires the relational intimacy given by the blessing of a father who is said only to love Esau. Upon meeting Esau after the Jabbok encounter, Jacob announces that he has been given everything: "'Please accept my gift that is brought to you, because God has dealt graciously with me, and because I have everything I want.' So he urged him, and he took it" (Gen 33:11). Jacob has always desired blessing, which he reiterates at Peniel: "I will not let you go, unless you bless me" (32:26). At Bethel, however, another dimension of Jacob's desire surfaces: "If God will be with me, and will keep me in this way that I go, and will give me bread to eat and clothing to wear, so that I come again to my father's house in peace, then the LORD shall be my God" (28:20-21). Jacob desires to return in peace (ושבתי בשלום). From the hollow verb שוב, Jacob's "return" may imply merely a geographical return to the home of his father; but the semantic range of שוב also allows for a return that reorients behavior (Holladay

1972, 362–64).¹⁵ The text remains unclear whether Jacob desires a (re)turn, a reorientation of the face, to something he has never known—a life of peace between him and Esau—or whether he simply wants to go back home. In his prayer to Yahweh, who he refers to as the "God of my father Abraham and God of my father Isaac" (Gen 32:9), Jacob also reiterates the desire he demonstrated at Bethel—that God הצילני ("deliver me"). The use of this *hiphil* imperative suggests a causative nuance to Jacob's plea—"cause me to be delivered from the hand of my brother, from the hand of Esau" (32:12). Now, Jacob's perpetual lateness—continually following from behind—cannot save him. He must meet his brother פנים אל־פנים ("face to face"). No longer will his duplicity, grasping, or following heel to toe deliver him from Esau; only this God of Abraham and God of Isaac can cause him to be delivered. His desire is also an expression of his lack. His hunger is for something that he cannot procure for himself; it exceeds his grasp. And yet there is in Jacob's mind's eye ... a face. For Fokkelman (1975, 206), it is the face—פנים—that he effusively labels "the most radiant key-word in the story of Jacob." Fokkelman avers that Jacob's "intentions" are found in the verse preceding the struggle, where Jacob's language is decidedly facial: "For he said to himself, 'Let me cover up his face (*pānāw*) with the present that goes before my face (*pānāy*). Afterwards I shall see his face (*pānāw*). Perhaps he will lift up my face (*pānāy*).' The present passed on before his face (*pānāw*)" (Gen 32:21) (Fokkelman 1975, 206). However, Fokkelman views Jacob's intentions at reconciliation as ultimately fruitless:

> For Jacob wants to see Esau's face after he himself has covered it up (the Hebraic metaphor for atonement).... Esau is meant to be overwhelmed by the present. How, then, is he to lift up Jacob's face (forgive)? If his face is covered up, can Jacob come and see eye to eye with him? Of course not. Such a reconciliation was impossible to begin with. (208)

---

15. Holladay offers this central meaning for שוב: "having moved in a particular direction, to move thereupon in the opposite direction, the implication being (unless there is evidence to the contrary) that one will arrive again at the initial point of departure" (1958, 53). While שוב is the word used in the Bethel text (Gen 28:20–21), theologically speaking, Jacob is not actually "returning." He is, instead, "facing," in keeping with the sense of פנים, whose etymological resonances, according to BDB 819, include not a (re)turning but rather a "turning," a movement inside and out.

Indeed, the impossibility of genuine reconciliation between them may be affirmed by Jacob's unwillingness to travel home with his brother after they meet (Gen 33:15–20). Moreover, as Gunn and Fewell claim, biblical characters speak like people in real life; they are also frequently prejudiced and self-serving. Public situations do not necessarily reveal the private person, and threatening situations can also color a character's speech (Gunn and Fewell 1993, 69). Here, the narrator's voice appears to dissuade a face-value reading of Jacob's words. Both Esau and the reader, Gunn and Fewell contend, are led by Jacob's speech to believe he will follow Esau to his home: "What we discover from this discrepancy between speech and action is that Jacob, for all his desire to placate Esau, is still the deceiver, concerned for his security, but hardly his integrity" (72).

As Levinas (1989b, 65) claims, each new meeting reconstitutes being. Even following the Jabbok encounter, Jacob's being is reinscribed, not as Israel, but as Jacob, deceiver. Esau's face, however, is merely one of the faces for which Jacob must acknowledge responsibility. Levinas's (1989a, 83) lengthy description is worth quoting in full:

> But, in its expression, in its mortality, the face before me summons me, calls for me, begs for me, as if the invisible death that must be faced by the Other, pure otherness, separated, in some way, from any whole, were my business. It is as if that invisible death, ignored by the Other, whom already it concerns by the nakedness of its face, were already "regarding" me prior to confronting me, and becoming the death that stares me in the face. The other man's death calls me into question, as if, by my possible future indifference, I had become the accomplice of the death to which the other, who cannot see it, is exposed; and as if, even before vowing myself to him, I had to answer for this death of the other, and to accompany the Other in his moral solitude. The Other becomes my neighbor precisely through the way the face summons me, calls for me, begs for me, and in so doing recalls my responsibility, and calls me into question.

Jacob's treatment of each of these faces is foregrounded at the Jabbok. In the face of Elohim/Ish, Jacob must answer for them all.

The Face of All Faces

Here, the Face that summons Jacob is the Face that represents all the human faces in the story. The face that summons Jacob is first Esau's face.

As a twin, Esau's face presents Jacob with a not-so-alien alterity. Esau's face is a face he recognizes. If the face that summons Jacob is a face that says, "Thou shalt not kill," here in the darkness of night Jacob is faced with the real possibility that he has, in fact, killed Esau symbolically. In his study of ethics in the book of Genesis, Burton Visotzky (1996, 148) avers, "The real blessing Jacob has robbed from Esau is his father.... Esau cries for his own loss of innocence.... He cries for the loss of his father, who appears to be an all-too-willing party to this deception.... He cries as he realizes that whatever blessing he may wrest from his father, it is time to leave home, it is no longer his." When Jacob deceives Isaac, the real victim is Esau. The face that summons Jacob second is Isaac's face, a face he has deceived, and one of pure nudity and vulnerability that he has exposed and violated. He has bid adieu to Isaac's face because his own existence has caused too much pain to stay, and if he stayed it would have caused additional pain, with one brother fulfilling the threat of killing the other.

The face that summons Jacob third is the face of Leah, unloved and held captive to a patriarchal system that she cannot escape but occasionally subverts (Gen 30:9, 16). The face that summons Jacob fourth is the face of Rachel, who summons him: "Give me children, or I shall die!" (30:2). As Fewell and Gunn (1993, 79) maintain, "Here lies the poignant trap of patriarchal motherhood: women face social death without children and physical death to bear children. The risks and the sorrows, the ambiguities and the ironies, are all but passed over in the rush to tell a man's story." Despite this reality, Jacob's answer is a dismissive rebuff: "Am I in the place of God, who has withheld from you the fruit of the womb?" (Gen 30:2). Despite the narrator's comment that Jacob loves Rachel, even prior to placing her in a caravan of the faceless, he appears unsympathetic to her plight. And while God has heard their cries, he too is implicated, like Jacob, whom he supports, in the women's struggles. Fewell and Gunn (1993, 79–80) affirm:

> While Jacob "struggles with beings both divine and human and yet prevails" (Gen. 32:28), Rachel and Leah merely struggle with each other. While Jacob confronts God face to face, Rachel and Leah can only confront each other. Which is the more profound struggle? Rachel says, "Struggles of God I have struggled with my sister and I have prevailed" (30:8). Indeed God has been there, opening and closing wombs, taking the side of the oppressed, but at the same time sanctioning their oppression. Just as Jacob declares to Esau, "Seeing your face is like seeing the face of God" (33:10), so too after his turbulent encounter with "the face

of God" (32:30), we must wonder, is there much difference between struggling with God and struggling with one's sister?

Furthermore, Visotzky (1996) raises questions about the sincerity of Jacob's love for Rachel in the first place. He points to a subtle inclusion of economics alongside the acquisition of Rachel as wife. Visotzky states: "The scene is even more subtle in its reportage, for Jacob does not only notice Rachel's beauty, he also notices Laban's flocks. It is a small but telling point.... This time Jacob, fleeing Canaan, counts Laban's wealth in flocks" (163). The face that summons Jacob fifth is the face of Laban, with whom he has been trapped in a codependent relationship of deception. As Visotzky adds, "Little does [Jacob] suspect, when greeted by Uncle Laban's kiss and hug, that he himself is being frisked and cased. As the rabbis said it many centuries ago, 'When Laban kisses you, count your teeth afterward'" (163–64).

The face that summons him last of all in the narrative is the Face of Elohim, a mysterious and dark countenance he encounters throughout the narrative and, most notably, one night at the Jabbok. In looking into the face of Elohim, Jacob looks into his own face, as Zornberg (1995, 240) affirms: "Jacob must expose himself to fear, to face-to-face encounter with what he most dreads. He must confront the nameless horror of the man who grips him, binds him arm and leg, if he is to acquire the partial freedom of a limping hero, who has learned his new name—and incidentally, the mirror identity of the face of his dread." In looking into the face of Elohim, Jacob looks into the Face of all faces. He is responsible for them all. Every face, whether loved for its "shapely beauty" or despised for its "weak eyes," wears the same expression, "Thou shalt not kill." He is responsible for their lives and their deaths before he can claim his own existence, his own being. He has worn, stolen, killed their lives, their faces. He is responsible for their deaths, for all the ways in which each of them has silently bid him not to kill. Here, Jacob is himself faced with the possibility of death.

"Prior to death there is always a last chance; this is what heroes seize, not death" (Levinas 1989d, 73). But Jacob is no hero. He looks into the Face of all faces and demands more than a last chance—he demands the blessing that has already been promised to him by the Other who has been behind him all along (Gen 32:27). He will ultimately receive this blessing of "everything." As he later implores Esau, "'Please accept my gift that is brought to you, because God has dealt graciously with me, and because I have everything I want.' So he urged him, and he took it" (33:11). God has, in fact, "favored" Jacob all along. Here in the darkness, with death staring him in the face, Jacob receives not death but, once again, the blessing he demands. Jacob does not get what he deserves—he receives grace instead. It is painful grace, but it is grace, nevertheless.

But grace is not given here without the expectation of some kind of response. Rather than bestowing an unambiguous blessing on Jacob and taking his leave, the Face lingers a while longer, leans in closer, and requires a response. In Derridian terms, perhaps Jacob's self-revelation was a kind of surrender: "To surrender to the other, and this is the impossible, would amount to giving oneself over in going toward the other, to coming toward the other but without crossing the threshold, and to respect, to loving even the invisibility that keeps the other inaccessible" (Derrida 1995b, 74). Scholars have variously spoken of a kind of conversion that Jacob undergoes in this encounter. It is surely not a conversion in the religious sense that leads to a moral change but rather another kind of conversion, a turning of face toward face.[16] A con*ver*sion is a turning toward the Other, just as in the Hebrew "face" (פנים) denotes a similar kind of movement, an inside motion (BDB, 819). This turning of face toward face in the midst of movement against (wrestling) and movement toward allows for the real blessing Jacob receives—a new name, Israel, God-striver and one who has striven with all the faces in the narrative, including his own. The blessing is not in knowing the name of the Face standing before him, for the Face rightly resists such signification. To pin down the name exactly, like assigning one Face to the Face Jacob wrestled, is to limit, reduce to a signifying trace. Here, in the dark, to save the name is to save the Face. It is, after all, Jacob's face that the Face of all faces is most concerned with. For Levinas (1985, 92), the Face of the Infinite is in fact a trace of all the faces. The possibility of this interaction engenders desire:

> In the access to the face there is certainly also an access to the idea of God.... "For my part, I think that the relation to the Infinite is not knowledge, but a Desire." A desire cannot be satisfied; a desire nourishes itself by its own hungers and is augmented by consummation; and desire is like a thought that thinks more than it thinks, or more than what it thinks.

---

16. For one could argue quite strongly that Jacob does not change much morally.

For Jacob, who has everything, this is the blessing of the face to face: to see into the Face of all faces and to desire the one thing he lacks—a face of his own. It is in the name change—and paradoxically, in the wound—that he is individuated from the faces he has sacrificed and worn. It is in the Face to face encounter that he is individuated and able to face Esau with a face of his own, recognizing in his estranged brother the Face of all faces: "Jacob said, 'No, please; if I find favor with you, then accept my present from my hand; for truly to see your face is like seeing the face of God—since you have received me with such favor'" (33:10). The Face of all faces has given a gift to one who has not deserved it—by showing, once again, favor. The Face of all faces is, after all, obligated—*such an act is necessary*. Nevertheless, for all the poetic possibilities offered at the Face of God, the realities of facing life with God on the other side of the Jabbok loom large. Jacob's language and behavior toward Esau are ambiguous, even following the Jabbok encounter; so too is the relationship between the nation and its god, who continues to hold the potential to kill or to offer blessing.

Nanette Stahl (1995) notes that in the context of Israelite history, the Peniel/Penuel encounter surely points to the ambiguity of this necessity, at times sensing that God is on Israel's side, truly orchestrating blessing, and at others fully aware of the trauma of the exile. Thus, Israel's narrative memory as one who strives with God, strives with humankind, and prevails is the hope of blessing; it is the hope of God's obligation. For Stahl and Michael Fishbane, the legal addendum (Gen 32:33) is a perennial reminder that Jacob/Israel has been made vulnerable in its most intimate of places; it is a staunch reminder and reflection of the ambiguity of Israel's relationship to God in the wake of exile. Stahl (1995, 85–86) writes,

> If the night is a symbol of danger and possible death, the rising sun that greets [Jacob] as he crosses the river (32:32) celebrates his transformation into Israel, eponymous father of God's chosen nation.... Yet the legal addendum does not confirm that transformation; rather it reverses the process, and calls into question that which had seemingly already been promised. Contradiction and opposition [wrestling] are thus present in both the narrative of the struggle and its legal etiological conclusion.

The rising sun is a representation of the hope for God's favor but an acknowledgment of the ambiguity of that favor in light of Israel's literary history. And, it should be added, it is an acknowledgment of this ambiguity in light of the larger postexilic reality the story represents.

3
The Wound

You oppose me to myself. How could I ever win this fight?

Defeat is the price agreed upon.
       —Edmond Jábes, *The Book of Questions*

The patriarch Jacob is often depicted as a man of victory—he wrestles with God and with men and prevails. Yet the Jabbok encounter does not conclude with an image of robust victory. Instead, a wounded Jacob is left limping. Near the end of his life, Israel's eponymous ancestor describes his days as few and evil (Gen 47:9). Moreover, the narrative does not deliver a burial notice for Jacob typical of the patriarchs.[1] He does not die "old and contented," nor is he buried at a "ripe old age."[2] The self-reflection of the

---

  1. Abraham's burial notice is described in the following way: "Abraham breathed his last and died in a good old age, an old man and full of years, and was gathered to his people. His sons Isaac and Ishmael buried him in the cave of Machpelah, in the field of Ephron son of Zohar the Hittite, east of Mamre, the field that Abraham purchased from the Hittites. There Abraham was buried, with his wife Sarah" (Gen 25:8–10). Similarly, Isaac's burial is described this way: "Now the days of Isaac were one hundred eighty years. And Isaac breathed his last; he died and was gathered to his people, old and full of days; and his sons Esau and Jacob buried him" (35:28–29). Jacob's burial notice, however, is terse by comparison, failing to describe his life as "old and contented" or that he died at a "ripe old age." Instead, the narrative describes Jacob's death in this way: "When Jacob ended his charge to his sons, he drew up his feet into the bed, breathed his last, and was gathered to his people" (49:33).

  2. While both Jacob and the narrative, on the one hand, depict his final days in this way, admittedly, a counterreading also exists. That Jacob lives to be 147 years old (Gen 47:28), dies surrounded by a superabundance of male heirs, and is buried with his ancestors (49:29–32) is also an inescapable narrative reality. By the standards of the ancient Near East, his is surely not just a good death but an idyllic death.

aged patriarch, as well as his narrative epitaph, depicts Jacob not as a man of victory but as a man of defeat. Jacob's is a life of deep suffering, and after the struggle is said and done, Jacob's wound remains.

Using the poststructuralist insights of Lacan, I examine three different wounds in the Jabbok story: those of the characters Jacob and Elohim (God)/Ish (man), and those of the community telling the story. First, I argue that Jacob is wounded *before* arriving at the Jabbok. In attempting to grasp at objects—birthrights, blessings, movable property, wives and children—and the identity of Esau, Jacob is cut or disassociated from himself. He is constrained by the desires of the visible others in the story world, as well as by the discourse of the Other—here the storytellers—who impose their desires on him. Jacob is wounded, full of holes, before being wounded at the Jabbok. Second, I maintain that, just as Jacob is full of holes, so too is Elohim/Ish. God displays a profound relationality at the Jabbok, grasping at Jacob to fill an invisible lack for he knows not what. The assailant's invisibility correlates to the impassibility, the impossibility, the invisible nature of his own deferred desire. Here God is not only wounded—God is the Wound.[3] In drawing on the socionarratological insights of Frank, I suggest that the wounds in the story are not only individual but also communal. For Frank (1997, 183), a wound serves as the source of suffering stories. Suffering stories in general—and this particular story of suffering—are told not only by individuals but by a community of wounded storytellers. Thus Jacob's wound is polyvalent—it is about the wounds sustained by a man, before and after the Jabbok encounter—and also a testimony by the Israelites of their deep *agōn*, their deep suffering, at the hands of one who is said to have inscribed them on the palms of his hands (Isa 49:16). Jacob's wound is the source of Israel's story, embodied in his individual body and memorialized through communal (non)practice (Gen 32:32).

Like the Jabbok text itself, Jacob's wound continues to testify, creating possibility for what Levinas and Frank have called a "half-opening."[4] This

---

3. In this chapter, when I capitalize *Wound*, I refer to Jacob's wrestling partner, who is named by the narrator as איש ("man") and by Jacob as אלהים ("God"). The character himself, however, resists such signification, choosing instead to be known not by a name but rather by an action—as one who wounds his wrestling partner. When I use a lowercase spelling of wound, I refer to the wound Jacob or other characters in the story sustain.

4. Frank draws on Levinas (1988, 158). Levinas queries: "Is not the evil of suffering—extreme passivity, impotence, abandonment and solitude—also the unassumable

half-opening does not attempt to suture the wounds of the man or the nation by (re)interpreting the Jabbok encounter as victorious. Instead, in drawing on Lacan and Frank, I allow Jacob's wound to remain open. A Lacanian excess continues to testify to the defeat of a man and the suffering of a nation.

Jacob's Wound

In his psychoanalytical analysis of the Jacob cycle, Klitsner (2009, 38) describes Jacob's story as a "struggle for wholeness." Klitsner's phrasing is aptly chosen, as Jacob and Esau "struggle together, kick and shove one another, crush one another," even in the womb, an iterative and violent action suggested by the *hithpolel* stem (יתרצצו, Gen 25:22). For Klitsner, wholeness and human autonomy are synonymous. He maintains that Jacob's struggle for human autonomy can be traced "by reading between the lines, by noting trauma, resistance, cognitive dissonance, and repression, and by discerning compulsive repetition, slips of the tongue, dreams as expressions of the unconscious, and the therapeutic effect of transference" (Klitsner 2009, 38). When viewed through this psychoanalytical lens, and specifically Lacanian thought, Jacob appears wounded even prior to the Jabbok encounter. Jacob's wound precludes him from taking hold of his own life *as Jacob*. Instead, he is a man "split in two," as his behavior and slips of the tongue suggest. It is this disintegration that the Wound uncovers at the Jabbok. In taking him to what Lacan (1977, 7) has called the "ecstatic limits of 'thou art that,'" in saying his name, "I am Jacob" (Gen 32:27), Jacob experiences an ironic reversal of his wounds, even as he is wounded once more. Name calling is a facing of his own wounding and of the ways in which he has wounded others. And it is a taking stock of this pattern of wounding and of being wounded that allows Jacob to receive both the Wound—God—and the wound that God offers to him—a limp that will remain with him for the rest of his life.

---

and thus the possibility of a half-opening, and more, precisely, the possibility that wherever a moan, a cry, a groan or a sigh happen there is the original call for aid, for curative help, for help from the other ego whose alterity, whose exteriority promises salvation?" In Frank's reading of Levinas, nameless suffering is not given meaning, but neither does that suffering remain useless. Frank says that while Levinas rightly avers that suffering remains useless, nameless, and untouched, suffering is also, in its call to others, not useless. For everyone rendered other by suffering, perhaps in that act of witness some nameless suffering is opened. It is, for both Levinas and Frank, the *possibility* of a half-opening.

Prior to the Jabbok struggle, however, Jacob both acquiesces to and colludes in behavior(s) that squelch his subjectivity. His actions are characteristic of his name: he attempts to grasp at objects—birthrights, blessings, movable property, wives, and children. None of these objects can quench desire, yet each of them *represents* the *objet petit a*. Dylan Evans (1996, 38) clarifies, "The *objet petit a* is not the object towards which desire tends, but the cause of desire. Desire is not in relation to an object, but a relation to a lack." Every *thing* that Jacob grasps demonstrates that he is lacking something deeper than the thing itself. Jacob grasps for things, which signifies his lack. Yet even in his grasping, Jacob's unconscious fears and desires manifest themselves. Each narrative step taken by Jacob deepens his wound, even as it transitions him, ironically, toward *devenir*, coming into being. Focalizing the unconscious demonstrates the polyvalence of Jacob's wound.

Lacan's (1977, 312) explication of the unconscious is worth quoting in full:

> The unconscious is *discours de l'Autre* (the discourse of the Other), in which the *de* is to be understood in the sense of the Latin *de* (objective determination): *de Alio in oratione* (completed by: *tua res agitor*). But we must also add that man's desire is the *désir de l'Autre* (the desire of the Other) in which the *de* provides what grammarians call the subjective determination, namely, that it is *qua* Other that he desires (which is what provides the true compass of human passion). That is why the question *of* the Other, which comes back to the subject from the place which he expects an oracular reply in some such form as "*che vuoi*?," "what do you want?," is the one that best leads him to the path of his own desire.

Discourse and desire are both part of Lacan's understanding of the unconscious. The discourse of the Other wounds the subject, causing an unavoidable alienation from the self. For Lacan, the Other is the symbolic order—the language a subject is born into and must learn to speak in order to articulate desire. The subject is trapped in these spoken and unspoken discourses. She is shaped not only by her nascent desires but especially through the imposed desires and demands of others. Caught in discourse yet severed from her own desire, the subject unfolds, be-comes, in the locus of the Other. This causes an unavoidable alienation; for Lacan, "alienation is destiny" (Homer 2005, 72). The weight of language's inscription on the subject is inescapable. On the other hand, the demand(s) and discourse(s) of the Other send the subject on a winding quest to discover

3. The Wound

desire, lack, and subjectivity. It is this lack—what Lacan (1977, 230) called the *manque à être* (want-to-be)—that sets the Jacob cycle in motion and undergirds the narrative as a whole.

The Jacob cycle opens with lack, ויעתר ("and he prayed," Gen 25:21), the pleading of Isaac on behalf of his barren wife. Rebekah, a barren ancestress, takes her place among matriarchs and other women whose wombs must be opened by Yahweh.[5] Jacob's story, like his body, is intertwined with Rebekah's at the deepest level. His body is entwined with her umbilical cord, and his life attempts to fulfill her lack. Klitsner views Rebekah's as a "consuming" love that severs Jacob from his own identity. He states, "Perhaps it is precisely the unconditional, and all-embracing character of her love that leaves Jacob with what we shall discern as a persistent sense of lack of entitlement. It is a love that is based on Rebekah's vision.... It is not a love that is dependent upon or reflective of Jacob's fulfillment of his autonomous self" (Klitsner 2009, 51–52). The consuming character of Rebekah's love precludes Jacob from self-actualization. Klitsner (52) adds, "It is therefore a love that leaves him hungry and desperate for another kind of love, for the blessing of a father who seems to love only Esau." For Lacan, every human subject is a wounded subject. Klitsner's use of hunger is an apt Lacanian description not only of Jacob's lack but also of the lack of each character in the story. In Rebekah's case, not even the birth of Jacob and Esau can satiate her lack. Not even the birth of another human being, a beloved child, can fill unconscious desire without some desire still remaining.

Throughout her story, Rebekah conveys both a hopefulness and a disdain about her life. When we first meet her, Rebekah demonstrates enthusiastic hospitality toward Isaac's servant. She provides water for both the servant and for his livestock, even running to fetch the servant's needs and eagerly offering for him to stay the night. For the servant, her actions are a divine sign that God has procured a wife for Isaac. Before even meeting Isaac, Rebekah agrees to marry him. Their union, as depicted by the Hebrew writer, is divinely ordained, and their relationship consoles Isaac after his father's death (Gen 24). Rebekah is brave, hospitable, and eager to be used by God. There is a clear hopefulness about setting out on an adventure with Isaac and his god. The rest of her life, however, is depicted

---

5. Sarah, Gen 21:1–2; Rachel, Gen 30:22–4; Hannah, 1 Sam 1:19–20; Ruth/Naomi, Ruth 4:13–14.

as a disappointment. More than once she laments the circumstances in her life, questioning why she is alive (25:22; 27:46). The narrator describes Isaac and Rebekah's collective life as "bitter" as a result of Esau's Hittite wives (26:34–35). Moreover, cultural custom dictated that the elder son receive the father's blessing, clearly a source of pain for Rebekah, who is said to love Jacob (25:28). Such is her desperation to procure the blessing for Jacob that she not only helps Jacob deceive his father but is also willing to be cursed for her actions (27:13). Her early story conveys a hopefulness about her life, yet the rest of the narrative betrays her deep disappointment. Her life has not turned out the way she thought it would, and her actions demonstrate her to be a person who is, like Jacob, willing to do what is necessary to get what she wants. Her duplicity is foiled, and she is never reunited with Jacob. No record is even given of her death. Strangely, her last narrative moment involves the death of her nurse (35:8). Through it all, it seems that not even Jacob, the son Rebekah is said to love, can completely fill her lack. So too Jacob's lack, like the wound that he will later receive, remains; and it is Esau's face that reveals Jacob's lack.

From the beginning of the Jacob cycle, Esau is a mirror for all that Jacob lacks. Jacob's lack propels the narrative forward, sending Jacob on a quest that is both actual and existential. Struggling against each other, Jacob and Esau are fraternal rivals and competitors for material resources from birth. In the words of Lacan, they are locked within a struggle where one cannot do without the other; yet at the same time, the relationship is conflictual (Homer 2005, 24). All subjects are both specular I's, private selves, as well as social I's, social selves (24). A Lacanian reading problematizes the construction of a private self, whether he is a character in a story or a person in real life. Subjectivity is always elusive. Characters may not be stable amalgams of consciousness but instead multiple signifiers crowding around a proper name. Yet Jacob, like every other *other*, is also a social self who is constructed by a narrator and contained in the story world. He is also representative of the community producing the story, whose demands and desires are foregrounded. The community preexists the characters, and the characters are the discourse of that community. Therefore the social I of the characters is polyvalent, existing on several levels, serving both the story being told and the community telling it.

Within the story world, however, Jacob and Esau are linked by more than an umbilical cord. As Homer (2005, 26) notes, "To exist is to be recognized an-other.… The other, then, becomes the guarantor of ourselves. We are at once dependent on the other as the guarantor of our own existence and a bitter rival to that same other." Jacob becomes the guarantor of Esau's existence through providing for a need that *can* be satisfied—his physical hunger (Gen 25:30). Both the narrator and Esau describe Esau's condition as עיף (faint, weary, 25:29, 30). Moreover, the use of the *hiphil* imperative הלעיטיני (cause me to eat greedily) suggests Esau's is a rapacious hunger, which must be assuaged immediately. Esau views himself as close to death—הולך למות ("walking toward death," 25:32). Nevertheless, Esau's hunger is a lack or need that can be satiated. For a moment, Jacob holds the key (or the stew) that Esau lacks. Jacob's hunger, however, cannot be quenched through a bowl of "red red stuff."

Jacob desires to be the fulfillment of *his father's desire*; Esau's existence threatens this. As the firstborn, Esau was promised the birthright (בכרה). The birthright granted him material blessing, as well as familial and spiritual authority (Sarna 1966, 184–85).[6] Reuben Ahroni notes that Israelite society accorded special status to the firstborn, man and beast alike. The firstborn was considered to be the sacred, exclusive possession of God; as such he was accorded spiritual and material privilege. Jacob's blessing of Reuben (Gen 49:3) and God's reference to Israel as firstborn son (Exod 4:22) both indicate a unique and intimate relationship (Ahroni 1980, 325). The firstborn also benefited monetarily: "He must acknowledge as firstborn the son of the one who is disliked, giving him a double portion of all that he has; since he is the first issue of his virility, the right of the firstborn is his" (Deut 21:17). Nahum Sarna (1966, 185) comments that this law in Deuteronomy indicates an earlier situation where the father could disregard primogeniture if he chose. Nevertheless, Sarna views the narrator's lack of comment on Jacob and Esau's barter as sanction for Jacob's behavior. Sarna (188) states,

> There is no doubt that the way Jacob acquired his brother's birthright could not have been considered either unusual or objectionable in the context of his times. As a matter of fact, there is every reason to believe that Jacob's dealings with Esau and his father represent a stage of moral-

---

6. Sarna notes that along with the firstfruits of the soil and the first male of herd and flock, the firstborn son was viewed as sacred to God. The firstborn son was the guarantor of the family's line. He preserved their ancestral heritage and was second only to the head of the family, whose successor he would become. The status of the firstborn, then, was two-sided: he was bound to the responsibilities and obligations of the family, yet he was also accorded the rights and privileges associated with his status. This status was formalized by the father's testimony blessing.

ity in which the successful application of shrewd opportunism was highly respected.

Whether Sarna's scholarly intuition is correct or not, the oracle preceding the brothers' birth indicates that Esau's subservience to Jacob was a foregone conclusion (Gen 25:23).

Beyond discussion of Jacob's morality, the larger issue involves what the birthright represents for Jacob as character and for the community whose interests this story serves. For a community of wounded storytellers, the tangible transaction of food for birthright demonstrates a deeper desire—for land, blessing, and relationship. These promises are (re)iterated to Abraham no less than three times (Gen 12:1-3; 15:1-5; 17:1-8), to Isaac in the one chapter of Genesis devoted solely to him (26:23-24), and to Jacob in the midst of distress (28:13-15). This repetition demonstrates a profound need for this wounded community to continue to remember and to lay claim to Yahweh's involvement with them. In the story world, when Jacob/Israel hears the promissory blessings repeated to him, the nation bearing his name, by whom and for whom this story is written, is able to find reassurance in their own suffering. By contrast, if the promises of God are made to Abraham, Isaac, and Esau, Jacob's blessing is indirect, and his name—and therefore the name of the nation itself—is of no lasting import. However, to be a direct heir of God's promissory blessing is to be deeply rooted in the land, sacredly connected to God, and remembered forever. To be a direct heir of God's promissory blessing is to be directly involved in all that God is doing. Jacob's grasping of the birthright demonstrates a community's unconscious desire to lay claim to a predetermined yet deferred fate (Gen 25:23). The repetition of these promissory blessings is, for the community, a *durcharbeiten*, a "working through" of their fears and trauma. As a character, however, Jacob is rendered vulnerable to the one who threatens his desire, Esau, as well as to the one able to respond to it, the Wound.

When Jacob barters soup for birthright and later proclaims himself *to be Esau*, he is cut or wounded and disassociated from himself. Jacob's self-(mis)identification as Esau is, in Lacanian thought, an example of the radical heteronomy that exists within every human subject (Lacan 1977, 172). Indeed, Lacan (172) asks, "Who, then, is this other to whom I am more attached than to myself, since, at the heart of my assent to my own identity it is still he who agitates me?" For Lacan (172), the presence of this other mediated between the subject and the double of the subject is a kind of counterpart. In the Jacob cycle, Esau is a counterpart, a proximate other, whose existence in the world of the Other—the world of discourse—always already threatens Jacob's subjectivity. This cut or wound in the story world also symbolizes what Lacan (299) calls a "cut in the discourse," the representative bar placed between signifier and signified. Jacob's woundedness—both prior to and after the Jabbok encounter—suggests a cut in the discourse of national (divine) blessing by throwing it into question and threatening its fulfillment. While Elohim/Ish threatens its fulfillment at the Jabbok encounter, for much of the Jacob cycle, Esau poses the threat. Narratively, this threat revolves around Esau's sacral connection to his father. Here, it is the boys' (m)other who responds to that threat. Narratively, the characters Rebekah, Jacob, and Yahweh function as tricksters. However, as a figure representative of a community and its interests, Rebekah is a symbolic other representative of the Other, the world of the discourse. The central desire for both the other(s) and the Other is to lay claim to land, blessing, and relationship. Within the patriarchal narratives, Rebekah is not the only figure who expresses anxiety that a (dis)elect character may receive the promise (Gen 15:2–3). In Abram's case, it is Yahweh who provides assurance that this will not occur. In the Jacob cycle, intervention comes through human autonomy.

The deception of Isaac is Rebekah's idea—it is her vision. Rebekah's words to Jacob are in the imperative: לך־נא (please let go) and a second-person causative translated as an imperative: והבאת (and you bring in, Gen 27:10). Her discourse demands. While Jacob makes some protestation (27:11–12), in the end, he follows her instructions and remains silent as she dresses him. As Lacan (1977, 264) observes, the Other has its own ideas about a person's needs. For Jacob, it is Rebekah's speech—the imperatives she makes to her son—that functions as the Other. Her discourse is that Other that makes its demands on him. Yet for Lacan (265) there seems to be a point of refusal, too: "In the final analysis, by refusing to satisfy the mother's demand, is not the child demanding that the mother should have a desire outside him, because the way towards the desire that he lacks is to be found there?" Despite his protestation, however, Jacob does not refuse his mother. He does not refuse the Other but instead remains trapped in that discourse. For Lacan (265), demand alienates even as it engenders desire: "Desire is produced in the beyond of the demand, in that, in articulating the life of the subject according to its conditions. Demand cuts off the need from that life. But desire is also hollowed within the demand, in that, as an unconditional demand of presence and absence, demand evokes the want-to-be." While the discourse of the (m)Other does engender desire, Jacob's desire recedes into the background. It is instead Jacob's "aggressivity" that is foregrounded in his protestations.

For Lacan (1977, 10), aggressivity is an image of corporal dislocation for the subject, measured, among other things, partly in unfinished sentences, verbal hesitations, inflections, and slips of the tongue. Lacan also says that unconscious desires manifest themselves in "gaps" or "ruptures" that structured the unconscious. Here, Lacan remained close to Freud, who believed the unconscious manifests itself in those moments where defense mechanisms are at their weakest—through dreams, in slips of the tongue when individuals say things they do not intend but that nevertheless reveal a great deal about them, through jokes, or through the symptoms of mental distress or illness. For Lacan, the unconscious manifests itself precisely in these "impediments" or "failures" where the speaking subject fails in her use of language (Homer 2005, 67–68). Following the usurpation of the בכרה (blessing), Klitsner views a "slip of the tongue" during Jacob's theft of the ברכה as indicative of his repressed moral conflict (2009, 141). Rabbi Yaakov Zvi Mecklenberg first noticed the puzzling use of the term "perhaps" (אולי) rather than "lest" (פן) in Gen 27:12. Mecklenberg states:

> "Perhaps my father will feel me": The word "פן—lest" implies that the speaker does not wish the matter to come to pass—it has a negative undertone, cf.: "lest he put forth his hand and take too of the tree of life" (Gen. 3:22) or "lest we be scattered about on the face of the earth" (Gen. 11:4).... Had Jacob wished to express the hope that his father *not* feel him, he should have said—"lest—פן—my father feel me." From here it would seem that Jacob did not favor the attempt to deceive his father and that he preferred to let the matter proceed without intervention.... Jacob hoped that his mother would cancel the attempt as a result of his plea. Thus, he said, "perhaps"—"אולי." The word *perhaps* (אולי) is used when the speaker *desires* the matter to come to pass. (Leibowitz 1973, 264–65)

Perhaps Mecklenberg's explanation is intended to exonerate the patriarch from the duplicity of his actions, casting him in a better light. For Klitsner, however, application of psychoanalytic thought yields a different reading. Klitsner (2009, 71) states, "Jacob's use of the inappropriate word betrays an unconscious discomfort that is revealed in such a hidden way to the reader precisely because it remains hidden to Jacob himself. For Jacob, it is a slip of the tongue that goes unnoticed by Rebecca, and by himself. For the biblical narrative, it is an intentionally artful 'slip of the pen,' gratefully noticed by the reader." Freudian and Lacanian thought would claim that, through an unconscious slip of the tongue, Jacob speaks truth without realizing it. Yet despite the repressed moral conflict proposed by Klitsner, Jacob dupes his father, twice repeating, "I am Esau" (Gen 27:19, 24). When Jacob veils his identity, he nevertheless reveals a fundamental Lacanian truth: any verbal self-disclosure can only be a disclosure of self-division (Bible and the Culture Collective 1995, 201). As the Bible and Culture Collective (202) affirms, "The I (*je*), even when it is God's *I*, must necessarily lag behind its speech; its speech precedes it only to misrepresent it." Jacob's speech effectively transfers the symbolic capital of the story world to himself. Outside the story world, however, birthright and blessing are merely signifiers. Lacan viewed a signifier as that which represents the subject for another signifier. Lacan (1977, 316) notes, "This signifier will therefore be the signifier for which all the other signifiers represent the subject: that is to say, in the absence of this signifier, all the other signifiers represent nothing, since nothing is represented only for something else." These signifiers of birthright and blessing fall short in representing desire. Lacan (300) views the subject's relation to the signifier as a relation that is embodied in an enunciation (*énonciation*), whose being trembles with the vacillation that comes back to its own statement (*enoncé*). The trembling statement "I am Esau," which procures the blessing, functions merely as a placeholder for desire. Jacob's desire is not verbalized here—the discourse could not contain it anyway, as Lacan notes that there is a limit to how far desire can be articulated in speech (Evans 1996, 37). His desire is never actually named—only hinted at, later at Bethel. For Lacan (1977, 301), desire is bound up with the desire of the (m)Other, but in this loop also lies the desire (on the part of the subject) to know. For now, however, the discourse of the (m)Other, coupled with the insufficiency of the signifiers, alienates Jacob as an autonomous subject.

Rebekah's demand alienates Jacob both psychically and geographically. Jacob's subsequent expulsion (ויצא, "and he left") simultaneously disassociates him from his identity, even as it puts him on a path toward recovering it. In his dream at Bethel, Klitsner notes another manifestation of Jacob's unconscious fear and desire. The repetition of the promissory blessing in Gen 28:13–15 startles Jacob from his sleep, causing him to proclaim Yahweh's presence there (28:16–17). When the morning dawns, however, Jacob offers a conditional vow—if God remains with him, protects him on the journey, gives him bread to eat and clothing to wear, and allows him to return safely to his father's house—Yahweh will be his God (28:20–22). When the sublime of the night gives way to the mundane of the morning, Jacob's daytime consciousness takes over. Klitsner (2009, 83) draws a distinction between the awakening (יקץ) and the arising (שכם), viewing them as two stages in the internalization of the dream. He notes,

> As will happen when one awakens suddenly in the night from a particularly vivid and portentous dream, one is struck with the power and novelty of the dream's insight.... But in the morning the same dream will have faded and what remains will have been translated into the context of one's reality, one's daytime consciousness. The lofty language of this epiphany will give way to the pragmatic attempt to integrate the dream into the categories of the here and now.

Through a Lacanian lens, Jacob's dream at Bethel and subsequent vow demonstrate a desire to find his place among the patriarchs, to return home, and to know the protective hand of God. The dream is an epiphany or theophany, representing Jacob's hopes and fears. Jacob hopes to experience blessing, entitlement, *as Jacob*. In the morning, however, the dream gives way to anxious realities. In this wilderness space, Jacob is geographically/physically alienated. He is also existentially alienated, cast off from all that he knows. This alienation, however, moves him toward subjectivity, as alienation is tied inextricably to desire (Homer 2005, 71).

Lacan maintains that the pain of separation fuels an individual's desire. Desire is not a need, because a need can be satisfied. Desire refers to something beyond basic human needs that cannot be satisfied. In grasping at object(s) and/or position, Jacob attempts to assuage an intangible, nameless desire with tangible objects. This is ultimately fruitless. Desire cannot be satisfied at all, and certainly not by grasping at things. Moreover, while the desire of the Other exceeds or escapes the subject, Lacan believes that something is always recoverable—the *objet a*, the object or cause of desire (Evans 1996, 128–29). Homer (2005, 87) describes Lacan's *objet a* poignantly:

> The *objet a* is not, therefore, an object we have lost, because then we would be able to find it and satisfy our desire. It is rather the constant sense we have, as subjects, that something is lacking or missing from our lives. We are always searching for fulfillment, for knowledge, for possessions, for love, and whenever we achieve these goals there is always something more we desire; we cannot quite pinpoint it but we know it is there.

3. The Wound

For Lacan, the *objet a* is closely connected to the Real. While Lacan's description of the Real shifted over time, for Lacan the Real is no(thing). The Real is not a material object in the world or human body, or even reality itself. Rather, the Real exists at the limit of the sociosymbolic universe and is constantly in tension with it, a support for social reality even as it undermines it (Homer 1995, 81). Moreover, the Real resists symbolization, the "traumatic kernel at the core of subjectivity." The Real is associated with the death drive and *jouissance* as the "ultimate, unspeakable limit of human existence" (Homer 2005, 94). Above all, however, Lacan associates the Real with trauma, derivative of the Greek word for wound (τραῦμα). The Real is a cut or wound. The Real is not necessarily a physical event but is instead a psychical event. A psychic trauma arises from the confrontation between an external stimulus and the subject's inability to understand and master these excitations. A psychological scar remains on the subject's unconscious that will resurface later in life (Homer 2005, 83). Lacan (1977, 299) states, "This cut in the signifying chain alone verifies the structure of the subject as discontinuity in the real." This discontinuity becomes a trauma, implying blockage or fixation in the process of signification, where a subject is fixed in an earlier phase of development. The memory continues to return, repeating the suffering continually. Moreover, the Real eludes language because that suffering cannot be put into words; there always remains a residue that cannot be transformed through language. This excess, this X, as Lacan calls it, is the Real. Lacan renders an encounter with the Real as impossible (Bible and Culture Collective 1995, 207); therefore, individuals are condemned to mourn the real for the rest of their lives (Homer 2005, 90). And, it should be added, this fate renders individuals vulnerable to that which they mourn, to that which they desire.

Jacob's wound(s) ultimately renders him vulnerable to the Wound, whom he beseeches at Bethel: ושבתי בשלום אל־בית אבי ("And I am brought back in peace to the house of my father," Gen 28:21a). He prays when he is most vulnerable—at night, on the run and exiled from all he knows. The encounter at the Jabbok is predicated on this prayer that expresses, perhaps for the first time, a bit of the Real Jacob that eludes Jacob's grasp. To pray for return בשלום ("in peace," "in safety," "in wholeness") is to pray for *tikkun olam*, the reparation of (Jacob's) world. The prayer encompasses a hoped-for reversal of all the alienation(s) Jacob has known—geographical/physical, interpersonal, and existential. Jacob is made vulnerable to the one he prays to—here referred to as the Wound but referenced by

Humphreys (2001, 2) as a "searching God," and, it should be added, a desiring God. This nebulous character wounds Jacob Otherwise at the Jabbok. However, Jacob is not only vulnerable to the Wound. In coming to Jacob at the Jabbok, the Wound is also vulnerable. Both the Wound's desire and Jacob's desire are foregrounded in the Jabbok encounter, where danger and intimacy meet in that place most tender to the touch—Jacob's wound. The physical wound Jacob will sustain as a result of the encounter is the outward mark of that agonistic struggle with the Wound.

The Wound

Lacan understood desire as something that was experienced not only by humans but by the divine as well. Here Lacan's understanding of the divine both converges with and diverges from traditional Judeo-Christian thought. For Lacan, the desire of God is not unlike the desire of the human. God's desire, like Jacob's, is not the desire of an object but of another's desire. As with Jacob, here too God's desire is the mark of an emptiness, a lack (Bible and Culture Collective 1995, 206). In Lacanian thought, what is most peculiar about the biblical God—here the assailant Jacob meets at the Jabbok—is the hole in his being, his lack, what Lacan called his "want-to-be" (*manqué-à-être*; Bible and Culture Collective 1995, 206). The assailant at the Jabbok is, in Lacanian terms, every bit as wounded as Jacob. His divinity or semidivinity (Elohim and Ish) does not diminish his desire. In fact, that he appears both human and divine may point to a kind of double dividedness, perhaps augmenting his desire. As the Bible and Culture Collective (1995, 207) puts it: "From the beginning of Genesis right up to the non-ending of Revelation ('Surely I am coming soon'—Rev. 22:20), the Jewish and Christian God is caught up in the unending circuit of desire, the realm of substitutions and deferrals." The being Jacob encounters at the Jabbok is at once one who has being, but, at a deeper level, one who also lacks being. His ability to experience desire at all, not unlike Jacob's own desire, *marks him as one full of holes*—in Lacanian thought, so full of holes is he that he can never be *whole*. Jacob's assailant, then, is not merely one who has wounds. As an emblem of human desire elevated to a transcendental position, he is the Wound itself. As two wounded beings meet one night at the Jabbok River, Lacanian thought raises questions about the possibility of an actual *encounter* between them.

Viewed through a Lacanian lens, several elements militate against referring to their encounter as anything more than a diaphanous disturbance.

First, Lacanian thought locates God—the Wound—in the *real*. Here the notion of God takes on a decidedly apophatic undertone. For Lacan, the real—or God—is "on the side of the ineffable," something to be encountered in the real, which is inaccessible (Bible and Culture Collective 1995, 207). For Lacan, the gods belong to the field of the real, and here the Hebrew god—the Wound—is no exception. As the Bible and Culture Collective (207) affirms, "For Lacan the real is unmasterable because it cannot be caught in the word. The function of Lacanian psychoanalysis, then, is an oddly 'miss-tical' one— that of staging 'an appointment to which we are always called with a real that eludes us.'" The real is therefore impossible, because it is impassible (207). Second, at the Jabbok, the real is impossible, not only because Jacob's assailant, as one semidivine, bears in himself his own impassibility but also because a hole punctuates their discourse. The language of the Wound is, in itself, *wounding*—"Why is it that you ask my name?" (Gen 32:29). The discourse is deferred, and, as Lacan would say, as a hole, the real can never be a whole (Bible and Culture Collective 1995, 208). The Wound speaks, but as Derrida (1995b, 59) would say, he does so in order not to say anything at all. The Wound speaks, yet that speech, as part of the Real, does not constitute a genuine encounter in or with the Real, as such an encounter is not possible. Moreover, as one wounded, the Wound has divested himself of a traditional Jewish/Christian notion of wholeness-holiness, which has also kept him unreal. If there can only be "bits-of-real," for Lacan, then there can also only be "bits-of-God" (Bible and Culture Collective 1995, 208–9), just as there are only bits of Jacob. In the world of the story, both are empty, wounded, expressing a desire for they know not what.

In some way, both Jacob and the Wound appear to choose each other to fill the nameless wound they feel. What happens between them is, to borrow a phrase from Landy (2001, 44), an "intimate disturbance." Jacob is chosen, for God knows what reason, seemingly even before he is born (Gen 25:23). The experience at the Jabbok is at once intimate and jarring, preceded by an expression of desire on Jacob's part—a prayer that the promises made to him at Bethel will come to fruition (32:9–12). Jacob's prayer at Bethel, admittedly framed around bargaining and quid pro quo, *also* expressed a desire for God's presence (28:20). This presence, seemingly with Jacob throughout the story, had already been promised to him the night before (28:15). This series of prayers and promises between them, then, precipitates the arrival of the Wound at the Jabbok. He comes to make good on his promise—he will *be with Jacob*. For the Wound, Jacob is the *objet petit a*, the leftover of his desire. He grasps at Jacob in much the same way that Jacob grasps at things.

The expression of mutual desire culminates in an experience that is both intimate and jarring. Jacob and the Wound wrestle, legs coiling and wrapping around each other, arms flailing and finding their way to faces obscured in the dark. It is nightfall—when lovers meet. It is secluded—where lovers hide: "And Jacob was left alone. And a man wrestled with him until the breaking of the dawn" (Gen 32:25). These are the realities of intimate encounter—an exchange of knowledge and the acknowledgment that some mystery still remains. The danger of desire is expressed, most surprisingly, in their *mutual vulnerability*. The Wound seeks and finds Jacob alone by the river and comes to spend the night with him, an expression of desire—"Jacob have I loved" (Mal 1:3; Rom 9:13). Whatever else may be said about Jacob's opponent, at the Jabbok he demonstrates a profound relationality, illuminating his desire for and vulnerability to the man he chooses to pursue, wound, and bless. Yet their wounds, and the isolating darkness in which they find themselves, wrap the scene in a decidedly apophatic gauze.

Despite its diaphanous gauze, the scene appears on the one hand, loving; and on the other hand, dangerous, even violent. Zornberg captures these dual sentiments well. She calls the encounter "both erotic and antagonistic," signaling the "love-hate ambiguities of the wrestler's grip" (Zornberg 1995, 250). Frederick Buechner (2006, 7) plays on this dynamic of intimacy and danger when he refers to Jacob's opponent as "beloved enemy." The confusion regarding their relationship is further compounded by the linguistic and phonetic instability of the text.

As early as Moses ben Nahman, exegetes have noted the linguistic and phonetic similarities between אבק (wrestle) and חבק (embrace). In the MT, the verb used to describe the encounter between Jacob and the divine being is ויאבק ("and he wrestled"), yet Nahman raised the possibility that the letter א may have been a ח. Relying on Targum Onqelos, Nahman's suggestion of a possible exchange of Hebrew consonants highlights what is already present in the text—a struggle that is both dangerous and intimate. Wenham (1994, 295) rightly notes that while אבק is said to be a by-form of חבק, there is nothing "friendly" about the encounter. The seminal poststructuralist reading of Barthes, which draws on the actantial analysis of Algirdas Julien Greimas, further underscores the dividedness—and therefore the violence—of the Wound in the story. For Greimas, an object is conveyed by a giver to a receiver. A subject carries out the action assisted by a helper, who is constrained by an opponent (Barthes 1966, 246–60). Barthes's own reading, when brought into conversation with Greimas's schema, reveals that the Wound is both helper and opponent.

The Wound is therefore divided within himself as to what his relationship to Jacob ought to be. He is, in Lacan's terminology, alienated, a "split subject" (Evans 1996, 9). For Lacan, divinity or semidivinity does not rescue the Wound from the fundamental reality of his condition—he is, like his actions, a mystery even to himself. Such a reality accords in part with the Hebrew mindset, which sees everyone, including the divine, as a mixture of good inclinations and bad inclinations. In both the Hebrew mind and in Lacanian thought, the splitting of the subject is recognized. As one who both enables Jacob to cross yet also blocks that crossing through violence, the Wound appears alienated, even from himself. As the Bible and Culture Collective (1995, 202) states, "The Judeo-Christian God is a hidden God—and he is hidden first of all from himself." Regardless of the ambiguous nature of the encounter, several scholars have proposed readings that foreground its intimate nature.

Brodie has compared the Jabbok encounter to betrothal-type scenes in the Hebrew Bible. Rather than resonance, Brodie's reading demonstrates "radical reversal." The meeting is not with a woman (as in meeting Rachel, Gen 29:1–30) but rather with God; and the result is not betrothal but blessing. Yet in Jacob's original journey from home (26:34–29:30), blessing and betrothal were intertwined. In the night struggle at the Jabbok, Brodie (2001, 321) notes several details that either mirror or reverse the idea of betrothal: the strange or foreign location; the scene-setting reference to wives and children; instead of a well, a river; togetherness through the night; the reference to the thigh (see Gen 31:25, 31–32; also 24:2, 9); and the final reference, typical of betrothal scenes, to eating (32:32). Brodie (2001, 321) concludes that the night struggle is not a betrothal—it is a radical changing of what betrothal means:

> Yet the concept of betrothal is important. Jacob's night of struggling, of confronting death, may indeed involve letting go of all that he holds dear. In that sense all his normal ties, his usual bonds of betrothal, are reversed, broken. Yet in that breaking there is another form of betrothal—an intimacy with God that gives blessing and enables him to emerge into the sunlight, ready for what is coming.

Brodie's analysis suggests an encounter where Jacob is drawn closer to his opponent in an intimate way.

Despite this intimacy, at the Jabbok the Wound resists signification—he will not say what or who he is. Jacob must intuit that on his own. While the Wound refuses self-disclosure, he does exhibit a deep desire to be with Jacob. He comes to him in order to spend the night with him. In coming to Jacob in this way, the Wound makes himself vulnerable to that which he desires—Jacob. Both are made vulnerable in the dark and dangerous intimacy of the encounter. The wound Jacob sustains at the Jabbok, however, serves to unite Jacob to his wrestling partner forever, even as he begs for release before the night turns to day (Gen 32:26).

Modern interpreters such as Hermann Gunkel, von Rad, and Claus Westermann offer a traditional response to the request for release—it is indicative of the story's folkloristic origins. The opponent's desire to depart before dawn is a regular feature of folktales, suggesting that Jacob encounters a Canaanite river god (Wenham 1994, 295). Otto Eissfeldt observes that the story identifies the opponent as El, the supreme Canaanite creator god (Wenham 1994, 295). In other dangerous encounters with the divine (Exod 4:24–26; Num 22:22–35; Josh 5:13–16), the unrecognized opponent is the Lord or the angel of the Lord. Often in Genesis, the Lord is equated with El. For Wenham, the reference to dawn indicates the struggle lasted for a long time and explains why Jacob was unaware of his foe's identity. Still, had he known his opponent was divine, Wenham (1994, 295) insists, he would not have engaged him in a fight. The midrash, however, states that Jacob's opponent demanded release in order to keep his appointment to sing in the heavenly choir. A similar request was made by Jupiter: "Why do you hold me? It is time. I want to get out of the city before daybreak" (Plautus, *Amph.* 532–533; Wenham 1994, 296). Following Rashbam, Hiskuni, and Abrabanel, the commentator Jacob paraphrases: "Let me go, for it is time for you to give up" (Wenham 1994, 296). Wenham (1994, 296), however, views the demand for release as a means to hide his identity, also hinting that no person can see God and live (Exod 33:20). Jacob's inability fully to know the Wound leaves his identity, like his own wound, felt but not seen.

Viewed through a Lacanian lens, the invisibility of Jacob's wound correlates to the phallus, which can only play its role when veiled (Lacan 1977, 288). The phallic signifier sets desire in motion, yet it is also the signifier of lack. The function of the phallus is to be permanently absent, permanently unavailable (Bible and Culture Collective 1995, 204). As the signifier of Jacob's lack, Jacob's wound is likewise felt but not visible, just like his assailant. Therefore, the demand for release is not solely about a desire to hide identity. Nor does it merely illuminate the intimacy of the encounter or the folkloristic origins of the story. Rather, the demand for release suggests that

Jacob must relinquish his grasp, allow himself to be wounded, in order to receive the blessing. For Jacob, real blessing cannot come through duplicity or running away but rather in relinquishing his grip on his own life. Jacob is a fighter who must allow himself to be defeated, to be wounded by the Wound. Jacob must relinquish his proclivity to grasp at tangible objects that cannot satiate intangible desire. What is required is to keep his body vulnerable and his desire open, to live with the open-endedness that is wrestling with God. Defeat is the price Jacob must pay for the blessing. For Buechner, defeat is the price agreed on.

For Buechner (2006, 6), Jacob must allow himself to be defeated in order to take hold of the blessing:

> The sense we have, which Jacob must have had, that the whole battle was from the beginning fated to end this way, that the stranger had simply held back until now, letting Jacob exert all his strength and almost win so that when he was defeated, he would know that he was truly defeated; so that he would know that not all the shrewdness, will, brute force that he could muster were enough to get this. Jacob will not release his grip, only now it is a grip not of violence but of need, like the grip of a drowning man.

In Buechner's estimation, Jacob sees in his opponent's face something more terrible than the face of death—the face of love. Jacob learns that blessing comes not through strength of cunning or force of will but rather as gift. Buechner (2006, 8) labels the encounter at the Jabbok a "magnificent defeat," noting that before giving everything, God demands Jacob's life. I am drawn to Buechner's beautiful theological reading. Nevertheless, I must acknowledge that in the world of the story, blessing is also paired with sustained uncertainty. Jacob is not given the name of his opponent. Something of this mystery is retained, opening space for continued desire. Like a wound that never heals, so too the story remains open, reiterated by a community of wounded storytellers.

Wounded Storytellers

Hugh O'Donnell states that there is always in every wrestling match a "trace that never goes away" (Moyers 1996, 296). For Jacob, that trace is the excess, the leftover of his wound, or the limp: "The sun rose upon him as he passed Penuel, limping because of his hip" (Gen 32:31). Scholars who have assessed Jacob's wound have often attempted to suture it, to close it, to proclaim him a man who has been made whole. Zornberg (1995, 241) notes that the midrashic literature viewed imagery of the sunlight as indicative of the healing Jacob experiences in the encounter. Something of the curative aspect of the encounter may also be suggested in an arcane etymology of the name Israel. Overwhelmingly, scholars have associated Israel with struggling or fighting (Wenham 1994, 295–96).[7] However, William Albright (1927, 159) suggests the name is related to Ethiopic and Arabic stems meaning "to heal," hence the word means "God heals." Interpreters who view Jacob's wound positively, however, tend to minimize his pain, focusing instead on the blessing he receives. For example, Brodie (2001, 332) states,

> Even the wound comes ultimately from the person who blesses. Thus the wound is contained, as it were, in a greater world of blessing. The opponent in the struggle is divine-human, but containing, integrating, the negative. By going through the night with this person, Jacob also achieves an integration. When the struggle is over, he may indeed be limping, but he is blessed, and the sun is shining on him.

While it is true that the one who wounds and the one who blesses are the same, Brodie's analysis minimizes the suffering associated with Jacob's wound. The "greater world of blessing" "contains" Jacob's wound, while his wound is all but erased. Similarly, Zornberg (1995, 218) avers that "to be whole, apparently, means to have been in great danger and to have been saved. Jacob's integrity has been significantly assailed on many levels, but losses have been recouped, injuries healed, the erosion of memory successfully fought." According to Edward Hirsch, Jacob's *agōn* serves a (re)creative purpose. The process is poetic. To cite Rainer Maria Rilke's poem "Der Angel," where a divine being comes at night to "test you with a fiercer grip" and "seize you as if they were creating you," such a transition can happen only if they would "break you out of your mold" (Rosenberg 1996, 185). Hirsch views this "breaking out of the mold" as necessary for the creation of something new, here, from Jacob to Israel. This (re)creation,

---

7. Wenham notes that the etymology of Israel offered by the text relates to שרה (struggle, fight). Other scholars, such as Geller (1982, 53), follow the Greek translators (LXX, Aquila, Symmachus) and the Vulgate and relate Israel's etymology to שרר ("to rule, be strong"). Similarly, Jacob (1958, 203) links Israel to ישר ("just, right"), comparing the other ancient poetic name Jeshurun (Deut 32:15; 33:5, 26).

like the poetic process, is an ugly one. Hirsch concludes: "The scandal of poetic originality is that the birth of something new is always unsightly; the work comes from a dark, relentless, internal, at times even demented struggle.... Steel is required—and courage—when the self is estranged, especially since one hopes to emerge with a new name, a consoling gift" (Rosenberg 1996, 187).

Other scholars view both Jacob's wound and limp as morally transformative in Jacob's life. Knight (1992, 454), for example, regards the limp as psychic and spiritual, as well as physical:

> For a tradition that speaks of the way of right living as *halakhah*, to be permanently hindered in one's walking could never mean just a simple physical wounding. The linguistic echoes penetrate far deeper. Right living, or "*halakhah*," is literally derived from the verb "to walk." The lingering limp of Jacob could not have been just in his legs. It would have reached every fiber of his identity as he stood before God, now as the "Godwrestler."... Similarly, the wound he bore thereafter, his limp, was bound to what he faced that night. Jacob would wrestle with that legacy, along with everything else, the rest of his life.... With Jacob's mixed legacy, his shame, like his fear, became neither a maudlin nor a paralyzing burden. Rather, like a limp, it was a wound that Jacob incorporated into his life and his walk with God and with others. Jacob was able to move on, but not without the signs of the struggle.

The "right living" suggested by Knight has been reiterated by scholars who have suggested Jacob's character changes as a result of the encounter. The limp—or Jacob's wound—renders a moral change in the formerly crooked man. Those scholars who argue for such a change approach the character of Jacob from one of two angles—either psychoanalytically or theologically. Jacob is a man who either transitions from disintegration and fragmentation to integration and wholeness, or from sinner to repentant saint. For Jesse Long, the chiastic structure of the Jacob cycle suggests that the "grasping Jacob" transitions to a more "giving Jacob."[8] However, the payoff of Long's chiasm hinges on a face-value reading of both Jacob's prayer to God preceding the encounter and his interaction with Esau the next day. In his prayer prior to the encounter, Jacob says קטנתי ("I am small," Gen 32:10), a statement Long views as Jacob's demonstration of humility. Long

---

8. See Long 2012, 56–57. Here Long gestures to the chiastic structure in Fishbane 1998, 42–58.

(2012, 59) asserts that the Jacob who prays at the Jabbok is different from the Jacob who bargained with God previously at Bethel. The next day, Esau meets Jacob and inquires about this entire "encampment," which belongs to Jacob. Jacob responds: ויאמר למצא־חן בעיני אדני ("And he said to find favor in the eyes of my lord," Gen 33:8). He states further that he wants his brother to accept מנחתי (my offering, Gen 33:10), כי חנני אלהים וכי יש־לי־כל ("because God has shown me favor and there is to me everything," Gen 33:11).

For Long, Jacob's prostration both before God and before Esau demonstrates his character change and fulfills the prophetic word spoken to Rebekah at the boys' birth. The elder shall serve the younger. Jacob will eventually be the greater son, his people the ones blessed by God (Gen 25:23). Long (2012, 60) concludes: "On the surface, the story does not work out as anticipated. In a reversal, bowing before his brother Esau, Jacob personifies the meaning of the oracle, the principle that the older one serves the younger. In this way, he earns the right to carry the name of his people 'Israel,' when he takes on the form of a servant." When Long (60) interprets these two scenes, he interprets the character of Jacob through a hermeneutic of grace, which enables him to say, "Jacob has wrestled with God and prevailed with the awareness before Him that 'I am small.'" Long's plain-sense reading does not take into account the complexities of characterization within narratives. Does not Jacob's (humble) prayer prior to the Jabbok encounter indicate that he stands to gain if God is on his side? Moreover, does not the giving of "presents," as well as the language of abasement before his brother, stem from fear of reprisal? Perhaps these are both indications that Jacob truly has changed. Perhaps, however, there is more to Jacob's response than Long's reading allows. Moreover, Long's interpretation assumes too easy a transition from the self-seeking Jacob to the humbled Jacob. Little else in Jacob's biography suggests that Jacob's relationship with God or with his brother changes much following the Jabbok encounter. In their next exchange of dialogue, Esau suggests that they journey together to Succoth. Once again, Jacob delays, lingering back, he says, for the sake of his family and flock. Ultimately, however, Jacob chooses not to follow his brother but instead to build an altar at Shechem (Gen 33:12–20). Did Jacob simply get lost along the way; was the limp too painful to travel the distance; or did he never actually intend to settle in Succoth? The text does not specify, and Jacob's reasons are left unstated. Like the Jabbok text itself, much ambiguity remains in Jacob's transition from his old life as a runaway to his new life as a settled man in his father's homeland. Long, however, does not stand alone in arguing for a moral change in Jacob's character.

Michael Abramsky (2010) interprets Jacob's encounter psychoanalytically and claims that Jacob moves from a preliminal stage of development to a liminal stage, and finally to a postliminal stage. In his psychoanalytic midrash of the Jacob story, Abramsky draws on insight from Freudian and Jungian psychoanalysis, mythology, and literary traditions to describe the change in Jacob's character. Borrowing from the tripartite system of Victor Turner and from the mythological work of Joseph Campbell, Abramsky calls the Jacob of the opening narrative preliminal. He is a man of the mundane world subject to the usual desires of power, greed, ignorance, and lust. He is an ordinary man troubled by conflicts; in stealing the birthright and the blessing, Jacob displays envy (107). These early conflicts in Jacob's life foster the development of a "deceptive personal core," which Jungian psychology refers to as the shadow. In psychoanalytic terms, the shadow is the inferior part of the personality. The repression of the shadow into the unconsciousness causes it to be splintered and then manifested in action. This shadow side is represented in Jacob's trickster personality—cerebral, clever, and goal oriented (108). This shadow side dominates his personality in the beginning, and, according to Abramsky (108), reinforces the evil inclination (*yetzer ha'ra*); his actions ultimately put distance between himself and God. According to Yiddish thought, *b'shert* ("predestination, fate") involves bringing the will or *ratzon* ("desire, life energy") into line with the *ratzon* of God ("obedience, submission"). Conflicts of this lower, preliminal stage block a person from recognizing his purpose. However, tragedy may open the heart to a vision of who God is and who God wants this person to be. Thus, the evolution of the soul involves climbing the ladder from the darkness of the ego to the realm of purpose and meaning (109).

By contrast, the liminal stage refers to a rite of passage where the protagonist must wrestle with who he is and who he may become. Here, the sense of identity dissolves; life is ambiguous and indeterminate. According to Abramsky, Jacob's transformation begins, as it does with most hero myths, with a journey. This journey sets the stage for transformation, and for Jacob, the inauguration of the journey and the transformation occurs at Bethel, where God shows Jacob *possibilities*. He can become a landowner, and his seed will father a nation, the same promise made to his grandfather Abraham. According to Mussar tradition, humankind moves toward wholeness (*sh'lemut*). God has planted seeds or potential, and the human must complete the work of creation (Abramsky 2010, 109). D.

Andrew Kille has stated that the placing and consecrating of a stone at Bethel suggests a beginning of God's temple and the beginning of Jacob's transformation. For Jung, stones represent the self, which may guide individuals into higher levels of being (Abramsky 2010, 110). Nevertheless, this liminal stage is mere *possibility*—the hero tries to grow by using wiles or becoming perfect in the way she expresses flaws. Here learning occurs gradually as the hero starts to relinquish old ways and to surrender to new realms of meaning (112). Indeed, psychoanalytic interpretation makes it clear—just as Bethel is incomplete without Peniel, so too transformation is incomplete without struggle. For Abramsky, Jacob's struggle at the Jabbok provides the ultimate transformation.

Like Abramsky, Walter Wink also views the wrestling as an internal, psychological dynamic. In order to achieve wholeness, the repressed and negative shadow side must be brought to light and acknowledged in order to be conquered and properly integrated into the personality. When Jacob faces his own treachery, deceit, and dishonesty, he conquers his "split-off side" and becomes whole (Abramsky 2010, 113). In Judaic thought, *teshuvah* ("repentance") carries a twofold meaning: to return or go back to one's origin or an authentic way of life after a period of absence; and to respond to a call originating outside oneself. Thus, God and humankind must partner together to bring the world to *tikkun olam* ("perfection" or "wholeness"; Abramsky 2010, 113). Abramsky's reading of the Jacob cycle through the lens of *teshuvah* entails three processes. First, Jacob had to recognize that his actions toward Esau were wrong, which involved insight or doing, rather than merely finding a more sophisticated means of deception. The acknowledgement of wrong entailed "constructive repentance" or real change. Second, *teshuvah* opens Jacob up to true authenticity through undoing the wrong. When Jacob both apologizes to Esau and attempts to give a portion of the wealth he has accumulated (Gen 33:8–11), this compensation begins to make the victim (Jacob) whole.[9] Third, Jacob loses the desire or seed, which began the destructive process; he accepts Esau as his father's heir and begins to establish his own unique identity as a patriarch (Abramsky 2010, 114). This wrestling match and the repentance it fosters transitions Jacob to the postliminal stage. Here, Jacob transforms from an ego-dominated stage characterized by anxiety-

---

9. Indeed, it might be argued that Jacob is wounded by his own deception. Thus the encounter at the Jabbok exchanges this wound for a wound that ultimately heals.

induced deception to a position of faith where he trusts God's wishes and protective hand (114).

For John Sanford (1981, 21), Jacob's transformation from ego-dominated to a person of faith hinges on three things: wilderness experience (or suffering), the experience of a power greater than himself at work in his life, and loving someone (Rachel) other than himself. Sanford views the entirety of Jacob's story through the lens of psychological development and Jacob's movement toward wholeness. Jacob's wholeness cannot be achieved apart from reconciliation with his brother; Jacob's wound can only be healed by facing his delayed, deferred confrontation with Esau. Jacob's wound, then, ultimately finds its healing in the hands of someone else—his twin brother. At the Jabbok, Jacob is wounded by his opponent, and according to Sanford, the struggle itself is the heart of the encounter. Moreover, the wound Jacob receives is not a "limiting" wound but rather a wound through which pours the life of God. Sanford states, "Such [wounded] persons are affected so deeply that they cannot return to their former selves, but constantly journey ahead through life, and every day of their lives they are forced to live with the realization that inner reality is but a hair-breadth away.... [The wound] is also a great blessing, for through such a wounded ego there pours the life of God" (42). For Jacob, perhaps wounding and blessing are one and the same. His limp represents the kind of fearful intimacy with God that no one else in the Hebrew Bible achieves, for only one who is known can be wrestled with.[10] And only one who knows he is wounded can be healed. Here the psychoanalytic reading of Sanford, which posits the possibility for the wounded to be healed, runs counter to a Lacanian interpretation. For Lacan, lack cannot be satiated; thus, a wound always remains. As Evans (1996, 99) writes, "No matter how many signifiers one adds to the signifying chain, the chain is always incomplete; it always lacks the signifier that could complete it." The missing signifier is constitutive of the subject (99).

Therefore, while it is clearly tempting to tie up the loose ends of Jacob's story, to proclaim that the wounded has been healed, a Lacanian reading of Jacob's limp suggests otherwise. About suffering, Frank (1997, 25) says, "One of our most difficult duties as human beings is to listen to the voices of those who suffer. The voices of the ill are easy to ignore.... These voices

---

10. Insight gained from private conversation with Dr. Gary Furr, senior pastor, Vestavia Hills Baptist Church, Birmingham, Alabama.

bespeak conditions of embodiment that most of us would rather forget our own vulnerability to. Listening is hard, but it is also a fundamental moral act." In tying up the loose ends of Jacob's story, have scholars failed to listen to it? Jacob's story is about a man who suffers and a story where victory and defeat are one and the same. After the struggle is said and done, Jacob's wound remains. Like his story, Jacob's wound is an excess that continues to speak. As such, the trace of the wrestling match exists on two levels—the inside and the outside. Jacob's wound is both a deep psychical pain associated with the wounds Jacob brought with him to the Jabbok—and a physical pain associated with the wound he sustained that particular night. Jacob's wound, then, blurs the boundary between what is known only to the man and what is revealed to and even embodied by the community. Jacob's wound is an embodied story, bearing implications both for the patriarch himself and also for the community; Jacob's wound becomes a source of stories about Israel's own woundedness, told obliquely. For Frank, it is precisely the communal element that renders Jacob's suffering useful. Jacob's wound was embodied by the wounded storytellers who memorialize it in their own bodies: "Therefore to this day the Israelites do not eat the thigh muscle that is on the hip socket, because he struck Jacob on the hip socket at the thigh muscle" (Gen 32:32). These wounded storytellers' relationship with God is, like Jacob's, an ambiguous one. They are, like their forefather, people whose wounds remain open. They are, like their forefather, people who struggle with God. And their story is, like their forefather's, a story of suffering.

Frank notes that suffering can be discussed in five key ways. First, suffering involves whole persons and thus requires a "rejection of the historical dualism of mind and body." The subject who suffers is a body-self. Second, suffering takes place when a state of severe distress threatens the "intactness" of a person. This distress can be immediate or imminent, real or perceived. Third, suffering can occur in relation to any aspect of the person. Fourth, suffering is a result of processes of resistance to the lived flow of experience. To suffer, a person must not only perceive a threat but must also resist that threat. Finally, suffering is social in nature. Suffering is both an existential universal and a novel experience culturally elaborated in distinct worlds (Frank 1997, 169–70). Central to the notion of suffering is telling the story as a form of resistance. In story, the "flow of experience" is reflected on and redirected. If torture—or suffering—defined by Elaine Scarry (1987) is "unmaking the world," then resistance through story becomes the remaking of the body-self. At a deeper level, a storyteller not only resists but also controls the telling of her experiences. Ultimately, the storyteller not only makes meaning out of suffering but also decides what kind of meaning is made by the story she tells.

Frank (1997, 180–82) illuminates four aspects of the story, which demonstrate that it is an "illness story" with ongoing usefulness. First, the self is formed through *uses of the body*. Jacob wrestles with his body, and he is wounded in his body. He leaves the Jabbok with a limp, (the stigmata of the encounter) and a new name (the blessing of the encounter). This blessing is bought with Jacob's wound. The self is found through the body, hence the body-self. Second, *the body-self is also a spiritual being*. Frank views Jacob's attacker as God and notes that Jacob's impulse toward him is curiously expressed as resistance. Jacob contests the divine. Frank notes that what is being contested is ambiguous. Is Jacob wrestling a blessing out of God, or is the angel wrestling the petitioner for a blessing out of Jacob? Or is Jacob wrestling *in order to be wounded*, since that wound will open him to the spiritual aspect of life he has resisted ever since he stole the blessing that belonged to his brother? Third, *the wounded, spiritual body exists in moments of immanence*. In his embodied resistance and through his wound, Jacob discovers that he has been on holy ground. Frank (1997, 181–82) notes, "The holiness of the ground is created in the wrestling that sanctifies that ground. Peniel is a place where Jacob may have thought God was absent; he learns in his wounding that God is present." Finally, *the spiritual body-self assumes an ongoing responsibility*. Jacob leaves the Jabbok in order to be(come) Israel. Frank avers that the "postmodern Jacob" never works out his resistance once and for all. The self must continue to wrestle and continue to be wounded in order to rediscover the ground it now stands on as sacred. For Frank, "to be is to wrestle with God" (182). The Jabbok encounter functions as a foundation story for ancient Israel, which will continue to be with God, continue to wrestle with God. Indeed, in the community of wounded storytellers meaning is made from the story.

What kind of meaning is being made, then, by the community telling the story of Jacob's encounter at the Jabbok? Given the ambiguity of the outcome—Jacob is purportedly victorious yet leaves with a limp—it is not difficult to imagine that the community is pointing, in part, to the instability of the patriarchy. This particular patriarch and what he represents—their own relationship with God—is inherently ambiguous. This subversion of patriarchy is expressed most notably in the legal addendum to the narrative (Gen 32:32). Immediately before crossing multiple thresholds—from past identity to future identity, and from liminal, wandering location back into the land—the eponymous ancestor of the nation is struck עַל־כַּף הַיָּרֵךְ (upon the calf of the thigh). The ירך is variously rendered as "thigh" or "loin" and as such signifies the site of a man's procreative power (see Gen 24:2–9; 46:26; 47:29; Exod 1:5; Judg 8:30). Stahl (1995, 81) has noted the crucial implications of the placement of Jacob's wound—it renders Jacob's connection to the Abrahamic covenant, embodied through the rite of circumcision, as wholly ambiguous. Stahl comments, "The legal addendum, which highlights the national implications of the struggle by invoking a taboo that alludes to the maiming of Jacob's genitals, his castration, also hints at the problematic nature of Jacob's legitimate right to his father's blessing. This shadow of doubt is transferred, through dietary abstention, to his progeny as well" (81). Moreover, after the encounter, Jacob does not father any additional children.

In response, the Israelites do not eat the גיד הנשה (sinew of the vein). Although נשה is a *hapax legomenon* in the Hebrew Bible, a subtle philological connection can be made with the closely related verb נשה (to forget). Moreover, a close philological connection also exists between גיד (sinew) and the verb נגד (to tell). Is the refusal to eat a memorial not to נשה but instead to זכר, to remember? Stahl (1995, 78) has observed that the law does not appear in either of the two series of dietary injunctions (Lev 11; Deut 14:3–21) or elsewhere in the Bible. For Stahl, this suggests that there might be aspects of the episode that the law memorializes (or remembers) but that biblical theology would rather keep at a distance. There is an element of taboo to the struggle, which future generations dare not replicate (Stahl 1995, 78). The wounded storytellers, then, appear to tell a story representing their profound ambivalence to the promises made to Abraham and Isaac regarding זרע (seed, offspring). In contrast to the portable practice of circumcision, here Jacob/Israel is memorialized not through practice but rather through the avoidance of it. Stahl notes,

> Memory, and by extension history, thus seem to be called into question in the dietary taboo whose very purpose is precisely to evoke memory and whose etiological frame is meant to give it historical resonance. On the one hand, the law affirms that Jacob's descendants did indeed become a nation among whose founding memories is their progenitor's encounter with the divine; on the other hand, the avoidance hints at partial obliteration of that memory. The threat of annihilation which hangs over the encounter—and which is seemingly overcome with Jacob's transformation into Israel—reappears in the legal addendum, casting a shadow over the destiny Jacob wrestled so hard to secure. (83)

The threat of annihilation hangs over Israel/Judah throughout its history, depicting its wound(s) as festering sores that are always open (Isa 1:5-6). God promises to "bind up the brokenhearted" (Isa 61:1; Pss 34:18; 147:3), yet Israel's literary (hi)story suggests otherwise. For both the man and the nation, the story is one of suffering, of defeat. For Frank, stories of suffering contain two sides—chaos and quest. Suffering stories demonstrate the threat of disintegration, called the chaos narrative, alongside the hope for a new integration of the body-self, called the quest narrative. Quest stories, according to Frank (1997, 171), reflect a confidence in what is waiting to emerge from suffering. Sandwiched between these two sides is the restitution story, which involves remaking the body in an image, derived either before the illness or elsewhere (87). However, the individual who is telling the restitution story is not necessarily the same individual who is ill, defeated. The purpose of such a story is to pronounce "good as new," a kind of "talisman against future sickness" (90). Such a story is not only projective—the future will not be disrupted by illness—but it is also protective, that the present illness is merely an aberration in an otherwise healthy life (90). Not only is such a story impossible, but it also deprives the subject of telling his own story. The "expert," or someone outside the subject's lived experience(s), tells the story. For Frank, the quest narrative is the only viable option: "The quest narrative recognizes ill people as responsible moral agents whose primary action is witness; its stories are necessary to restore the moral agency that other stories sacrifice" (134). A quest story allows agency through a subject's (self) testimony and moral responsibility as part of a community of those who suffer. The dual imagery inherent in the Jabbok text—sunlight, indicating some peace or resolution might be achieved, alongside a limp, the excess of a wound—suggests that Israel's story is about both the chaos of communal disintegration and the quest to wrestle honestly and to make meaning out of suffering. For a people who frequently reside in wilderness, for a people who are more often on the move than settled in the land, the encounter at the Jabbok represents the ambiguity inherent in their struggle with God and the perceived instability of that relationship. Their grasp on life, on the land, on God, is tenuous and always already wounded and wounding. The wound is already there before the story is (re)told—a story with an invisible assailant and an invisible wound. The story remains, like Jacob's wound, half-open.

The invisibility of Jacob's wound—and of the assailant—gestures not only to identity but also to elements of space and time in the story. In darkness the assailant makes himself (un)known, and it is in darkness where

Jacob sustains his wound. Therefore to walk heel to toe with Jacob into the darkened space of encounter becomes a necessary part of reading the story.

4
The Dark

At the Jabbok, Jacob is left in the dark. Yet it is not only at the Jabbok where Jacob finds himself in darkness. Examination of the Jacob cycle (Gen 25–50) demonstrates that the narrative frequently situates Jacob in darkness; he experiences both attachment and detachment in darkness. Jacob is attached to Rebekah in the darkness of her womb. Later in the story, Rebekah uses the blindness or darkness of her husband's eyes to aid her deception (Gen 27:1–29). Also, in the darkness of exile, dispersion—ויצא (and he left, 28:10)—Jacob is isolated and detached from his origins. At Bethel, the dark night functions as both aporia—a disjunction or blocking of the divine presence—and the annunciation that the divine is present. Later, Jacob is deceived in the darkness of the night and in the marriage bed (29:21–30). And at the Jabbok, with darkness as proximate temporal and spatial companion, Jacob sees the face of God and lives. In many places and temporal spaces in Jacob's life—the birth canal, theophanous sites such as Bethel and the Jabbok, and the marriage canopy—darkness hovers and settles, unsettlingly, like a stranger in a home. Further, in darkness God is both revealed *and* concealed in Jacob's life. As the most critical moment in Jacob's life, the Jabbok encounter functions as a dark mirror through which his whole life is (un)reflected.

Pairing the Jacob cycle with the theoretical insights of Bakhtin and Gary Saul Morson demonstrates that the Dark is an intersection of time and space that the narrative uses strategically. In the Dark, the identities of the characters unfold. The darkness is about spaces—geographical terrain—and faces, the identities of the characters. Here, Bakhtin's (1990) concept of the chronotope demonstrates that the Dark "authors" and is "authored by" those individuals who traverse it, sojourn in it, and are inhabited by it. Therefore, darkness is not limited to time and space but also reveals/conceals the faces of the characters. The Jacob cycle in general and the Jabbok scene in particular demonstrates "loose play" and the surprise of "eventness." Therefore, human and divine agency in/with the Dark becomes "momentous" in the formation of identity (Morson 1994, 22). Multiple possibilities are laid out, raising the question of the moral agency of its characters. Consequently, I explore both the darkness of geographical space and the darkness of the faces hidden in the shadows.

Dark Spaces and Dark Faces in the Jacob Cycle

Rebekah's womb is the first dark space in the story. The womb is a dark space, which gestates life yet is also a site of struggle. As one who carries the struggle in her body, Rebekah's life is endangered, even as that struggle produces life after the requisite period of time (Gen 25:24). Rebekah's womb is an example of Bakhtin's chronotope, or "time space." Bakhtin (1981, 84) explains,

> In the literary artistic chronotope, spatial and temporal indicators are fused into one carefully thought-out, concrete whole. Time, as it were, thickens, takes on flesh, becomes artistically visible; likewise, space becomes charged and responsive to the movements of time, plot and history. This intersection of axes and fusion of indicators characterizes the artistic chronotope.

Time becomes thick, takes on flesh, as Rebekah's body thickens. With the thickening of her body, the plot of the story also thickens. The narrative is shaped by the embodied struggle of Rebekah. Her struggle, the narrative relays, is not limited to the normal pains of childbirth. Rather, her embodied struggle is actualized in the struggles of two nations who are housed in the time space of her womb: "And Yahweh said to her, 'Two peoples are in your womb and two peoples are in your belly. And people will be divided from people and one people will be stronger than the other; and the chief (one) will serve the insignificant (one)'" (Gen 25:23, author's translation).[1]

---

1. Heard (2001, 98–101) explains the complexities involved in translating Yahweh's oracle to Rebekah. He notes that the last line of 25:23 is usually read, "The older will serve the younger" (as by Alter 1996, 127; Dicou 1994, 175; Dillmann 1897, 195; Driver 1915, 245; Fewell and Gunn 1993, 74; Gunkel 1997, 289; Hamilton 1994, 177; Hendel 1987, 11; Kunin 1995, 5; von Rad 1973, 264; Skinner 1930, 359; Speiser 1964, 193; Syrèn 1992, 82; Turner 1990, 119; Wenham 1994, 175; Westermann 1985, 411; ASV, NJPS, KJV, NEB, NIV, NJB, NRSV, RSV). Syntactically, Heard says, the case is

Yahweh's prophecy does not explain the why of that struggle. The birthing process—the transition from the dark womb—provides a hint. Attendant midwives can see that Jacob is gripping Esau's heel. The struggle of the two nations is embodied in the bodies of Jacob and Esau.

By order of their birth, Esau is to inherit the rights of primogeniture. The conflict this engenders revolves around the ways in which human life has been institutionalized among the Hebrew people. Brueggemann (2010, 290) states:

> Primogeniture is not simply one rule among many. It is the linchpin of an entire social and legal system, which defines rights and privileges and provides a way around internecine disputes. But the same practice which protects the order of society is also a way of destining some to advantage and others to disadvantage. That world of privilege and denial is here disrupted by the God of blessing who will sojourn with the "low and despised" (cf. Luke 7:34). This narrative, then, is a radically revolutionary announcement. It dares to call into question a conventional settlement of power. The governing oracle and the narrative, which flows from it are not disinterested. They are an attempt to arrange the blessings in an alternative way. And with that attempt, painful possibilities are reopened. Many things are placed in jeopardy.

Key here is this notion of the possibilities that are (re)opened in the time space of Rebekah's womb. While Humphreys (2001, 157) has referred to the words of Yahweh's oracle as "great and enigmatic," John Anderson (2011, 50) has noted perceptibly that the "trickster oracle" is the key to unlocking the Jacob cycle. This oracle demonstrates that the characters in the Jacob cycle are not locked in a deterministic (story) world. William James's description of determinism, cited in Morson (1994, 83), delineates the contours of a deterministic (story) world:

> The future has no ambiguous possibilities *hidden in its womb*: the part we call the present is compatible with only one totality. Any other future complement than the one fixed from eternity is impossible. The whole is in each and every part, and welds it with the rest into an absolute unity, an iron block, in which *there can be no equivocation or shadow of turning*. (emphasis added)

---

not closed. The syntax of the entire clause must be considered, as a lack of explicit case markers requires other recourse to consider subject and object of the verb יעבד.

Here, the world described by James would warrant carrying out the predetermined patterns of birth order. As firstborn, Esau would receive the requisite allotment of resources and be sacredly connected to God, and no "equivocation or shadow of turning" could undermine that tradition (Sarna 1966, 184–85). The narrative would be predetermined and the future of characters predestined. The element of surprise would be removed. Here, however, the oracle portends a different story altogether. While not addressing the two boys directly, Yahweh's prophecy hints that the Deuteronomistic tradition ought to be held loosely. In the words of Bakhtin, a surprising "loophole" may break the expected "rhythm" of the story (Morson 1994, 90). Or it may not. Possibilities are (re)opened. In a reading that follows closely the theoretical insight of Bakhtin, Morson draws a distinction between determinism and the loose play of time offered by the indeterminist. Morson states, "The determinist asks us to accept a singular world, the indeterminist a world in which there is a 'certain pluralism'—what James calls an excess, and Bakhtin a surplus of possibilities" (83–84). What is envisioned by the indeterminist, Morson adds, is not chaos but instead some loose play (84). In this time space, Yahweh reveals that Rebekah's womb is a charged space. The womb is a site of creation that harks back to Creation. Darkness in the depths, a surplus of water, and space made habitable are elements in the birthing process of creation and in the birthing process of Rebekah's children. Jacob and Esau gestate in the dark of Rebekah's womb, where fecundity and struggle twist together. So too the stuff of creation gestates in a dark that is at once rife with possibilities and loose play, and also a site of struggle. The dark space of creation is a space, like Rebekah's womb, that must be made habitable. And it is a space, like Rebekah's womb, that gestates, waits for a particular time before giving birth.

Both Rebekah's womb and the womb of precreation are night watches, fertile time spaces. In the words of Levinas (1989c, 31), this is clearly not wasted time: "There is a nocturnal space, but it is no longer empty space, the transparency which both separates us from things and gives access to them, by which they are given. Darkness fills it like a content; it is full, but full of the nothingness of everything." Similarly, darkness will fill the time space of both Bethel and the Jabbok. Just as the creative stuff of creation is water, deep and darkness, spirit and spoken word and the face of תהום, so too the company Jacob keeps at the Jabbok is with night and sun, stream and face.

In the looseness of this created (story) world, the surplus of possibilities also creates space for the moral choices of the characters to be scrutinized. The ways in which characters play in the looseness of time becomes an important part of the discussion. A character's agency—his or her ability to act in moral or amoral ways—is foregrounded in the indeterministic (story) world. In the episode immediately following the transition from the womb, the moral choices of the characters are thrown into question.

Waiting in the Shadows

As the events of the narrative unfold, Jacob frequently (dis)appears in the shadows. Jacob's character is authored in the dark chronotope of the family tents, which he "keeps" (Gen 25:27; Speiser 1964, 193–94). The family tents function as another kind of dark womb that offers him protection from the world outside. Even as he keeps the tents, there is a sense in which the tents also keep him. The participle ישב (dwelling, remaining, Gen 25:27) suggests Jacob's occupation of this time space is ongoing. Jacob remains in darkness for a long time. Zornberg's (1995, 164) examination of the Zohar reveals an uncertainty to the way in which Jacob is authored there: "There is a suggestion that Jacob is born without a strong *personal* bent of his own. The early years of his maturity are spent in the created worlds of his father and grandfather; he is engaged in a search for God *by indirection*." Indeed, the author's description of Jacob suggests his subjectivity is intricately connected to someone else—Esau (Gen 25:26). He gestates in the darkness of Rebekah's womb, transitions into the world of Esau's shadow, and dwells in the shade of the family tents. The world of shadows in which he lives also suggests an ominousness to his character, according to Speiser (1964, 193–94). Similarly, David Zucker (1986, 404) states that there is a sense here of "keeping secrets, keeping his own counsel, plotting, scheming, allying himself with the darkness of the tent versus the more open-field approach of brother Esau."

By contrast, Esau occupies a duality of spaces, transitioning out of the field and back to home and hearth. The spaces occupied by Esau are in keeping with the time space of adolescence, where character is developed in quests outside the home, even as it continues to be nurtured inside it. Transitions between inside and outside mark the transition from child to adult. For Esau, this is an embodied movement, a chronotopic world, in which eventness can take place. In the words of Bakhtin (1981, 250), "[Chronotopes] are the organizing centers for the fundamental narrative events of the novel. The chronotope is the place where the knots of the narrative are tied and untied." In both tying himself to the knots of the tents and untying himself through moving outside them, Esau opens himself up to the element of surprise, "eventness." As Morson (1994, 22) states, "For there to be eventness, there must be alternatives. Eventful events are performed in a world in which there are multiple possibilities, in which some things that could happen do not. In such a world, time ramifies and its possibilities multiply." In transitioning from outside the tents and back, Esau is presented with many possible outcomes. As the narrative demonstrates, not all the possible outcomes are favorable. Transitioning out of the family tents, like transitioning out of the womb, opens individuals up to dark possibilities and dark choices. Someone else is always waiting in the shadows. Esau's sojourn into Jacob's tent of shadows results in the exchange of birthright for stew (Gen 25:29–34). All the while, God (dis) appears absent from the scene. If God is anywhere at all, it is in the shadows. In the world of the story, God's agency is, like the human characters to whom he relates, also called into question.

For Bakhtin (1993, 10), the eventness of being implies moral reflection on individuals' actions. Each act of being serves as an "answerable act or deed," juxtaposed to other unrealized behaviors. Jacob could have respected the rights of primogeniture. Esau could have, as well. Jacob could have given a gift without demand of reciprocity. Isaac and Rebekah could have created a family life where neither child was favored over the other. The community could have constructed its moral and ethical framework around חסד. Instead of remaining an ethical and theological ideal, the community could have taken steps to actualize fidelity to God and to neighbor. God could have shown up in this moment but did not, indicating, perhaps, his support of Jacob's actions. As Anderson (2011, 50) quips, "God is not a disinterested bystander or someone who withdraws and spasmodically appears when it is convenient for his characterization (that is, when there are no deceptions occurring) but is a figure deeply woven into the fabric of the story." From the birth canal to Bethel to Peniel, God works through human agency to act as Jacob's patron. For Anderson, there is no divine circumlocution but instead divine centrality. If such is the case, then God is also implicated here. Inaction is as open to critique as action.

All of these unrealized possibilities, however, are framed with the presupposition that Jacob's action is *immoral*. This is not necessarily the case. Jacob's action is not necessarily immoral. How much mutability existed with primogeniture remains unclear. As Sarna points, there is reason to think Jacob's actions are viewed favorably. For Sarna, there is no doubt that the way Jacob acquired his brother's birthright could not have been considered either unusual or objectionable in the context of his times. Sarna (1966, 188) claims there is every reason to believe Jacob's dealings with Esau represent a stage of morality where shrewd opportunism was highly respected.

In almost the same breath, however, Sarna states outright that Jacob's dealings, both here and in the next episode involving Isaac and Esau, *are* immoral. Sarna (1966, 184) avers, "The biographical details of Jacob's life read like a catalogue of misfortunes…. All the foregoing makes quite clear Scripture's condemnation of Jacob's moral lapse in his treatment of his brother and father. In fact, an explicit denunciation could hardly have been more effective or more scathing than this unhappy biography." Sarna's comments regarding Jacob's behavior are helpful for considering his agency in these events and framing it morally. However, his statements cannot be substantiated textually. In the absence of comment from the narrator or judgment by God, we are left uncertain whether Jacob's actions would be honored or excoriated by the community. Sarna's comments, moreover, do not take into consideration a likely postexilic date for the text. If the story was composed during the period after the exile, then the reality of the exiles is reflected in the character of Jacob. The appropriation of the birthright by Jacob may symbolize the competition for resources between the returnees and remainees, who would have been represented by Jacob and Esau, respectively. Therefore, morality and moral agency exists on two levels, in the poetics of the story world through the actions of its characters and in the rhetoricians behind that narrative who seek to frame it in particular ways. Fewell's (2015, 79–96) point is apt: narrative discourse operates as a moral agent in creating space for the community to reflect on its own ethics and behavior. While the rhetoric of the story—the way it is constructed and remembered—receives merely a gesture here, the final chapter titled, "The Crossing," deals with this in additional detail.

The next scene in the Jacob cycle (Gen 27) demonstrates that each of the characters sojourns in the dark. A dark authorship hovers over the narrative, authoring each of the characters who are situated in it. For Isaac, his body acts as a chronotope: "When Isaac was old and his eyes were dim so that he could not see" (Gen 27:1a). The darkness covering Isaac's aged eyes is a time space where Isaac is enveloped in a dark vulnerability. His field of vision, however, is not only blurred or darkened by old age. His field of vision has been dark around the edges from the start of the narrative, where he is said to love only Esau (25:28). His ongoing blindness, the love for only one child, frames the giving of the blessing to Esau as a foregone conclusion. Isaac's preference imposes a rhythm to the story that resembles Bakhtin's notion of authorship, described by Morson (1994, 90) as a "controlling presence at every moment." Time may shadow his eyes here, but it is his preference that shadows the narrative. Similarly, Rebekah's preference also darkens, blurs, her field of vision. Her preference also shadows the narrative. Indeed, the potential for conflict between husband and wife is even *fore*shadowed from the start (Gen 25:28). Here too Jacob waits in the shadows, caught between the (over) protective love of his mother and his continued sojourn in the darkness of the family tents. That darkness authors him, like a child, to follow his mother's instructions with minimal protest. Rebekah dresses Jacob in Esau's clothes; she covers his smooth skin with the skins of kids. Rebekah does all of this before the face of God (27:7). When the aged father asks Jacob whether he is Esau, twice Jacob responds, "I am" (27:18-19; 24). Wenham notes that Jacob's response is an overcompensation of identity. The normal reply in Hebrew to Isaac's question would have been "Esau am I," but Jacob instead employs the more assertive form, "I am Esau" (Wenham 1994, 208). Jacob's masquerading and his staunch assertion that he is Esau, coupled with the darkness of Isaac's bleary eyes, completes the deception. Jacob, once again, supplants Esau. Once again, God has (dis)appeared from the scene. God is either nowhere to be found, or God is hidden in plain sight. Either way, this act of deception functions as a transition in Jacob's life. For the first time, there is movement. Movement from darkness to darkness authors him in a different way—he is awakened to possibility. His exile from the shadows of the family tents casts (side) shadows on the narrative.

Sleeping and Waking in the (Side) Shadows

Jacob's expulsion is a transition from everything familiar—ויצא ("and he left"; Gen 28:10). Jacob leaves Beersheba, a place with strong patriarchal associations—places where his father and grandfather often stayed (22:19; 26:23, 33). Beersheba is also associated with security (21:31; 26:26-33), divine assurance (26:24), and patriarchal worship or the presence of God (21:33; 26:25; 46:1; Walton 2003, 42-43). Walton notes that Beersheba is a place as near to anywhere that Jacob might call home. Walton (2003, 42-43) continues, "Thus the reminder that Jacob is leaving this place, emphasizing the sense of absence he is to feel—from place, from family, and from God." Two reasons are given for Jacob's dispersion—the need to find an acceptable wife (Gen 27:46–28:2) and fear of Esau's anger (Gen 27:42–45). In his midrash, Rashi states that the leaving of a righteous person from a place *makes an imprint* (Zornberg 1995, 181). Given the relationship between יעקב (Jacob) and עקב (heel or footprint; BDB 784), it is likely that Jacob left his imprint—his footprints—throughout Beer-sheba. Similarly, the memory of the footprints of יעקב has been imprinted on the mind of the Israelite audience throughout the long stretch of patriarchal narrative. Yet Zornberg (1995, 181) notes that the void in Beer-sheba following Jacob's absence may have been felt within Jacob as well: "Rashi speaks of a void left behind Jacob as he begins his journey. But perhaps the void is *in* Jacob, as well. As he 'goes out' of his place, a vacuum separates him from his origins, a kind of necessary detachment." Zornberg adds:

> In leaving home, Jacob goes out into exile. This is an exile not only from his geographical home but, in some radical sense, from himself. His going out makes an imprint on himself: how is he to know himself in that strange country, that darkness of exile? As he begins his journey, the sun sets (Gen. 28:11); when he returns, twenty years later, the narrative describes a sunrise (Gen. 32:32). Both these markers of time, the Midrash suggests, are functions of Jacob's personal sense of time. Between these two points, there is darkness, the Dark Night of the Soul. (185)

For Jacob, the darkness of exile, the darkness of the place to which he is exiled, is the thing on which personal transformation may hinge. Prior to that transformation, however, Rashi notes that fourteen years of elapsed time must be accounted for. Rashi claims that during the fourteen years prior to Jacob's arrival at Bethel, he hid himself in the House of Study of Eber. While he was going to the House of Laban, he was learning Torah from Eber. Due to the merit of the Torah, Jacob was not punished for those years spent away from his father (Scherman and Zlotowitz 1995, 306–7). Even in the midrash, the image of Jacob's containment suggests sequestering in scholarly darkness, a kind of womblike protection from the world. Darkness protects—even overprotects, like his (m)other.

At Bethel, however, the dark acts as a companion both to Jacob, who sleeps under its heavy cover, and to Yahweh (and his heavenly consort), who appears in the midst of it. Jacob's exile transitions him from the chronotope of womb and tent to what Bakhtin refers to as the chronotope of the threshold. This chronotope is connected with a "breaking point" in life, the moment of "crisis," the decision that changes a life. As such the threshold chronotope is "highly charged with emotion and value" (Bakhtin 1981, 248). Bakhtin viewed this particular chronotope as linking naturally to encounter, even to mystery time (248–49). Beersheba may be a (time) space *associated with God*, but it is the time space of Bethel where Jacob encounters God. Significantly, Bethel is time space away from home and out of the shadows, even as it is enveloped in the shadows of the night. Yet it is a moment of crisis, a moment of psychic disintegration away from home and hearth, where, in his sleep, Jacob is awakened to (side) shadows. Morson (1994, 117–18) delineates between foreshadowing and sideshadowing, noting:

> Whereas foreshadowing works by revealing apparent alternatives to be mere illusions, sideshadowing conveys the sense that actual events might just as well not have happened. In an open universe, the illusion is inevitability itself. Alternatives always abound, and, more often than not, what exists need not have existed. *Something else* was possible, and sideshadowing is used to create a sense of that "something else." Instead of casting a foreshadow from the future, it casts a shadow "from the side," that is, from the other possibilities. Along with an event, we see its alternatives; with each present, another possible present. Sideshadows conjure the ghostly presence of might-have-beens or might-bes. While we see what did happen, we also see the image of what else might have happened. In this way, the hypothetical shows through the actual and so achieves its own shadowy kind of existence in the text.

At Bethel, the night falls "unexpectedly," Zornberg notes. When Jacob comes to that place, she notes that he "collides" with it. Suddenly, before he knows it, the place takes him over (Moyers 1996, 290). In his remarks on the Bethel episode, Rashi notes Jacob stays at Bethel "because the sun had set." Rashi states, "It should have written, 'And the sun had set, and he spent the night there' because the sun had set implies that the sun set for him, suddenly, not in its normal time, so that he should spend the night there" (Moyers 1996, 311). Indeed, this is no normal time but instead a threshold chronotope where a dark God authors a set of possibilities heretofore hidden in the shadows.

Until Bethel, the presence of God in Jacob's life is marked by a kind of semipresence or even absence. God is presumably behind the scenes, foretelling Jacob's usurpation of Esau (Gen 25:23), and invoked in Isaac's blessing (27:28–29). However, Jacob has not yet met God face to face, nor does he claim God for himself, as evidenced by his reply to Isaac: "But Isaac said to his son, "How is it that you have found it so quickly, my son?" He answered, "Because *the Lord your God* granted me success" (27:20). This is the God of Jacob's father. This is not yet Jacob's God. But in this "certain place" (28:10), after the sun had set and the night had fallen, he takes one of the stones "of the place" (28:11), puts his head down and lays down "in that place" (28:11), sees a vision of God, proclaims that "the Lord is in this place" (28:16), notes "how fearsome is this place" (28:17, author's translation); and calls "the name of that place" Bethel (28:19, author's translation), the house of God.[2] Before the narrative places Jacob at Bethel, however, the place already contained the dark footprints of worshipers gone by. Israel's literary history demonstrates that long before the writing of the Bethel episode, Bethel was already haunted by worshipers.

In the eighth century during Amos and Hosea's prophetic careers, Bethel was an important sanctuary (Amos 5:5; 7:10–13; Hos 10:5). And before its excoriation by the prophets as a place of seduction, Bethel had been a sacred site for assembly (Judg 20:18, 26; 21:2; 1 Sam 7:16; Vawter 1977, 311). Bethel remained until King Josiah's Deuteronomistic reform, which obliterated country shrines and priesthoods in favor of Jerusalem-centered worship (2 Kgs 23:15). Vawter (1977, 312, emphasis original) states, "Somehow, Bethel is envisioned as a quintessential meeting place of God and man [sic]—exactly what a shrine or sanctuary is supposed to be—a place where God's *messengers* are constantly *going up and down* bearing petitions and responses, therefore a *gateway to heaven*." When he happens upon this place, Jacob leaves his own dark footprints there. Here, in this darkened place of holiness, Jacob encounters the divine absence that henceforth promises divine presence. What might be expected of such a theophany—judgment for Jacob's multiple moral infractions—is absent. What is present, instead, is the promise of presence.

> And the Lord stood beside him and said, "I am the Lord, the God of Abraham your father and the God of Isaac; the land on which you lie I will give to you and to your offspring; and your offspring shall be like the dust of the earth, and you shall spread abroad to the west and to the east and to the north and to the south; and all the families of the earth

---

2. Alter (2008, 149) notes that this repetition of a term is generally a thematic marker in biblical narrative.

shall be blessed in you and in your offspring. Know that *I am with you and will keep you wherever you go*, and will bring you back to this land; for *I will not leave you* until I have done what I have promised you." (Gen 28:13–15)

Fokkelman (1975, 122) notes that this nocturnal encounter is the pivoting point between two family entanglements—the one with Esau, from which he has just escaped, and the one with Laban, which he will experience immediately following the night at Bethel. Fokkelman states, "In that darkness the light of revelation shines suddenly and surprisingly. The vertical dimension which Rebekah was allowed to glimpse during her pregnancy is now opened up for Jacob himself. Election and blessing prevail over judgment and punishment" (121). Fokkelman's theological comments are apt, yet his phrasing further exemplifies the binary of light and dark, where the light shines (in spite of) the dark, offering something better. Similarly, Anderson (2011, 82–83) maintains that if God intends to reprimand Jacob for his moral infractions, ironically, the chosen mode of punishment is not rebuke but a "litany of unconditional promises." Moreover, the Bethel oracle's reference to Abraham rather than to Isaac indicates Yahweh's sidestepping around Isaac, who has also been deceived, whose god Jacob claimed made him lucky (Gen 27:20). Yahweh's rhetorical return to Abraham indicates that the promise rightly belongs to Jacob. Finally, parallels exist between God's promise to Jacob in Genesis 28:14 and God's promise of the land to Abram in 13:14–15. These associations bypass Isaac and reinforce Yahweh's annoyance at Isaac's preferential treatment for Esau; or they may signal profound changes in intergenerational identity and associated blessings, the transference of wealth. Either way, Anderson (2011, 33) concludes, "The compound effect of these narrative cues demonstrates that God views Jacob and his duplicitous actions positively." Thus, throughout the unfolding of the narrative, human agency, whether through Rebekah or Jacob himself, is always undergirded by an unseen face who has, through his oracle, suggested a script. In the wake of that script, however, human choice has been "momentous" (Morson 1994, 22). The rest of Jacob's life, Fokkelman agrees, occurs amid this continuing election and under the guise of God's presence. Moreover, it appears that presence is not dependent on location, even though place is critical to how Jacob's story unfolds, including Jacob's encounter with the deity both at Bethel and at the Jabbok. The presence of God in Jacob's life henceforth will not hinge on visiting particular holy places. God's presence will not depend on Jacob's pilgrimage but on his own person. This is significant in considering that those producing the story—the returnees—must discover that the presence of God is portable. Even in exile, the presence of God makes itself felt through prophetic utterances (e.g., throughout Second Isaiah, e.g., Isa 43) that promise deliverance and return. Therefore, the portability of the presence of God is significant for Jacob individually and for the postexilic returnees whom he symbolizes. The promise made to Jacob at Bethel, then, is a familiar ringing in the ears for the community producing this story.

Here, Jacob responds with a prayer: "Then Jacob made a vow, saying, 'If God will be with me, and will keep me in this way that I go, and will give me bread to eat and clothing to wear, so that I come again to my father's house in peace, then the LORD shall be my God'" (Gen 28:20–21). Jacob's response to God's beneficence is conditional. Jacob, ever the wrestler, struggles rhetorically with God, bargaining with God just as he did with the famished Esau (Alter 2008, 151). While this dark side of Jacob persists, so does his quest to move from disintegration to integration. To return safe means to return in peace or in wholeness. Rashi interprets בשלום as "whole from sin," free from any defect caused by sin. Here, Rashi also demonstrates clear displeasure with Laban, claiming that בשלום also means not learning from the ways of Laban (Scherman and Zlotowitz 1995, 316). Safe return is his hope for the journey and it is the essence of Jacob's prayer. The promise from God is *presence*; the *possibility* Jacob yearns for is wholeness. Jacob turns the aporia of darkness into an occasion for night prayer, the first night prayer in the Hebrew Bible. In her explication of Pirqe Rabbi Eliezer's midrash, Zornberg (1995, 188) notes, "[Jacob] intended to pray in daylight, in the mode of all human prayer till then, drawing strength from the light of the sun; but God put out the lights and Jacob discovers a *new possibility—almost an impossibility*, an oxymoron, as the *Sefat Emet* conceives it—called the Evening Prayer" (emphasis added). The aporia of darkness is the aporia of God, and in his prayer, Jacob turns the impossibility of God into the possibility of presence. And yet, prayer in general strains itself, as Derrida (1995b, 56) says: "For this particular prayer asks nothing, all the while asking more than everything. This prayer asks God to give himself rather than his gifts." When Jacob prays for peace, and God promises presence, both speak of *possibility* in the face of *impossibility*. The aporia is the dark, which partially hinders Jacob's movement, yet it is the precise thing that allows for excess. Rashi notes that it is this night prayer that gives Jacob light-footedness. When Jacob lifts his feet and goes to the land of the easterners, his heart lifts his feet and it becomes easy to walk (Scherman and Zlotowitz 1995, 317). Bill Moyers links Jacob's light-footedness with the binding of the feet of Isaac (Gen 22:9). Moyers (1996, 294) claims that after lying all night in the place where his father was bound hand and foot, unable to use his legs, Jacob discovers a "certain energy," even in relation to the "haunted family" from which he hails.

Moreover, Jacob has turned the *impossibility* of what the Hebrew Bible says about such encounters—"You cannot see my face; for no one shall see me and live" (Exod 33:20)—into a *possibility* that such an encounter might occur not only in the sleeping but in the waking as well. The possibility of such an encounter must unsay what is impossible in the text in order to say what is possible of the God behind and beyond the text. Derrida (1995b, 59) states,

> And the language of ab-negation or of renunciation is not negative: not only because it does not state in the mode of descriptive predication and of the indicative proposition simply affected with a negation, but because it denounces as much as it renounces; and it denounces, enjoining; it prescribes overflowing this insufficiency; it mandates, *it necessitates* doing the impossible, necessitates going (*Geh*, Go!) where one cannot go.

This episode at Bethel foreshadows the encounter later at the Jabbok where Jacob meets God face to face, cracking open the *no* inscribed on the face of the Hebrew Bible, this aporia, into excess. Seemingly, the Hebrew Bible's inscribed "no" on the Face of all faces, and on the face of the page, is perhaps more contingent on the face of the human than on the face of God.[3] Here, at Bethel, Jacob's face is still hidden behind a mask of disintegration, running from the face of Esau, even as masquerading as that face is the reason for his footprints. Later, Jacob will meet God face to face, individuating him from his brother (Gen 33:10). For now, however, this dark encounter offers the *possibility* for an encounter of greater intimacy.

The final dark event leading up to the Jabbok encounter begins in "broad daylight" (Gen 29:7) and ends with darkness: "Jacob kept Laban the

---

3. One may hear resonances here with the central question of C. S. Lewis's (1956) final novel, *Till We Have Faces*: "How can the gods meet us face to face until we have faces?"

Aramean in the dark, not telling him that he was fleeing" (31:20 NJPS).[4] When Jacob arrives in broad daylight at the door of his uncle Laban, he is deceived by Laban through the darkness. After Jacob works for him for seven years, Laban promises to give Rachel to Jacob in marriage. After spending the night together, Jacob awakens to find himself in bed with the wrong woman—Rachel's sister, Leah. Zornberg (1995, 211) states, "[Leah] takes Rachel's place under the marriage canopy; and in the darkness, in which forms and structures become fluid, in which transformations, fantastic combinations, and splittings become possible, Leah *becomes* Rachel." Leah becomes Rachel in the same way that Jacob *became Esau* before the face of his father, Isaac. Yet this time, Jacob is deceived though the darkness. Zucker (1986, 407) states, "Darkness is essential to Laban's 'putting one over' on Jacob. The wedding feast lasts well into the evening, for it was only 'when evening came' (Gen. 29:23) that Laban brought Leah to Jacob, and it is, ironically, in the contrasting light of morning that the new husband sees that he has been outmaneuvered." This time, the darkness acts as a protective cover not for Jacob but for Leah. The nocturnal time space of the marriage bed supposedly transitions her as one covered by the protection of a father to one covered by the protection of a husband. Here, the dark deception is underscored by the emphasis on Leah's eyes—described as "weak," harking back to Isaac's blind eyes, which Jacob used to his advantage in order to deceive. Soon thereafter, the relationship between Jacob and Laban disintegrates, with each one keeping the other in the dark about the sheep and the goats they were breeding. Jacob notices that Laban's face is not with him as it had been in the past (Gen 31:2, 5). Jacob takes his wives and other possessions, keeping Laban the Aramaean in the dark as he leaves Laban's house (31:20). The God who promised to be present with Jacob appears to Laban at night and warns him not to harm Jacob (31:24, 29). The two make a pact not to harm each other. And Jacob sets his face toward the Mount Gilead and toward Edom, the home of his brother (31:21).

Side Shadows at the Jabbok

At the Jabbok, the darkness is present/absent in several ways: through dust and dark, which render seeing the visage of God (im)possible;

---

4. While the NJPS translates the Hebrew of the phrase as keeping Laban in the dark, the Hebrew deals with stealing the heart of Laban.

through the self-concealing and ambiguous nature of Elohim/Ish; and through the apophatic gestures of silence, isolation, and trembling that characterize the encounter.

To begin, at the beginning, when darkness was on the face of the ארץ ("earth, dirt, land") two men kicked up some dust together by the River Jabbok. Rashi was the first interpreter to notice darkness on the surface of the text. Rashi notes that Menachem explains that ויאבק (and he wrestled) means "and a man became dusted." According to Menachem and Rashi, Jacob and his assailant would have raised dust with their feet through their movements. Rashi further amends Menachem's interpretation by drawing on Aramaic. Rashi states, "It appears to me that it means 'and he became bound up' and it is an Aramaic word, like 'after they became bound up with it,' and 'tied them in a bow,' which means 'tying in a bow'; for it is the way of two people who are struggling to topple each other that one hugs and ties up the other with his arms" (Scherman and Zlotowitz 1995, 370). Being bound and kicking up dust at the Jabbok recalls the earlier episode at Bethel, also in darkness, where Rashi again draws on an image of darkness in relation to the promissory blessings of God. In his night prayer just prior to the Jabbok encounter, Jacob reminds God: "Yet you have said, 'I will surely do you good, and make your offspring as the sand of the sea, which cannot be counted because of their number'" (Gen 32:12). Rashi rightly notes that the word used by Yahweh at Bethel is עפר ("dust"; Scherman and Zlotowitz 1995, 364). While Rashi's reminder may seem like splitting philological hairs, here his midrash evokes the connection between darkness (both the dark night and the dust) and the promissory blessings of God. These promises are made to Jacob in the darkness at Bethel; they are prayed for in the dark prior to their wrestling match; and later they are actualized in the dark at the Jabbok. Therefore, it appears that at the Jabbok, Jacob and his assailant are doing more than kicking up the dust—they are also kicking up the promises. Theirs is a physical and psychological negotiation of what has already been promised, with darkness as proximate companion. Similarly, the Zohar also draws on the imagery of dust in order to underscore the apophatic nature of the episode.

The Zohar views the assailant as the demonic angel of Esau (named Samael) and compares the dust or powder with the Shekinah or ash the rabbis mention in the midrash: "What is the difference between them? Ash, residue of fire, never generating fruit; dust, yielding all fruit, totality of above and below.... But ash never generates fruit or vegetation, so *va-ye'aveq*, and he wrestled, arriving with that *avaq*, ash, riding upon it, to contest against Jacob" (Matt 2006, 28). For the rabbis, the dark ash symbolizes Lilith, the demonic feminine, who is barren, while dust symbolizes Shekinah, who receives all emanation and bears life below (28). The wrestling until the break of dawn (Gen 32:26) symbolizes the night of exile that Israel endured. "For now exile resembles night—it is night!—and that ash rules over Israel, who lie in alien dust, until morning rises and day brightens. Then Israel will prevail; to them will be granted the kingdom, since they are the holy ones of the Most High" (Matt 2006, 29). Esau, then, in the rabbinic mind, stands in variously for the demonic wrestling opponent Lilith, who wages war in darkness, the tragedy of the exile, and later, as a polemic against Christianity. Thus, in the rabbinic mind, Israel (the man and the nation) wrestles with a formidable opponent whom he/it will eventually overcome. The darkness of the exile preoccupied the rabbinic mind, prompting the rabbis to make theo-political statements regarding the assailant's identity.

For Keller, the scene prompts a different kind of political reading. In her theo-political interpretation of the encounter, Keller (2003, 230–31) states:

> If we face the shadow in the night—whether we call it Other, angel, Elohim, problem, sibling—we may find ourselves moved by a strange eros. This "wrestling" (*va-ye' avek*), as Rashi comments, "is the way of two people who strain to push each other down to the ground—they embrace and struggle with each other" (*hovko ve-ovko*; Gen. 32:24). Limping into the next day, ultimately wounded ("touched in the hollow of the thigh"), the place of this nocturnal struggle has opened up: it is called *Peni'el*. Face of godhood.

Keller notes that the image of the dark evokes fecundity—that which is birthed, begotten in dust or dirt. What is birthed, it seems, is actually a rebirth, though certainly not of Jacob. Rather, the dark allows for a rebirth or unearthing of promises already made in the dark. In the dark they are (con)tested amid arms and limbs and fears and a wrestle and embrace that (dis)appear markedly similar. Could it be that both Elohim/Ish and Jacob are (re)born on this night to the possibilities inherent in the promises? As Hirsch has said, the element of the dark is crucial to interpretation of the Jabbok text. Hirsch's literary, poetic reading of the Jabbok encounter connects to what William Wordsworth termed "spots of time," as well as Virginia Woolf's "moments of being" and James Joyce's "epiphanies." Hirsch states,

> Psychologically, everything must happen under the eerie cover of darkness because Jacob's experience is unsightly, epiphanic, and prophetic, an event out of time. The linear flow and narrative momentum of the overarching story—Jacob's return to his homeland and reconciliation with his brother—are radically interrupted; indeed, what we think of as chronological or historical time is completely ruptured on this night of nights.... He is now a solitary traveler left on the edge of a deep gorge. The nocturnal setting is so crucial because he has moved outside the arena of what can be apprehended by daylight and has entered the realm of the visionary. He has moved from eyesight to vision. The dangerous encounter that follows is the pivotal moment—the turning point—in Jacob's life. The great archaic genius of the Yahwist was to literalize in a human figure the encounter with the Otherworld. (Rosenberg 1996, 183–84)

As a specific time space, the darkness of the Jabbok demonstrates the unfinished nature of the story, embodied in the bodies of Jacob and the antagonist. In what Bakhtin (1981, 99) has called the "chronotopic motif of meeting," at the Jabbok the "inner unfinalizability" of these characters is foregrounded (Morson 1994, 92). Here they "act into the open future," one without teleology, a suspension of time in which the promises made to Jacob at Bethel are radically and grotesquely called into question (99–100). The dark at Bethel had authored Jacob to trust in the provision of God. In that dark chronotope the promises he needed to hear were uttered. Just prior to the moment of meeting at the Jabbok, he offers a night prayer beseeching God to remember those promises. Darkness there, as in Rebekah's womb and in the tents he kept, had been protective. At the Jabbok, however, a radical reauthoring of darkness takes place. Here, the darkness becomes a space where the anxieties of his waking life are heightened. This mysterious man may kill him, just as Esau may. The promises made to him at Bethel are of no use if he does not make it through the night. The assurance offered in the dark at Bethel is removed at the Jabbok. This time space is a disintegration, a rupturing akin to the darkness of exile he felt so long ago (Gen 28:10) and akin to, it would seem, the darkness of exile for the nation he comes to represent.

Equally critical to this time space is not only the darkness but also the isolation of the protagonist and the relative silence of the antagonist. A familiar trifecta of apophasis hovers over the scene at the Jabbok: darkness, isolation, and relative silence. The darkness of this time space, on the one hand, appears to act as a protective shield for Jacob's mortality (Exod

33:20), even as the presence of that darkness heightens the anxiety of the moment. The dark renders the Face of all faces (in)visible. Derrida posits two variations of (in)visibility. First, Derrida refers to the visible in-visible, an invisible of the order of the visible that one keeps in secret by keeping out of sight. Like a veil over a face, a surface is concealed beneath another. Whatever one conceals in this way becomes invisible but remains within the order of visibility. Derrida also refers to absolute invisibility; this absolutely nonvisible refers to whatever falls outside the register of sight: the sonorous, the musical, the vocal or phonic, but also the tactile and odoriferous. Desire also falls into this category, where "seeing in secret" moves secrecy beyond the secret (Derrida 1995a, 90). For Derrida, this is evocative of the *mysterium tremendum*. Elohim/Ish looks at Jacob, facing him, while Jacob must only hear him—"What is your name?" (Gen 32:29). Most often, Derrida claims, this *mysterium tremendum*, here, Elohim/Ish or the Face of all faces, is heard through the voice of another—angel, prophet, messiah, or postman. "God looks at me and I don't see him and it is on the basis of this gaze that singles me out and my responsibility comes into being" (Derrida 1995b, 91). As Derrida claims, this is dissymmetrical—the gaze sees Jacob without Jacob seeing it look at him.

There is, of course, something of trembling within this encounter with the *mysterium tremendum*, with this Face and his frequent companion, darkness. An encounter with this Face of all faces holds the potentiality or portend(iality) for death. It is violence and fraternal fear, after all, that this apophatic text narrates (Gen 32:7, 25, 28). For Jacob, the *mysterium tremendum* is both human and divine, as his wrestling partner attests: "For you have striven with Elohim and with Anashim" (32:28, author's translation). Both his proximate wrestling partner at the Jabbok and Esau, who he will face the next day, are reasons to tremble. He trembles because he faces, on the one hand, the (un)known—"Are these the shadows of the things that will be, or are they shadows of things that may be, only?" (Dickens 1986). Does Jacob's trembling portend a certain death at Esau's hand? Jacob's future—the stuff of life and death—is concealed in darkness. Jacob is left in the dark. His future is a secret to him. Derrida (1995b, 53–54) writes:

> A secret always *makes* you tremble. Not simply quiver or shiver, which also happens sometimes but tremble. A quiver can of course manifest fear, anguish, apprehension of death; as when one quivers in advance, in anticipation of what is to come.... A quiver is not always very serious, it

> is sometimes discreet, barely discernable, somewhat epiphenomenal. It prepares for, rather than follows the event.... On the other hand, trembling, at least as a signal or symptom, is something that has already taken place.... It suggests that violence is going to break out again, that some traumatism will insist on being repeated. Most often we neither know what is coming upon us nor see its origin; it therefore remains a secret.

Trembling takes place, Derrida states, because Jacob is afraid of what already makes him afraid. He has been threatened, the sound of it still ringing in his ears (Gen 27:41–45). He waits, not only for the repetition of the threat (32:7), but ultimately for what has been forestalled—the possibility of his own death. Thus, he trembles not only because the threat may be repeated but because it may be actualized. More immediately, however, Jacob trembles because in the concealed face of his opponent, death stares him in the face. The dark, death, and this man-God all share the same face, one who, in Derridian terms, appears (un)like the *kryptō*.

For Derrida, the *kryptō* refers to the concealed, dissimulated, secret clandestine. The *kryptō* is that which extends beyond the visible, making its home in the field of secrecy beyond the nonvisible to that which *resists deciphering*. Rather than being merely invisible, the *kryptō* or secret is illegible or undecipherable (Derrida 1995b, 89–90). That is, it is purely apophatic, that which resists—"Why do you ask my name?" (Gen 32:29). This refusal to (self-)disclose, coupled with the darkness as his companion, keeps the secret. Darkness and silence cloak the conversation—and conversation partner—in mystery. Darkness, isolation, and silence function as aporia, blocking movement. Derrida's comments on the Akedah are equally apt for the verbal resistance displayed by the Face of all faces at the Jabbok. This Face speaks. He says a lot. As Derrida (1995b, 59) puts it: "Speaking in order not to say anything is always the best technique for keeping a secret." But even if the Face of all faces says everything, he need only keep silent on a single thing to conclude that he has not spoken. The silence impregnates the whole discourse. The Face speaks and he resists speaking. He responds without responding, in the form of a question (Gen 32:29). He responds indirectly. The Face speaks in order not to say anything about the essential thing that he must keep secret—namely, his identity, his Name and Face.

But why this dark apophasis, this heavy silence? For Derrida, the face of death and the face of love appear to be one and the same. In speaking about Abraham's role in the Akedah, Derrida (1995b, 65) (un)says:

4. The Dark

Abraham comes to hate those closest to him by keeping silent, he comes to hate his only beloved son by consenting to put him to death. He hates them not out of hatred, of course, but out of love. He doesn't hate them any less for that, on the contrary. Abraham must love his son absolutely to come to the point where he will grant him death, to commit what ethics would call hatred and murder.

Certainly, the Jabbok encounter is not the only occurrence of a spasmodic action on the part of this Face toward one of his chosen just prior to an event of significance (see Exod 4:24–26). Is the weapon wielded by the darkness and the Face it conceals something akin to love, a kind of holy, preparatory purgation? Is this "beloved enemy," as Buechner (2006, 7) calls him, the "face of love"? For Derrida, it appears that God—the name of the absolute other *as* other and *as* unique—wields not only the flint knife of Abraham, or in the case of Jacob, the power to kill, but paradox, scandal, and aporia. The dark functions as the "bottomless collapse," that place where everything else "bottoms out." What remains is a Face who has left his darkened signature. And it is a Face that might, along with Derrida (1995b, 68), claim the following: "I offer a gift of death, I betray, I don't need to raise my knife over my son on Mount Moriah for that. Day and night, at every instant, on all the Mount Moriahs of this world, I am doing that, raising my knife over what I love and must love, over those to whom I owe absolute fidelity, incommensurably." Derrida's day and night, and more aptly, the night at the Jabbok, functions as merism for Jacob's whole life. From the dark time space of the womb to the possibilities awakened in the dark at Bethel, that elusive presence, that *kryptō*, has left dark footprints, a dark signature of presence, over Jacob's whole life. Jacob's response is something of the apophatic, too, some measure of *Gelassenheit*: "Surely the LORD is in this place—and I did not know it!" (Gen 28:16), and, "For I have seen God face to face, and yet my life is preserved" (32:30). Life is offered in the Face of death. Reconciliation is offered in the Face of hatred (33:4). And darkness has (un)shaded into the morning (32:31).

In spite of the sunrise at the end of the story, which signals hope and a new beginning, the dark and ambiguous nature of the Face at the Jabbok remains a cause for scholarly and theological trembling. Christian interpreters past and present have found the picture of God at the Jabbok to be unsettling. In his transcanonical examination of the Jabbok encounter, Tongue traces scholars' own wrestling matches with the text. He begins with Hosea's canonical midrash, through Rashi's interpretations in the eleventh and twelfth centuries, through the Reformation, all the way to contemporary retellings. Unsurprisingly, for Reformers such as John Calvin and Martin Luther, Jacob's wrestling partner was thought to be some iteration of the divine, whether God or Jesus. Their anxiety about this God was palpable, as Tongue (2014, 176) attests:

> Luther and Calvin seem to have little difficulty imagining the assailant as God Himself, incarnate as the unrecognized Son, rather than merely a man or an angel. This fits with the theologies which they are trying to construct around the paradoxical relationships between the Christian and a God able to destroy and bless, to discipline and to love, *whilst remaining dark and obscure.* (emphasis added)

Tongue's survey reveals not merely anxiety surrounding the nature and character of God as revealed in the text. The history of interpretation also demonstrates a certain tendency among Christian readers to deflect the darker elements. Luther and Calvin's foregrounding of blessing and love are paradigmatic of this tendency, as was the tendency to focus on the other darker elements of the text—Jacob's own dark character finding reformation in a dark night of the soul, for example. Indeed, their psychological struggle with the darkness of the text appears to mirror in intensity the physical struggle between Jacob and Elohim/Ish.

Tongue (2014, 174) notes that for Calvin in particular, a deep paradoxical need existed for an adversary to prove Jacob's faith. It was, in Calvin's words, "an occasion to exhibit, as on a field of battle, an example and proof of our strength and firmness.... But this could not be done without an adversary, *for what advantage would it be to fight with a shadow?*" (Tongue 2014, 174, emphasis added). And yet fighting with a shadow, or a shadowy figure, is exactly what Jacob does, for how can a face properly be seen in darkness? Even as Jacob exclaims that he has looked upon God and lived, how much of God does he actually see? For Calvin's theological vision, the adversary has to be more than Josephus's phantom (Tongue 2014, 174). In order to prove one's faith it must be tested against a God who "not only exhorts us to be strong, but supplies us also with arms, endues us with strength, and also fights himself, in a manner, with us, and is powerful in us, and enables us to overcome our temptations" (Tongue 2014, 174).

For Luther, however, Calvin's interpretation of God as conqueror is deeply problematic, for Calvin's interpretation (and therefore Calvin's

God and the story Calvin (re)tells is, as Tongue (2014, 175) puts it, "dark with ambiguities." Luther seems fascinated with the "dark side of God," as he links the Jabbok encounter with the Akedah (Tongue 2014, 174–75). Luther states that the Jabbok encounter, as well as the binding of Isaac, indicates "a dark side to the nature of God, an aspect of his character which seems to want to annihilate his own promises, and which can be resisted only by clinging more firmly to these promises" (Pelikan and Oswald 1970, 146–47). The obscurity and paradoxes involved in the nocturnal wrestling match appeal to the "imaginative faculties, especially, for the Reformation mind, with the implied stakes of 'wrestling' a blessing from *an obscured and terrifying God*" (Tongue 2014, 175, emphasis added). Obscured and terrifying are apt descriptions of the Face's endarkenment in the Jabbok encounter. The Face remains both obscure—(apo)phatic for what is visible and knowable—and terrifying for the way he attacks the person he has promised to bless. Ultimately, the Reformers struggled with the notion that the God who appeared at the Jabbok was not, perhaps, the same God who appeared to them in their prayer closets. Certainly, this remains a challenge even for contemporary (religious) interpreters who dust off their Hebrew Bibles and read a difficult text about a dark God who nearly kills the same person he has promised to bless.

Wilson challenges Wessner's (2000, 169–77) positive assessment of this encounter, arguing that instead of blessing it produces *both* blessing *and* fear. Nevertheless, Wilson's (2009, 114) conclusion is still positive, using vocabulary not found in the text itself: "Ultimately, this divine encounter transforms, even sanctifies, the person(s) involved and prepares the persons for divine service, bearing witness to the awesomeness and holiness of Yahweh." Wilson's assessment is also an implicit stamp of approval on the character of God. Rather than allowing the dark and unruly portrayal of God present in the text to stand on its own, Wilson's interpretation domesticates God.

However, other scholars such as Otto Kaiser and Norman Whybray provide alternative images of a Face who appears anything but domesticated. If God's Face is in view at all, for these scholars it appears dark, immoral, or altogether unruly. In his examination of three difficult narratives in the Pentateuch (Gen 22:1–19; Exod 4:24–26; Gen 32:22–32), Kaiser draws on the tension between *deus absconditus* and *deus revelatus*. When speaking about the near sacrifice of Isaac, Kaiser (2000, 77) holds in tension the "dark God" who, on the one hand, threatens to destroy the meaning of life; and the "revealed God,"[5] who is working to fulfill the promises he has made (Gen 12:1–3; 15:1–21; 17:1–16). This tension between a revealed God who makes promises and a dark God who threatens the promises he makes certainly finds resonance in the near sacrifice of Isaac and is present explicitly in the *panim el panim* (face to face) encounter at the Jabbok. Not even prayer, Kaiser (2000, 81) maintains, appears to pacify or protect from a dark God who attacks the patriarch at night. Jacob's night prayer in Gen 32:10–13 does appear effective in that it saves him from violent encounter with Esau. However, his prayer does not save him from violent attack from Elohim/Ish. Rather, it is prayer that appears to stimulate it. Indeed, it is only after Jacob prays that he is attacked and is forever marked by God. Kaiser (81) affirms:

> The context makes it clear that prayer in fact does not protect a person from such an encounter with the dark God.... Whoever has encountered God will remain marked by him, even after having won the struggle with fear in prayer. Prayer itself thus mediates between the *deus absconditus* and the *deus revelatus*, between the God who delivers human beings over to their own fears and anxieties and the God who nonetheless promises his presence as the foundation of the basic trust from which they live (Gen. 28:15; 31:3; 32:10).

For Kaiser (2000, 81), this tension between *deus absconditus* and *deus revelatus* demonstrates the "struggle for certainty" of God's "sustaining, sheltering presence." For Kaiser every theodicy ultimately deconstructs itself. Indeed, Jacob's God, or the god who wrestles with him, appears at once enshrouded in darkness, hidden, and yet also paradoxically and even violently present. This God is a kind of hyperpresence, even as it must be admitted that this is a God who is still hidden. To use Terrien's (2000) terms, this God is *self-concealing*.

In his theological monograph, Balentine traces the hiding of the face of God in the Old Testament. The phrase פנים סתר ("hide the face") occurs twenty-nine times in the Hebrew Bible: four times in the Pentateuch,

---

5. Kaiser (2001, 73) states explicitly: "Our entire human experience militates against understanding God only as the beneficent, revealed God devoted to human beings in his salvific will. If indeed he is Lord of all reality, then his nature also includes unpredictability, inaccessibility, and hiddenness, for everything that lives also suffers. Only an understanding that conceives his revealed nature together with this hidden quality preserves his comprehensive divinity."

twelve times in the Psalms, eleven times in the Prophets, and twice in the wisdom literature (Exod 3:6; Deut 31:17, 18; 32:20; Pss 10:11; 13:2; 22:25; 27:9; 30:8; 44:25; 51:11; 69:18; 88:15; 102:3; 104:29; 143:7; Isa 8:17; 50:6; 53:3; 54:8; 59:2; 64:6; Ezek 39:23, 24, 29; Mic 3:4; Jer 33:5; Job 13:24; 34:29). Balentine (2000, 164) says the reason for the hiding of God's face is to demonstrate that Israel's God will not brook unfaithfulness; if Israel does not adhere to God's demands on their loyalty, they cannot expect the benefit of his presence. Yet, as the Jacob cycle demonstrates, God appears more than willing to brook the unfaithfulness and deception of Jacob, even acting as a trickster himself while Jacob is in the womb. Moreover, despite the nature of Jacob's character, God continues implicitly to sanction his success (Gen 27:26–38; 28:13–22; 30:25–43; 31:24). Still, it must be noted that Jacob's success does not necessarily mean that God is present to him in an intimate way. Balentine (2000, 171) maintains that this problem of the presence of God appears in virtually every stratum of the Old Testament.[6] For Terrien, the full force of the Hebrew reflexive must be noted (e.g., Isa 45:15, a "self-concealing God"). For Terrien, this terminology reflects more accurately the Hebraic understanding of divine hiddenness—an active and sustained hiding with an emphasis on divine freedom and sovereignty, the "presence of an absence." Precisely this "elusive presence," Terrien (2000) thinks, provides the key to understanding not only the Hebrew Bible but the Bible as a whole. However, scholars are divided as to just how present or absent this Face may be in the Jacob cycle. Is this

---

6. Balentine states that in the early narratives of the wandering in the wilderness, it is the lack of food and water that prompts Israel to question God's presence. In the lament psalms, it is the experience of unjust suffering that leads the worshiper to accuse God of being capricious in his treatment of his people. In the Prophets, the experience of God's hiddenness is identified with God's departure from Jerusalem. And in the wisdom literature, the hiddenness of God's activities arises out of the fragmentary nature of human understanding. Indeed, Balentine (2000, 171–72) contends: "Israel's struggle with God's hiddenness ought not to be treated as if it were merely a footnote to an otherwise optimistic and unshakeable faith. The evidence of the present study would hardly support such an understanding. It indicates instead that Israel was repeatedly plagued by the experience of God's hiddenness. Time and again the disparity between religious convictions and the realities of actual experience brought the issue into the forefront of Israel's thought.… What calls for chief mention here is the fact that the experience of God's hiddenness, just as the experience of his presence, is an integral part of Israelite faith. Both experiences derive from the nature of God himself. He is both hidden and present, both near and far away."

Face one who lingers behind Jacob at every step, haunting his footsteps all the way through? Is this Face one who is maddeningly absent, thus forcing human agency to propel events forward throughout the narrative? Is this a Face that is present, even hyperpresent (and violently so), but only at the Jabbok?

For Humphreys, a further complication arises when attempting to (un)cover the Face at the Jabbok—the fact that the Face at Bethel appears markedly different from the Face at the Jabbok. While there was a certain mysterious quality about the first encounter at Bethel, for Humphreys this encounter was clearly constructed around God's promise of support, protection, and safe return. By contrast, the פנים אל פנים ("face to face") at the Jabbok takes on a dark and mysterious quality in significant ways; it is not clear at times just who is who as the episode unfolds, opening with the laconic "And a man wrestled with him until the rising of the dawn" (Gen 32:24, author's translation; Humphreys 2001, 191). The Face is at once איש and Elohim, man and God. Humphreys (191) questions whether this transformation represents Jacob's own developing awareness of who and what this figure is—from man to God. Jacob's life of struggle with all around him, then, is finally also a life of extended struggle with God. This struggle with God seems in part a struggle to release God from the rhetorical grip of his prayer and wrestling partner. Humphreys notes that at certain key moments in the narrative (Gen 29:31; 30:22; 31:3, 24), God does act in ways that further Jacob's desires and fulfills the promises made in Genesis 28:13–15. Nevertheless, God is most fully present in what others say of God—Leah and Rachel, Laban, and especially Jacob. In each instance, Humphreys asserts, God is spoken of in ways that serve the interests of the one speaking of God. God is a character constructed in the stories these characters tell. This is a God constructed by Jacob, a God who facilitates Jacob's good and who serves Jacob's needs. This is a God in danger of becoming "Jacob's God," and, as Humphreys (2001, 194) notes, perhaps the Jabbok encounter is God's opportunity to confront Jacob; it is a time for God to reconstruct Jacob. In this way, it seems both God and Jacob are in the process of be-coming; each character's markings on the other may change the other. Indeed, Jacob's wrestling match at the Jabbok River appears to work on both levels, leaving him physically wounded (Gen 32:32) yet also allowing him to confront his brother without fear (33:1–3) (Humphreys 2001, 194). Nevertheless, the dark God that appears at the Jabbok is not an isolated incident in the Hebrew Bible. Several intertexts also demonstrate the dark nature of this God.

While Whybray does not discuss the Jabbok encounter specifically, the texts he does examine (portions of the primeval history in Gen 1–11; 18; and Job 1–2) uncover a Face that, for him, appears all too willing to act in an immoral or amoral way. For Whybray (1996, 89), these narratives constitute a small part of a much larger problem—namely, can one properly speak of a consistent view of God in the Hebrew Bible? Whybray's presentation variously presents this Face as one who is vulnerable, an anthropomorphic construction that is pre-Yahwistic; and at other times amoral or immoral, a depiction derived from folklore that glorifies Moses (Exod 32; Num 11; 14). In such depictions, the human (be it Moses, Abraham, or someone else) is depicted as more righteous than the god that human represents. Whybray draws on seminal scholars Gunkel and John Skinner, who raised similar questions about the nature of the divine character. Gunkel asks, "What can one expect of human judges if the highest judge does not care for justice?" and Skinner likewise, "Unrighteousness in the Supreme Ruler of the world would make piety impossible" (Whybray 1989, 102). In each of these stories stand two facets of the character of God that are difficult to reconcile: on the one hand, the caring God whose loving guidance of his people, though it may necessitate severe discipline, is tempered with mercy; and on the other an "irrational god" who loses patience with his people and is ready even to destroy them (117). In speaking of the Joban prologue specifically, Athalya Brenner calls this a dark side of God that has not yet been conquered (Whybray 1989, 111). In particular, the Face at the Jabbok is indeed a dark one, one embraced and concealed in the dark. The Face is one as blank and as black as the dark itself, one undecipherable yet who has nevertheless left a dark signature on the place and the page.

The Trope of the Blank

I find it necessary to end again at the beginning, when darkness was on the face of the deep. In the end, the dark is still on the face of the page, as Fokkelman (1975, 222) observes: "The ending is most ambiguous: Jacob passes as a delivered man, but is lame. Looking back we see that the entire event has been imbued with ambiguity. The adversary's identity, the issue of the struggle, the 'striving' in v. 29, asking for one another's names: all these elements can be and must be looked at from two sides." To put it darkly, the ending is itself a type of apophasis—it says, says otherwise, and ultimately resists finality. The ending is like a blank page continuing to be written on and then erased. In *The Breaking of the Vessels*, literary critic Harold Bloom traces what he calls "the trope of the blank" from the poetry of John Milton to Wallace Stevens. Derived from the French *blanc*, for "white," blanc is also, paradoxically, related to the word *black*. Both black and blank share the same root, meaning "to shine or flash" (Zornberg 1995, 361). To be assailed by the blank is to draw near to the printed page as if there were no words on it at all. Readers are struck by the pages' density, emptiness, or unintelligibility. Words become no words, and the page is unreadable. Stevens (1990, 267) puts it well: "It is difficult to read. The page is dark. Yet he knows what it is that he expects. The page is blank or a frame without a glass, or a glass that is empty when he looks." To put it simply, the Face is glimpsed through a page darkly. Brought out of the dark yet kept by it still, the Jabbok and all the faces that haunt it recede into the night.

For the community constructing and remembering this text, the picture of Jacob, who knows the displacement of darkness, who receives deferred promises in that dark displacement/exile, and whose relationship to the divine is obscure or dark symbolizes their reality of exile following the Babylonian conquest. The Jabbok story symbolizes the darkness of their exile, of their present, and possibly of their future. The story functions as midrash, a continued searching, which is itself apophatic.

5
THE CROSSING

For the community constructing the Jabbok story, exile and return are at the heart of their shared experience. They understand the darkness of exile and the complexity of crossing home. Because Jacob is the character they have constructed to embody their story, Jacob must also transition from displacement (ויצא, "and he left") to crossing over into the land (ויעבר, "and he crossed"). Just as Jacob has experienced exile in the story world, so too he must experience a coming home. In order to do that, he must cross over a dangerous place—the Jabbok River. The community telling the story emplots their fears and concerns, their prejudices and complicated inter-relationships, on their own crossing and returning home. Therefore, Jacob's crossing of the Jabbok River contains elements of the community's own fears of fraternal retaliation, prejudicial and suspicious fraternal reconciliations, and complex relationship to God and to the land. For the community constructing this story, their past is traumatic and their present tenuous. The narrative's emphasis on tension, struggle, and trickery in the Jacob cycle is one discernible way the community can work through its traumatic past. These tensions also demonstrate the multiple and, at times, contrasting ways in which that past can be remembered. Therefore, the Jabbok story is no casual, disinterested recollection of a shared past. Rather, the story is an example of how wounded storytellers construct a past based on present needs and future anxieties. The Jabbok text—and the Jacob cycle generally—functions as a hinge between the community's past, present, and future.

Drawing on the remarks of Fewell (2016, 4), biblical narratives such as this one work on several levels: they express in story form what happens in bodies, narrating anxieties and trauma; they help communities rebuild what has been lost; they express preoccupation with boundaries; they use trickster characters to disrupt what is culturally normative; they tell a community's troubles and narrate shattered assumptions; and they vacillate between tradition and new ways in which Yahweh may be working in the world. Jacob's crossing of the Jabbok River and subsequent settling in the land is an apt reminder of the multiple concurrent work that biblical narratives can do. Here, Mieke Bal offers a helpful word in need of a minor corrective. Bal states the following: "The people with whom literature is concerned are not real people. They are *fabricated creatures* made up from fantasy, imitation, memory: *paper people, without flesh and blood*" (Elliott 2011, 59–97, emphases added). Here it is necessary to alter Bal's statements slightly—even if they were fabricated creatures, Jacob and Esau are not without historical valence. They are still conduits for the makers of meaning in the Israelite community. Jacob and Esau are crafted in the hands of narrators, and they are contained in the pages of narrative. Here the focus is not on what *is* or *is not* historical, as Scott Elliott (2011, 67–68) explains:

> Narrative forces the negotiation of boundaries between truth and mendacity to take place elsewhere. What seems like a relatively clear-cut dichotomy between fact and fiction is in fact a mirage. For instance, everything we know about historical (read "real") figures has been garnered through a series of encounters—narrated. Even firsthand experience is recounted through the telling of stories, stories that have, at their heart, an interest in explanation, which is to say meaning-making.

Biblical narrative and cultural/collective memory studies are necessary conversation partners in the discussion of Jacob's crossing. Pairing the Jacob cycle with collective/cultural memory studies, as well as the socionarratological insights of Frank (2010, 20), demonstrates that the Jabbok functions as a usable past in the wake of communal trauma. The Jabbok story and its characters represent that trauma and situate communal identity through crossing, maintaining, and reifying boundaries. Such a conversation raises questions about the sunrise happy ending of the story, emphasizing what it meant for the postexilic community to work through their trauma and to lay claim to land that was at once home and not-home. Such a conversation highlights the exilic community's preoccupation with boundaries through the figure of Esau and his progenitors, the Edomites. And such a conversation spotlights the complexity of peaceful reconciliation between the returnees and the remainees in postexilic Yehud.

In this chapter, I put biblical narrative into conversation with cultural/collective memory studies in order to do what these storytellers have done—to work through all of these complicated questions of identity, boundary reification, and the long journey home.

Constructing Esau and the Edomites

Within the narrative, Rebekah's womb is the first threshold to be crossed and the site where fraternal conflict gestates: "And Yahweh said to her, 'Two peoples are in your womb and two peoples are in your belly. And people will be divided from people and one people will be stronger than the other; and the chief (one) will serve the insignificant (one)'" (Gen 25:23) As Heard (2001, 98–99) notes, scholars typically translate the last line "the older will serve the younger."[1] He avers that syntactically, the case is not closed, noting the ambiguity involved in who will serve whom. The syntax of the entire clause must be considered. A lack of explicit case markers requires other recourse to consider subject and object of the verb יעבד ("he will serve"). Heard claims the translation choice "the older will serve the younger" contradicts the most frequent constructions of Hebrew grammar; while "the younger will serve the older" pits Israelite ethnic pride vis-à-vis Edom. On the other hand, Heard states, seeking a resolution by translating the phrase "one people will be stronger than the other" also fails to close the case. The odd syntax of subject-verb-object (or as containing an unmarked nominative absolute), verse 23bβ predicts Jacob's purchase of Esau's birthright (Gen 25) and the theft of his blessing (Gen 27). Moreover, for Heard, Jacob's actions receive a "veneer of divine approval, or at least of divine foreknowledge." Therefore, Jacob's subservient attitude toward Esau later in the narrative (Gen 33) appears contrary to the divine oracle (Heard 2001, 100). However, if read according to the more natural syntax of object-verb-subject, the oracle predicts Esau's preeminence, inverting the relationship of Jacob's actions to the divine will specified above. This second reading, Heard (100) maintains, renders Jacob's purchase of the birthright and theft of the blessing contrary to the oracle; his later subservient attitude toward Esau, then, gains a "sense of divine approval."

In the end, however, Heard (2001, 100) concludes: "By using the ambiguous *noun-verb-noun* pattern with no additional markers, the narrator has essentially compelled readers to make their own decisions about the sense of v. 23bβ." For Rashi, the vagueness of the oracle in Gen 25 means that sometimes one brother would prevail, sometimes the other: "They will not be equal in power, when one rises the other falls" (Scherman and Zlotowitz 1995, 275).

---

1. See further p. 104 n 1.

This scholarly disagreement over seemingly grammatical minutiae leads, obviously, to arguments that are theological in nature. Equally important, though, is that both this disagreement and the midrashic contributions of Rashi demonstrate the point that collective memory studies attempts to make—communities form multiple, even contrasting, memories to suit their present needs. The tension, struggle, and trickery of Jacob pays off not only for him as a character; it pays off for the community attempting to transform their past into a usable present. Because the past is amorphous, it is amenable to intervention. The past remains an authority, but the nature of its authority shifts. Jan Assmann's (2006, 3) comments on the emotive aspects of memory are apt: "Remembering means pushing other things into the background, making distinctions, obliterating many things in order to shed light on others. This brings horizon and perspective into individual memory spaces, and these perspectives are emotionally mediated." Some memories are not always usable, and societies may not want to remember them. Yair Zakovitch (2012, 16) maintains that the verse's contrary readings reflect the vicissitudes that would characterize future power relations between the nations of Edom and Israel. Following Zakovitch, I suggest that this slippery text has wide explanatory power. The slipperiness of the text elucidates the power not only of remembering but also of forgetting, of foregrounding or privileging one character and allowing another to recede into the background.

Specifically, the prenatal oracle points beyond two brothers to the two nations they represent, Israel and Edom. Heard (2001, 100) notes that a prenatal oracle often "shapes readers' expectations and evaluations of the entire forthcoming narrative and, indeed, the entire relationship between Israel and Edom reflected in the Hebrew Bible." Specifically it is the narrative's construction of Esau that reveals Israel's collective cultural memory concerning Edom, as Frank (2010, 3) notes: "Stories breathe life not only into individuals but also into groups that assemble around telling and believing certain stories."

For a culture whose thinking and writing are often centered on תולדות ("generations, ancestries"), preservation of this particular characterization of Esau would have been vital. Doing so helped to fashion Israel's own identity as those expressly *not Edom*. Communities establish identity as much around who they are *not* as they do around who they *are*. Here Jürgen Reulecke's comments on generationality-generativity-memory are useful. The term *generationality* expresses the twofold meaning of a תולדות or generation. On the one hand, Reulecke states, generationality refers to characteristics resulting from shared experience that individuals or larger generational units collectively claim for themselves. On the other hand, generationality can also refer to the "bundle of characteristics resulting from shared experiences which are ascribed to such units from the outside" (Reulecke 2010, 119). As Reulecke has noted, narratives, institutions, and other works can be passed down as an intentional or unintentional legacy bequeathed to successive generations. These later generations may then choose to reject, reinterpret, or erase them (123). Here, however, narrative does serve as an "expressed intention" to pass down a particular memorialization of Edom vis-à-vis Esau. The Jacob cycle is a text that delights in trickster antics, even as it denigrates the diselect.

The narrative, for example, makes no moral judgment on Jacob's actions and instead highlights the crudeness of Esau's character: "Esau said to Jacob, 'Let me eat some of that red stuff, for I am famished!' (Therefore he was called Edom)" (Gen 25:30). Rather than using the ordinary Hebrew word for stew (נזיד), Esau instead points to the stew and says, "this red stuff" (אדום-אדום). Vawter notes the link between אדום (Edom) and the red land or land or red clay, just as man, the אדם, had been formed from the red earth (Gen 2:7). In the only other story about the birth of twins in the Hebrew Bible, the author also sees red. Perez and Zerah are sons of Jacob's son Judah (Gen 38:27–30). The root of Zerah means "to shine," and the story relates it to the "crimson thread" (see Isa 1:18) that was tied to Zerah's hand. The name derivation, Zakovitch avers, better suits Edom. However, Zerah is also the name of an Edomite clan, and a further link between these intertexts (Gen 36:17; 1 Chr 1:37; Zakovitch 2012, 19). Zakovitch (2012, 20) states: "Apparently, then, in the popular, orally transmitted version of Jacob and Esau's birth, the midwife tied a red thread to the hand of Esau-Edom, who was about to be born, but Jacob cheated and successfully pushed his way out first—as is now told about Perez." The secondary physical description of Esau as "hairy" links him to Seir, the name of the region where Esau makes his home (Gen 32:4). In both instances, Vawter claims, geography—a territorial boundary—constructs Esau's identity. Esau's physical characteristics draw attention to it, as hairiness or shagginess appears to be a mark of incivility. Vawter (1977, 288) states, "The author's wordplays go beyond mere cleverness and insinuate a bias against [Esau] from the beginning."

Moreover, the verb used for gulping down (לעט) occurs nowhere else in the Hebrew Bible. In Rabbinic Hebrew, it is reserved for the feeding of animals (Alter 2008, 131).² Beyond these linguistic cues, the rapidity of Esau's actions in Gen 25:34—he eats and drinks, he rises and goes away, and he belittles his birthright—is not accidental. Instead, this is an intentional decision on the part of the Hebrew writer to characterize Esau as impetuous and vulgar.

Not all scholars, however, agree that this linguistic evidence points to the vulgarity of Esau's character. Heard, for example, does not view the connection to postbiblical Hebrew as strong enough to make confident statements about the intentions behind the author's characterization of Esau. Heard (2001, 104) claims that interpreters such as Skinner, Speiser, Wenham, and Alter overreach because of their overall tendency to denigrate Esau, rather than from sound lexicography. Given the political complications between the nations represented by Jacob and Esau, however, scholars who view Esau's negative characterization as intentional are surely correct. While unwilling to make such claims himself, Heard does allow that the narrator's punning etiology may function at a higher level of abstraction. Heard (105) states, "Esau eats some of Jacob's stew, that is, Edom (*ʾĕdôm*) eats 'red' (*ʾādōm*). The narrator may be hinting that, by overestimating his hunger (if that is what Esau did) and underestimating the value of his birthright (if Esau did so), Esau in effect ate himself up."

Perhaps the vulgarity of the narrator's presentation of Esau allows for the writer to demonstrate how Jacob can circumvent the rights of primogeniture. Here Jacob functions as a trickster character, disrupting what is culturally normative. Jacob supplants Esau by taking his birthright. This birthright, as the story will later show, is intimately tied to the father's blessing. Leslie Brisman (1990, 68), among many others, notes the close connection in Hebrew between בכרה ("birthright") and ברכה ("blessing"). The flipping of two letters occurs just two chapters later, when Jacob supplants Esau for the second time, acquiring not only the birthright but also the blessing. Once again, the narrative makes no moral comment on Jacob's conduct, instead concluding the episode with another indicator of Rebekah's disdain for Esau: "Then Rebekah said to Isaac, 'I am weary of

---

2. Alter notes Abba ben David's contention that Rabbinic Hebrew developed from a biblical vernacular excluded from literary usage: the writer would have introduced the vernacular term for animal feeding to suggest Esau's coarsely appetitive character. Even if one allows for semantic evolution, however, Alter says that the presumption that it was always a cruder term for eating than the standard biblical one remains a safe bet.

my life because of the Hittite women. If Jacob marries one of the Hittite women such as these, one of the women of the land, what good will my life be to me?'" (Gen 27:46) Her disgust follows the narrator's comment earlier that when Esau was forty years old, he took to wife Judith daughter of Beeri the Hittite, and Basemath daughter of Elon the Hittite. These women are a source of "bitterness" to Isaac and Rebekah (26:34–35). Here again, the unusual placement of this narrative comment—immediately preceding Jacob's deception—may function as justification for favoring the one brother over the other. In Midrash Rabbah, the rabbis' whimsical presentation of Esau's marriages demonstrates their preference for Jacob: "So for forty years Esau used to ensnare married women and violate them, yet when he attained forty years he compared himself to his father, saying, 'As my father was forty years old when he married, so I will marry at the age of forty.' Hence it is written, "And when Esau was forty years hold, he took to wife" (Friedman 1986, 581). Vawter (1977, 297) notes that in the Priestly account no rivalry exists between Jacob and Esau. Nevertheless, the Priestly writer also views Esau as "debased" on the basis of his choice of wife. Still, Heard (2001, 182–83) insists that the characterization of Esau (and, by extension, other diselect characters in Genesis) is "shot through with ambiguities," and the answers to such questions are resolved only by "acts of readerly will." Esau is characterized negatively, in other words, because a particular reader or readers prefer to read him in that way. Nevertheless, whether Esau (or Lot or Ishmael) is read positively or negatively does not appear to matter: "Even on the most positive possible readings, Lot, Ishmael, and Esau remove themselves or are removed by Yahweh from their (potential) place among Abraham's descendants and from any share or claim or historic right in Canaan" (Heard 2001, 182–83).

For Vawter, the perpetual hostility and political back-and-forth between the two nations is demonstrated in Isaac's blessing of Esau, which Vawter (1977, 305) calls an "afterthought in the narrative." Isaac tells Esau:

> Then his father Isaac answered him:
> "See, away from the fatness of the earth shall your home be,
> and away from the dew of heaven on high.
> By your sword you shall live,
> and you shall serve your brother;
> but when you break loose,
> you shall break his yoke from your neck." (Gen 27:39–40)

Vawter (1977, 305–6) notes the connection between the Edomites and the Ishmaelites (Gen 16:12), both peoples depicted as "warlike, brawling people inhabiting a harsh and inhospitable land, whose further destiny is one of subjection to others." On the face of it, Vawter claims, Isaac's blessing appears to envision a time when the Edomites have regained their independence from Israel and Judah, beyond the Davidic and Solomonic purview attributed to the Yahwist.

In Carr's diachronic analysis of the fractures in Genesis, he also views the relationship between Jacob and Esau as indicative of the political anxieties between the two nations they represent. Carr (1996, 297) divides Genesis into the "pre-promise traditions" that stand at the beginning of the redactional process—an independent primeval history—the Jacob and Joseph compositions, and the successive Israelite and Judean editions of the Jacob-Joseph narrative. Carr views the Jacob story as the composition with the clearest distinction between the authorial hand and his "precursor traditions" (Gen 25; 27–31) and the broader Jacob story (28:20–22; 31:4–16, 24, 29). Many of these precursor materials, which appear to celebrate the trickster, would have been utilized by northern resistance movements to Davidic-Solomonic power structures. Carr (1996, 298) claims that the later additions, which bend these trickster materials into a Jacob story, introduced a number of important shifts that anticipate a new power structure centered in the north. For Carr (298), the author of the Jacob story focused on introducing a highly "political form of theology" into the narrative he created, one that closely linked Jacob with the northern cult cites such as the royal sanctuary at Bethel, the early capital at Penuel, to Shechem, Mahanaim, Succoth, and all the way to Ephrath. In what Carr refers to as the "proto-Genesis Abraham story," the author appears to have crafted the story of Jacob to parallel the story of Abraham. The prepromise story of Jacob links to the ancestral traditions of Genesis and affirms a particular social structure (299). However, when the reigns of David and Solomon become a bad memory in the north, the author writes a sequel to Jacob's and Esau's interaction, one that inverts their relationship. With this sequel in place, the final word is of Jacob's self-subjugation to the Edom he once overcame (see Gen 25:23–33:20). Carr (1996, 299) claims that the variety of these readings attests to the existence of one of the many fractures in Genesis. For Carr, the combined Jacob-Joseph story originates in the Northern Kingdom, with Isaac's blessing featuring Jacob competing with a southerner (Esau/Edom). The origins of this tradition probably derive from the south, articulating David's right to dominate Edom. However, while Gen 27 establishes the dominance of an "all-Israelite hero" (Jacob) over a neighboring group (Edom), Gen 48 focuses more exclusively on the precedence of one northern group over another, Ephraim over Manasseh. Thus, the originally southern model of Gen 27 has been appropriated to articulate northern intergroup power relationships (Carr 1996, 302).

The payoff for Carr is political and theological, revolving not merely around Israel and Judah's past but, more importantly, around their present and future. The proto-Genesis composition emphasizes divine promise and blessing. This composition insists on God's will to execute the promise, as Carr (1996, 306) affirms:

> This kind of marshalling of cultural resources—personal piety and royal ideology—and theological defense of the reliability of the promise is not required when the narrative future is the audience's present. Rather, it occurs when the author must build a bridge from a given narrative to a future that does not yet exist for the narrative's audience.

Thus, the various building blocks of Genesis are, for Carr, not etiological tales but rather served to provide assurance and comfort to generations of Israelites/Judahites/Yehudites who struggled to feel connected to a God who kept his promises.

For Jacob's ancestors, no generation needed to lay claim to these promises more than exilic and postexilic Israel. Laying claim to these promises, however, exacerbated the need to reinscribe boundaries between Israel and Edom, therefore inscribing a clear boundary between those God (s)elected and those he (dis)elected. This inscription of boundaries is indeed a kind of script—and, it should be added, one that is given additional cultural and theological weight when placed on the lips of the prophets. The survey below of postexilic prophetic texts demonstrates that narrative memory can serve multiple interpretations and exist in multiple places. Narrative memory is both multiple and portable. The prophetic (re)tellings illustrate diverse chains of memory, which situate tension between Israel and Edom in the present moment of the postexilic community.

In the exilic period, the enmity between the rival nations was exacerbated by the Edomites' collaboration with the Babylonians, as Ps 137 attests: "Remember, O Lord, against the Edomites the day of Jerusalem's fall, how they said, 'Tear it down! Tear it down! Down to its foundations!'" (Ps 137:7). Lamentations, which mourns the destruction of the first temple, expresses a similar sentiment:

> Rejoice and be glad, O daughter Edom,
> you that live in the land of Uz;
> but to you also the cup shall pass;
> you shall become drunk and strip yourself bare.
> The punishment of your iniquity, O daughter Zion, is accomplished,
> he will keep you in exile no longer; but your iniquity, O daughter Edom,
> he will punish,
> he will uncover your sins. (Lam 4:21–22)

Edom's sins include their refusal to cross to Jacob/Israel, in addition to their exultation over Israel's distress during the Babylonian conquest. In recalling their sin, the postexilic prophet Malachi uses language of borders/territory and peoplehood to denote Esau's wickedness—גבול רשעה (wicked territory, Mal 1:4). Even their borders are evil. As a result, they are העם אשר־זעם יהוה עד־עולם ("the people with whom the LORD is indignant with forever," Mal 1:4). Here the language revolves around a particular people—a people who will be "damned forever," sharply juxtaposed to Israel, whom Yahweh covenants to bless forever. Zakovitch links the scene back to the birthright story of the two boys. He notes that the birthright story describes Rebekah's love for Jacob (and Isaac's love for Esau), yet in Malachi's prophecy it is God who loves Jacob and hates Esau, "from which we realize that it was not Jacob's actions that precipitated his fate but God himself" (Zakovitch 2012, 27). For Zakovitch, God has (s)elected a particular family member, from before the boys' birth.

Obadiah also utilizes the language of family—"For the slaughter and violence done to your brother Jacob, shame shall cover you, and you shall be cut off forever" (Obad 10), and "But you should not have gloated over your brother on the day of his misfortune" (Obad 12). The prophet uses familial language to highlight the incomprehensible nature of Edom's crimes. Here too Esau and Jacob are juxtaposed, as the prophet draws on familiar remnant language: "The house of Jacob shall be a fire, the house of Joseph a flame, and the house of Esau stubble; they shall burn them and consume them, and there shall be no survivor of the house of Esau; for the LORD has spoken" (Obad 18). According to Zakovitch, it is not merely that no survivor is left in Esau's house—it is also that Esau's name is "most despised" (Obad 2). Zakovitch views the prophet's use of מאד ("very") as a not-so-subtle link to Edom, with the same letters rearranged. Obadiah believes the Edomites' status as "most despised" is intended as a permanent attribute, tied to their name (see Jer 49:15; Zakovitch 2012, 26). For Zakovitch, Jeremiah's prophecy that Edom will be קטן

("little") demonstrates that God was responsible for reversing the order of the brothers, transforming Jacob, who is described as Rebekah's younger (קטן) son (Gen 27:42), into the firstborn and Esau into the קטן. Furthermore, the use of בגוים ("among the nations") harks back to the birth story and to the words of the oracle—שני גוים ("two nations," 25:23)—and is a reminder that it was God's intention from the beginning that Esau serve his brother. Moreover, Jeremiah's use of the word בזוי ("despised") relates to the end of the birthright episode, where "Esau despised his birthright" (Gen 25:34). Because Esau despised his birthright, Zakovitch (2012, 27) claims, it is only fitting that he should be despised. The prophet's use of "younger" (קטן) also links directly back to Jacob's self-abasement before Esau, suggesting its reversal (Gen 32:11). The prophetic adaptation(s) of the birth narrative suggests the permeability of the boundary of Rebekah's womb. The crossing of the threshold of Rebekah's womb did not indicate a once-for-all decision about who would be צעיר ("little, insignificant"). This boundary, it appears, was a malleable one, based on a nebulous combination of divine will and human autonomy. The prophets function as eis/exegetes for the unfolding of the boys' (hi)story. Outside the prophetic corpus, the narrative in Num 20 offers a final biblical portrait of the Edomites.

The story in Num 20 attests to the reification of brotherly boundaries, demonstrating that at no time was the relationship between Israel and Edom congenial—it was always contentious. On their way from Kadesh to Moab, the children of Israel request access through Edom. Moses instructs the מלאכים ("messengers") to say the following: אמר אחיך ישראל אתה ידעת את כל־התלאה אשר מצאתנו ("your brother Israel says, you yourselves know all the hardship that we found," Num 20:14b). Their oppression in Egypt is then recounted. The rhetoric, intended to persuade a crossing, is framed around language of brotherhood and oppression. In describing the relationships among the Israelites, the language is typically familial: בני־ישראל ("sons of Israel") is a common expression. Here, brothers should help brothers, particularly when considering their reality as an oppressed group, one that has known תלאה ("weariness, hardship"). The request is clearly stated in terms of crossing, and the mood is volitional: נעברה־נא בארצך ("please let us cross into your land," Num 20:17a). The messengers also inscribe their own boundaries on the intended crossing: לא נעבר בשדה ובכרם ולא נשתה מי באר דרך המלך נלך לא נטה ימין ושמאול עד אשר־נעבר גבולך ("we will not cross into field and into vineyards and we will not drink waters of Beersheba. We will stay on the king's highway; we will not stretch the right hand and left hand until we have crossed your boundary," Num 20:17b).

The term גבול and its various cognates, such as גבל and גבולה, refer variously to borders, boundaries, and territories of lands or people. In the case of גבל the nuance of twisting or winding is included (BDB, 147–48). Here, the territorial restrictions the Israelites place on themselves when crossing Edomite territory appear insufficient. The Edomites alone will maintain the boundaries between the brothering nations: ויאמר אליו אדום לא תעבר בי פן־בחרב אצא לקראתך ("and Edom said to him, you shall not cross us, lest we will go out against you with the sword," Num 20:18). If that boundary is crossed, it will be reinscribed with bloodshed, and the Edomite army will protect the boundary. The language is aggressive and final: "you shall not cross."

Zakovitch views the episode as Esau's/Edom's revenge. Because Jacob demanded payment in exchange for satiating Esau's hunger and thirst (Gen 25:31), Zakovitch claims, the request for drinking water in the Numbers narrative (and for crossing at all) is refused. Zakovitch (2012, 25) states, "Since, according to Genesis, the brothers made peace with one another after Jacob returned from Haran, it is clear that the writer of Numbers wanted to portray Edom negatively. The story represents the enmity that existed between the two nations in the period in which it was written." Here, too, the book of Numbers offers what appears to be a final word regarding Edom's fate: "Edom will become a possession, Seir a possession of its enemies, while Israel does valiantly. One out of Jacob shall rule, and destroy the survivors of Ir" (Num 24:18–19). Total erasure is hoped for and propagandized.

On closer inspection of the denouement of the Jabbok text, however, total erasure does not occur. Esau and Edom are not wiped out (Gen 36). Nor, however, does the Jacob-Esau story completely resolve itself in peaceful side-by-side habitation or by a fair distribution of wealth and resources. Brodie's (2001, 322) comments underscore the ambiguity of the scene: "On the one hand, Jacob is announcing his life's achievement, telling how his time with Laban has earned him great wealth. On the other hand ... Esau is coming with 400 men.... Jacob's achievements, however great, look fragile. He is at a crossroads." After having crossed a physical and theological boundary, Jacob must still attend to the anthropological. He must still meet his brother face to face. He does so through the giving of gifts. In his first protestation that Jacob's מנחה ("present, offering, gift") is unnecessary, Esau states, יש־לי רב ("I have a lot," Gen 33:9). Jacob's seemingly gracious response highlights the economic disparity between the two men: יֶשׁ־לִי־כֹל ("I have everything," 33:11). Here, as is often the case in the narrative, Jacob attributes his success to God's favor (see 27:20; 31:7, 9, 42). Jacob, as the one (s)elected from birth, receives the promissory blessings, as did his father and grandfather. He is also the beneficiary of material largesse. Esau, like the (dis)elect character Ishmael, has been provided for, but the hush money silences both characters; both recede into the narrative background, while the stories of Abraham, Isaac, and Jacob are foregrounded. The narrative depicts God providing for Ishmael, at the level of both immediate need and skillful longevity (21:15–22). Through the character of Isaac, the narrative likewise offers a begrudging blessing to Esau (27:30–40) and provides him with a host of descendants (Gen 36). Politically and theologically, however, the Lord is depicted as having chosen Isaac over Ishmael and Jacob over Esau. The Lord is working out his purposes of blessing the nation of Israel, promised generations prior (12:1–3) through Isaac and Jacob. While Ishmael and Esau will be (begrudgingly) provided for, it is not their stories that the biblical author(s) are interested in telling. It is not their (narrative) lives that will advance the narrative of Yahweh's blessing to Israel. In the narrative that the biblical authors construct, Isaac is the child of Yahweh's promise, and Jacob is the character who will represent Yahweh's blessing in the (narrative) world.

This final scene, when juxtaposed to the narrative in Numbers and the prophetic corpus surveyed above, demonstrates the multiple ways in which stories are adapted and remembered. Astrid Erll refers to this disparity of memory as "modes of remembering" in culture. Memories of past events can vary greatly; this holds true not only for *what* is remembered but also for *how* it is remembered. Myth, religious memory, political history, trauma, family remembrance, and generational memories are each different modes of referring to the past (Erll and Nünning 2010, 7). The Jabbok text and its narrative denouement is just one mode among many literary remembrances concerning Israel and Edom. These remembrances—narrations of things past—are also projections of future hopes and anxieties.

Beyond the literary remembrances of the biblical narrative itself, historians have traced when tensions arise between the two nations, Israel and Edom. This historical work around the Israel-Edom relationship helps to clarify why Esau's character is depicted in such a negative way. Scholars disagree about when tensions arise between Israel and Edom/Idumea. Consequently, scholars also differ on exactly how the characters of Jacob and Esau represent those tensions. Israel Finkelstein situates the tension between the two nations in late monarchic times, declaring that the relations between the two brothers, the fathers of Israel and Edom, "reflect a clear case of seventh century perceptions in more ancient costume" (Finkelstein, Mazar, and Schmidt 2007). Assyrian sources attest to Edom's emergence as a fully developed state in the eighth century BCE. Finkelstein claims that, prior to the eighth century, Judah was an isolated and sparsely populated kingdom. In terms of wealth, territory, and military might, Judah could not compare to the north. After the Assyrian Empire dominated the Northern Kingdom in 720 BCE, Judah grew, developing a sense of its own importance and divine destiny. Therefore, Judah envisioned its survival as evidence of God's intentions from the time of the patriarchs, indicating that Judah should rule over the land of Israel (Finkelstein and Mazar 2007). Diana Edelman confirms that Edom rose to prominence only after Israel had disappeared as a kingdom. Likewise, Edelman (2013, 49) places the political rivalry between Judah and Edom at the end of the monarchy in the north until the conquest of Idumea by the Maccabees. The placement of the Edomites in this particular historical moment is critical to understanding the ways in which they are linked to the Babylonian conquest and remembered in the biblical record. As Juan Manuel Tebes has noted, the burden of guilt for Judah's exile has been placed, almost exclusively, on the Babylonians. However, there are some biblical passages, Tebes (2011, 220) argues, that allude to the involvement of a southern Transjordanian people, the Edomites, descendants of Esau. The biblical texts that Tebes cites offer contradictory details regarding the fall of Judah and the destruction of the temple.

Tebes cites 2 Kgs 25, which situates the Babylonian siege on the tenth of Tebeth (early January 587 BCE) and its end on the ninth of Tammuz (end of July 586 BCE), totaling eighteen months of siege. Here the Babylonians are the only cause of Judah's collapse, with no mention of the Edomites (see Jer 39:1; 52:4; Ezek 24:1; Tebes 2011, 222). Jeremiah 39 and 52 detail Zedekiah's flight and captivity, again with no negative mention of the Edomites. The only reference is Jer 40, which notes that the Babylonians appointed the Judean Gedaliah as governor, and groups of Judeans escaped to the land of Edom. Tebes (2011, 224) contends, "Although it could be argued that feelings of sorrow among the Edomites for the Judeans' fate could somehow have superseded the 'national' rivalry between Judah and Edom, there is no question that Jeremiah would likely have alluded here to an Edomite intervention during Nebuchadnezzar's attack had it occurred." In surveying the MT as well as the versions in the LXX, Tebes notes that the Judean historical memory was in constant flux and that important details such as the chronological sequence of events, as well as the role of the Edomites, belong to later editorial layers (227). Second Chronicles 36 also details the destruction, laying blame for it squarely on the Babylonians, this time with a decidedly "divine punishment" motif (Tebes 2011, 227).

By contrast, Obadiah, Lamentations, Psalms, Amos, Joel, and Ezekiel do refer to Edom negatively (e.g., Obad 11; Lam 4:21–22; Ps 137:7). Tebes states that it is possible that Edom celebrated, if not favored, the fall of their bitter enemy. They possibly refused asylum to Judean refugees. Also possible, they may have benefited territorially and economically as a result. In the end, there is no evidence that this actually took place (Tebes 2011, 230). However, the buildup of their purported crimes continued to accrue throughout biblical and extrabiblical literature. First Esdras 4:43–45, for example, places blame for the burning of the temple on the Edomites (Tebes 2011, 231). Some scholars read these texts at face value, arguing for the involvement of the Edomites in the downfall of the temple. Edelman (1995, 28) claims, "Unless the Edomites were extremely myopic, they saw the Babylonians coming and recognized that their survival meant disassociation from Jerusalem." Likewise, John Lindsay (1999, 72) suggests that Edom and Babylon were close collaborators against Judah. Basing his comments on the so-called stab-in-the-back traditions of modern defeated nations, Tebes (2011, 232) claims that ire toward the Edomites was based not on *actual* behavior but instead on *perceived* behavior. Stab-in-the-back traditions included six major themes: (1) cultural nationalism, a "golden age" of cultural creativity; (2) feelings of humiliation, embarrassment, and vengeance; (3) jingoism, xenophobia, and racism; (4) "lost cause" legends; (5) the "divine punishment" theme; and (6) stab-in-the-back myths (235–36).

Taken to its logical conclusion, then, the payoff for Tebes's argument lies in the scapegoating of Edom. Archaeological records have provided evidence for the appearance of material culture similar to those found in contemporary settlements of southern Transjordan, considered to be the homeland of the Edomites. This archaeological research has unearthed locally manufactured wares, "Edomite" pottery and cultic objects concentrated in Ḥorvat Qitmit and Tel Malḥata in the Beersheba Valley and ʿEn Ḥaṣeva in the Arabah (Tebes 2011, 241). The Edomites supposedly crossed the Wadi Arabah in two-wave movements, allowing for a slow and persistent influx of people, with material culture and folklore coming from Edom and reaching southern Judah beginning in the eighth century BCE (Tebes 2011, 243). Moreover, the lax administration of the Persians allowed for an influx of southern Transjordanian population into the Negev and areas farther north, suggesting that they assembled into and adopted the culture of the local people (248–49). The payoff for Tebes is to situate the Edomites as the "people of the land" over against the "Golah" returnees. The Edomites, then, become a primary source of xenophobia for the Jewish elite. In conclusion, Tebes argues:

> I would argue that the Edomites were a main focus of the Golah's xenophobia and that the myth of the stab-in-the back was its main theme. The "blame Edom" theme reads as an artful piece of propaganda of political importance. Although evidence of their direct involvement in the attack on Jerusalem is absent, Judean folklore soon after—as is already evident in Obad. 11—developed the notion that the Edomite jubilation had to do with an actual participation in the fall of the city. The presence of Edomites in southern Judah and probably Jerusalem in the late Judean kingdom served to reinforce the idea that the Edomites, close neighbors that were considered their "brothers" according to the customary use of kinship terminology for describing political and geographic realities, were a treacherous people that stabbed Judah in the back at its weakest moment. (250)

If Tebes's instincts are right, then the construction of Esau as inherently unworthy of the birthright and blessing makes sense historically.[3] The narrative's construction of Esau highlights Israel's collective cultural memory concerning Edom. Consequently, the character of Esau is not without historical valence. This link from historicity to rhetoricity is an important one, as Assmann (1997, 8–9) has remarked:

> Unlike history proper, mnemohistory is concerned not with the past as such, but only with the past as it is remembered. It surveys the story-lines of tradition, the webs of intertextuality, the diachronic continuities and discontinuities of reading the past.... The past is not simply "received" by

---

3. For an intriguing counterreading to Tebes's argument, see the creative work of Mario Liverani (2005), who views the patriarchal traditions as "invented history." His reading, like Tebes's, also views the patriarchal narratives through the lens of the Golah/am ha-aretz. The main difference is that Liverani argues that the narratives depict peaceful coexistence rather than scapegoating of Esau and the Edomites.

the present. The present is "haunted" by the past and the past is modeled, invented, reinvented, and reconstructed by the present.

The precise role of the Edomites in the wake of the Babylonian captivity continues to stay in the mist of history. The scholarly survey around the issue demonstrates the diversity of thought among historians. While we may not resolve these questions historically, what we do have is a biblical narrative that, across the board, portrays Esau's character and subsequent descendants in a negative light.

Indeed, as cultural/collective memory studies have shown, no memory is ever purely individual, nor do societies remember literally. Memory is always shaped by collective contexts. Individuals remember in sociocultural contexts, and they reconstruct their past creatively and selectively according to their culture's present needs (Erll and Nünning 2010, 5). A close connection exists, for example, between a nation's version of its past and its national identity. This link extends, Erll claims, to John Locke, who believed there was no such thing as an "essential identity."[4] Instead, identity is constructed and reconstructed by "acts of memory, by remembering who one was and by setting this past Self in relation to the present Self" (Erll and Nünning 2010, 6). The past, then, may be past, but it is a useable past, and the stories that are told "make life social" (Frank 2010, 20). The Jabbok text serves, to appropriate Frank's comment, as a "story [for Israel] to grow up on" (7). Indeed, it is growing up, the maturation of boys into adulthood—and fledgling nations into fighting ones—that the Jacob cycle narrates. Whatever else may be said, what is clear is this: while Jacob and Esau are twins, they are not the same. Jacob, for all his trickster antics and morally questionable behavior, is the (s)elect character, given birthright and blessing. Esau is foolish enough to trade what is rightly his for a bowl of stew, and subsequent narratives and prophetic texts "remember" his descendants as contentious, (dis)elect, and unloved by Yahweh.

Crossing Laban and the Aramaeans

In the story world, Esau is not the only character with whom Jacob must contend. His expulsion from his father's house puts him in the role of a fugitive fighting for resources, reliant on his wits to survive economically.

---

4. For Locke's original discussion of identity, personality, and memory, see John Locke (2016), *An Essay Concerning Human Understanding*.

While his family appears to possess material means (Gen 12:16, 20; 13:1–6; 14:21–24; 20:14–16), Isaac sends Jacob off with nothing more than a blessing and the promise that the birthright will transfer to him after his death. He leaves his home as a pariah; he will later return as a man of significant wealth. Jacob leaves Beersheba and crosses into Haran. Upon his arrival in the land of the easterners, Jacob discovers more than a comely shepherdess—he also discovers an abundance of sheep, a sign of wealth and later the focal point of Laban and Jacob's duplicity (29:10). In Laban, Jacob faces someone much like himself—wily and willing to do what it takes to orchestrate things in his favor.

Laban responds to Jacob's arrival with great emotion—he hugs Jacob and kisses him and takes him into his house, calling Jacob "the bone of his bones and flesh of his flesh" (29:13–14), a statement reminiscent of the bond between the אדם (man) and his wife (2:23). Nevertheless, in their first meeting, their conversation foreshadows the precariousness of their relationship: "Then Laban said to Jacob, 'Because you are my kinsman, should you therefore serve me for nothing? Tell me, what shall your wages be?'" (29:15) As Wenham (1994, 234) notes perceptibly, while Laban's question sounds amiable, the mention of working and pay introduces a "jarring note." In his discussion of the quest for the historical Israel, Finkelstein traces not only the historical valence of Esau but of Laban as well. The attention given to the Aramaeans in the Jacob stories demonstrates their importance as a people who were sometimes ally, sometimes enemy. Therefore the stories about Jacob and Laban metaphorically express the "complex and often stormy relations" between Iron II Israel and Aram (Finkelstein and Mazar 2007, 47). Similarly, Edelman (2013, 49) avers: "It would be logical to posit that the stories dealing with Jacob's outwitting of his 'uncle,' in spite of Laban's attempt to exploit him, may have been based on older folktales reflecting the political tensions between the kingdom of Israel and the adjoining Aramean kingdoms in the mid-ninth century BCE."

Textually speaking, the key terms עבד (he served) and משכרת (wages) will figure prominently in the narratives that follow (Gen 29:18, 20, 25, 27, 30; 30:26, 29; 31:6, 16, 32, 33; 41; 31:7, 41), and, for Wenham (1994, 234), are "laden with echoes of the exploitation Jacob suffered at Laban's hands." Jacob's agreement to work for Laban rather than offer monetary payment for Rachel underscores his position as a poor man with fractured family ties; he is without resources himself and unable to ask his father to pay the bride price. Since casual laborers received between one-half and one shekel a month in old Babylonian times, Jacob offered a sizable marriage

5. The Crossing 149

gift in exchange for his marriage to Rachel (Wenham 1994, 235). After Jacob is duped by Laban and pays off his debt, however, the issues of service and wages are again raised.

In Jacob's demand to leave, he uses the term עבד (he served) no less than three times, a reminder of Laban's exploitation. Jacob's use of first-person pronominal suffixes is also a rhetorical reminder that the women and children are *his property* that *he has worked for*. They are now a demonstration of *his wealth, his success*, rather than Laban's: "Give me *my wives* and *my children*, for which I served you, and I will go; you know about *my service* to you" (Gen 30:26). In demanding to leave, Jacob implies that he is more than a poor man and more than a slave—he is an industrious man who is crossing Laban's land to go back to his own. He is a man who is (re)turning to receive an inheritance (28:4, 13; Wenham 1994, 254). The legal situation between the two men, however, appears muddled, as it is unclear whether Jacob should be viewed as Laban's slave. The book of the covenant stipulates that a slave who is given a wife by a master must leave her and any children behind when he leaves his master's service after six years (Exod 21:3–6). If the slave did not wish to part from his family, he would remain a slave. Wenham says that it is unclear whether this law was to apply in Jacob's case. Jacob's repeated use of עבד could imply slave labor, even as Gen 29:15 insinuates the opposite; as Laban's nephew, Jacob was offered wages. Because he was a kinsman it was hoped that Laban would treat him kindly (Lev 25:35–36). Certainly, Wenham (1994, 254) says, Gen 31:43 could imply that Laban viewed Jacob as a slave rather than as a son-in-law. Nevertheless, Jacob links Laban's newfound wealth to his service: "For you had little before I came, and it has increased abundantly; and the LORD has blessed you wherever I turned. But now when shall I provide for my own household also?" (30:30 NRSV). Jacob's crossing over Laban's borders yields wealth for Laban, which Jacob eventually appropriates.

Jacob's wealth, it seems, exceeds even Laban's: ויפרץ האיש מאד מאד ויהי־לו צאן רבות ושפחות ועבדים וגמלים וחמרים ("and the man grew exceedingly exceedingly; and there was to him sheep and many maidservants and servants and camels and male asses," Gen 30:43). Jacob's wealth, it seems, borders on conspicuous consumption and arouses the ire of Laban's sons. The sons' rhetoric revolves around their father's work (עשה) and their father's glory (כבד, Gen 31). These things, the sons claim, Jacob has לקח (taken). A convenient appearance of Yahweh compels Jacob to change course, to cross back into his father's land (31:3). In his attempt to persuade Rachel and Leah to leave their father's house,

Jacob uses rhetoric of propagandistic piety—"And said to them, 'I see that your father does not regard me as favorably as he did before. But the God of my father has been with me.... Thus God has taken away the livestock of your father, and given them to me'" (31:5, 9 NRSV). Wenham (1994, 271) states, "In other words, God has not simply transferred the herds from Laban to Jacob; he has done them a favor, giving them a much better life!"

The women side with Jacob, owner of wealth and the presumed recipient of God's favor (Gen 31:16a). Jacob appeals to his completed service and to the favor of God as reasons for his departing with this wealth (31:38–42). He accuses Laban of attempting to send him away empty-handed (31:42). The use of שלח (he sent) recalls Pharaoh's sending Israel away from Egypt (Exod 3:20) and the promise to Moses that Israel would not leave empty-handed (3:21). Wenham notes that the same collocation of "send away ... empty-handed" is also found in Deut 15:13–14, which insists that after six years' service a slave shall not be sent away empty-handed. Instead, "you shall furnish him liberally out of your flock...; as the LORD your God has blessed you, you shall give to him" (Wenham 1994, 278).

Jacob arrives in Haran penniless; he leaves with wealth and the blessing of God. Before Jacob leaves, however, a boundary is established between him and Laban. A גל (wave, billow, heap) and a מצבה (pillar, stump) is set up between the two men, and a promise centered on establishing and maintaining a boundary—אם־אני לא־אעבר אליך ("I shall not cross to you") and ואם־אתה לא־תעבר אלי ("you shall not cross to me") ... לרעה ("for evil"). The two men seal their mutual (crossing) agreement with a meal typical of covenant making (Gen 31:53–54). Finkelstein avers that the biblical description of the tensions between Jacob and Laban and their establishment of this boundary east of the Jordan seems to reflect the "territorial partition" between Aram and Israel in the ninth or eighth century BCE (Finkelstein and Mazar 2007, 47). Narratively, Jacob's crossing from one threshold (his father's house) into another (his uncle's house) has transitioned him from a penniless fugitive to a man of conspicuous consumption, blessed by God, on his way back to the land that has been promised to him. Before taking hold of the promise, however, he must attempt reconciliation with Esau.

Crossing God and Humans

Jacob takes his first tentative steps toward peace with Esau through the use of obsequious language and the offer of obsequious gifts. Jacob's language centers, as it did with Laban, around servitude. The appellation לאדני ("my lord," with the inseparable preposition ל), coupled with Jacob's self-construction as עבדך ("your servant") indicates a posture of humility, whether real or contrived. Whether Jacob actually feels humbled before Esau is not the point. His rhetoric is intended to manipulate Esau, garnering his favor and, Jacob hopes, saving him from the promise Esau made long ago to kill his brother (Gen 27:41). Jacob knows that if ever there was "a time to kill" (Eccl 3:3), this is Esau's opportunity. The language Jacob uses is one protective step toward a dangerous crossing. Moreover, the language of servitude harks back to the oracle at the boys' birth, also centered on servitude (Gen 25:23). Fearing—and perhaps misunderstanding—Esau's response of sending four hundred men toward him, Jacob prays. This prayer is the next tentative step toward crossing over to his brother. Wenham (1994, 291) questions how Jacob's "frenetic activity" can "square with his pious prayer," yet Wenham's reading interprets too graciously Jacob's character here. Similarly, Brodie (2001, 324) says, "The prayer was real—it changed him." However, it is not clear whether this is piety at work or something more akin to a foxhole prayer begging for mercy from a God he has already bargained with once (Gen 28:20–22).

In the next stage of the crossing, Jacob sends a מנחה, which can signify either a "present" or an "offering." Wenham (1994, 292) notes that in secular contexts, a present is often a "gift that ingratiates," a "sweetener" (Gen 43:11; Judg 3:15). Here too Jacob presents himself as Esau's servant, again hoping to incur favor (Gen 32:21–22). Yet his meeting with Esau is forestalled by a crossing of another kind—this time the physical crossing of the Jabbok River.

Vawter, using the earlier scholarship of James Frazer, provides a sobering reminder that Jacob undertakes no mere "casual crossing" of the מעבר יבק ("ford of the Jabbok"). Instead, Frazer states:

> The gorge is, in the highest degree, wild and picturesque. On either hand the cliffs rise almost perpendicularly to a great height; you look up the precipices or steep declivities to the skyline far above. At the bottom of this mighty chasm, the Jabbok flows with a powerful current, its blue-grey water fringed and hidden, even at a short distance, by a dense jungle

of tall oleanders, whose crimson blossoms add a glow of colour to the glen in early summer. The Blue River, for such is its modern name, runs fast and strong. Even in ordinary times, the water reaches to the horses' girths, and sometimes the stream is quite unfordable, the flood washing grass and bushes high up the banks on either hand. (Vawter 1977, 348–49)

In highlighting the dangers in crossing the Jabbok, Vawter and Frazer's comments underscore the hyperbolic nature of the biblical account. McKay (1987, 7) notes, "The itinerary itself, and particularly the river crossing, stretch the imagination to the breaking point. The gorge of the Jabbok is extremely deep, and the idea of crossing it at night with a crowd of people and herds of animals is extraordinary." For McKay, the physical danger and hyperbolic insinuations of the text are purposeful, representing the symbolic transformation Jacob undergoes. The fight and the crossing of the river function together as a *rite de passage* for Jacob, marking a change from herdsman entrepreneur to respected leader of the tribe (7). The crossing, then, is polyvalent, functioning both geographically and symbolically. In expanding the scope of the geography beyond the physical to the symbol, McKay claims, the ambiguities and confusion of the text—what she calls the "missing piece"—are (slightly) clarified. McKay draws on the work of David Pocock, who argues for two geographies, the physical and symbolic (or moral). This two-sided paradigm is linked to disputes between north and south and the impossible nature of Jacob's itinerary. McKay and Pocock acknowledge that in many Genesis traditions, people coming from the north are considered to be of lineal purity, even though people from the south are depicted as more prosperous. In Genesis, Pocock (1975, 273–84) points to twin themes of inheritance by irregular means and bias in favor of those who are bred in the north. In the story of Esau, McKay claims that the "theft" of the birthright and blessing means that Jacob has to flee for safety to the north, where he acquires family and numerous possessions. After Jacob travels southward to meet Esau, however, the geography of his travels stops making sense (McKay 1987, 8). Jacob either travels on the wrong side of the Jabbok or, having to cross it twice, loops back when the narrative says he continues on in the same direction (8). For this reason, McKay says that trying to make literal sense of the itinerary is impossible, and even Pocock's insights do not solve the geographical problems. His scheme requires the separation of the fight from crossing the Jabbok. The crossing must take place in a southward direction during the flight from Laban, and in a northward direction when Jacob makes his way to Succoth. Thus, McKay claims, "getting the geography right" was unimportant to the purposes of the narrator as he constructed the story (8). For McKay, the purpose of the story as told by the narrator was to situate it in the perspective of the postexilic community, those returning to the land:

> Thus the story would have among its aims—as it was told—the creation of a hopeful attitude towards a long, hazardous journey south, with enough expression given to the difficulties to be met to make them appear both real, and yet containable and defeatable; the provision of an image of the future in a new land where former exiles would be welcome and live prosperously.... The narrator accomplished his task in something under a hundred words, and spelled out again to his hearers his belief that their race alone was permitted to hold God to a close, intense commitment, upon which they could rely totally. (11)

McKay's overall argument successfully foregrounds the Jabbok encounter as a means for Israel to use its past. However, her construction of the postexilic community's relationship to God does not capture the complexity of a character who appears to break the boundaries he establishes. Here, Barthes's seminal structuralist analysis underscores the complexities of the role of God in the story.

Barthes's essay meanders between structuralist binaries and poststructuralist unraveling of binaries. Barthes seeks the (dis/un)closure of the text, reading not for where the text comes from (historical criticism), nor for how it is made (structuralism). Instead, Barthes's (1988, 247) aim is to discern how it is "unmade, how it explodes, disseminates: according to what coded avenues it *goes*." For Barthes, the "coded avenues" wend through three primary *Leitworten*: the crossing, the struggle, and the name (change). In the narrative preamble to the Jabbok encounter, Barthes (1988, 249) notes a double schema in Gen 32:23–25, where crossing functions as follows: in verse 23, Jacob rises, collects, and crosses; in verses 24–25, Jacob collects, sends across, and remains alone. Here, not only does Jacob rise, but the discourse also gets underway; what is said must be distinguished from what is not said (Barthes 1988, 249). According to Barthes, the crossing can be read in two different ways. First, Jacob himself crosses the ford, if need be, after having made several trips. The wrestling therefore occurs on the left bank of the stream (he is coming from the north), after having definitively crossed over. In this case, Barthes claims, "sending across" is to be read as "crossing oneself." Second, Jacob sends across but does not cross himself. He wrestles on the right bank of the Jabbok *before crossing*. In these two possible readings, Barthes notes two "pressures of readability." If Jacob remains alone *before* having crossed the Jabbok, then Barthes claims the episode must be read as folklore—Jacob desires trial by combat (e.g., with a dragon or spirit of the river) so that he can overcome it and be victorious. Conversely, if Jacob and his tribe have crossed and he remains alone on the right side of the stream (of the country where he wants to go), the crossing is without "structural finality," even though it acquires a "religious finality." If Jacob is alone, it is to *mark himself* in solitude, the "familiar setting apart of the chosen of God" (Barthes 1988, 250). For Barthes (251), the jagged narrative—or what Carr calls "fractures"—must be the "mingled vestige of two stories," one more archaic, which renders the crossing itself as a test, and the other more "realistic," attaching geographical significance to Jacob's journey by mentioning the places he passes through. In other words, Barthes refuses to decide between mythology and etiology. He argues for both instead. When including the wrestling and the naming in his sequence, Barthes expands the scope of the reading. This allows for two additional possibilities: sending the others across, not crossing oneself, wrestling and naming, and having crossed (Gen 32:32); or sending the others across, crossing oneself, wrestling and naming, and continuing (32:32). Of this pressured readability, Barthes (1988, 251) claims, "The theologian would no doubt be distressed by this indecision; the exegete would acknowledge it, hoping that some element, factual or argumentative, would allow him to bring it to an end; the textual analyst, it must be said, if I may judge my own impression, will savor this sort of *friction* between two intelligibilities."

When broadening the discussion of Jacob's crossing beyond Barthes's seminal textual analysis to structuralist interpretations, the role of God at the crossing assumes an even more jarring tone.

In considering Algirdas Greimas's actantial analysis, for example, Barthes notes that the actants are "filled" as follows: Jacob is the *subject* (of the demand, of the search, of the action); the *object* (of this same demand, search, action) is the crossing of the guarded, forbidden place, the Jabbok; the *sender*, who puts into circulation the stake of the search (the crossing), is God; the *receiver* is again Jacob; the *opponent* (the one or ones who hamper the subject in his search) is God (who guards the crossing); the *helper* (the one who assists the subject) is Jacob, who aids himself by his own strength. Barthes notes that the formula here is readily apparent, and that the subject be identified with the receiver is typical enough. What is paradoxical—even scandalous—is that God functions as both the sender and the opponent. For Barthes (1988, 257), the scandalous nature of God's dual role is only matched by the scandalous nature of God's defeat. While it is true that Jacob does prevail over אלהים (God) and אנשים (men), Jacob's opponent does possess enough strength to permanently wrench Jacob's hip out of joint (Gen 32:25), suggesting that he allows himself to be defeated. The "defeat" of Jacob's opponent is ambiguous, as is the establishment and/or crossing of boundaries between the human and the divine. A brief survey of stories outside the Jacob cycle also demonstrates the reality of a divine character who "sends," "opposes," permits, or encourages the crossing of social/ethical/geographical boundaries.

Excursus: Crossing the Divine

Within the Primeval History (Gen 1–11) alone, several stories indicate that the divine character feels anxiety about the human crossing into the boundary of the divine. By contrast, the divine character appears to transgress the boundaries he establishes. While אלהים (God) does make the אדם (man) in his own image (Gen 1:26), physical boundaries are also enforced to separate God from (hu)man. The first creation story is as much about separation as it is about creation, with בדל ("he divided, separated") as a theme word throughout (1:4, 6, 7, 18). Scholars such as van Wolde (2009) argue that the semantic range of ברא should be expanded beyond "creation" to "separation." While the first creation story is based on the categorizing instincts of the Priestly writer, the second creation story also displays a deep ambivalence about the human "crossing" the divine. Yahweh Elohim does walk in the same space as the man and his wife, yet he also erects a boundary—a place they must not cross (Gen 2:16–17). Once they cross that boundary, the anxieties of Yahweh Elohim are expressed: "Then the LORD God said, 'See, the man has become like one of us, knowing good and evil; and now, he might reach out his hand and take also from the tree of life, and eat, and live forever'" (3:22). Two primary fears are expressed—that the man know טוב ורע (a merism for knowing everything) and that he might וחי לעלם ("live forever"). After Yahweh Elohim expels them from the garden, another boundary is erected, which will guard the way back to the place they crossed (3:24).

This boundary between the human(s) and the divine must be protected, and the human(s) must not cross it.

Anxieties about the human and the divine coming into contact also occur prior to the flood (Gen 6:1-4) and at the tower of Babel (11:1-9). In the precursor to the flood story, the בני־אלהים ("sons of God") see the בנות האדם ("daughters of man") and take them as wives. Three remarkable images—בני־אלהים ("the sons of God"), the הנפלים (Nephilim), and the הגברים (warriors, mighty ones)—demonstrate for van Wolde (1994, 69) the smallness of this narrative universe. The "sons of God" may correlate to any of the following: godlike Sethites, while the daughters of men are ungodlike Canaanites; dynastic rulers or powerful kings from before the flood and the many women they took into their harems; or godlike creatures who are members not of the class of "man" but of the class "god" or of the members of the heavenly court (69). The mixing of these two classes of human and (semi)divine leads Yahweh to construct a temporal boundary on the flesh (בשר) of the (hu)man. For Brevard Childs, בשר (flesh) denotes the temporal, corruptible, and weak side of human nature, which contrasts with the life-giving force of the רוח (spirit; van Wolde 1994, 69). Flesh is the carrier of the unethical virus: God's sons and the daughters of men have behaved so badly that their wickedness is located in their flesh. Moreover, the spatial placement of Gen 6:1-4—immediately before Yahweh's decision to destroy the earth with a flood—has led to, as van Wolde (1994, 69) says, an overall "negative picture" of Gen 6:1-4.

Ultimately, van Wolde proposes a positive assessment of the story. Debates about whether the story serves as catalyst for the flood or whether the actions of these human and semidivine creatures are to be viewed ethically or unethically ultimately blur the point. This small pericope prescribes a boundary that is not crossable for the human but fully crossable for the divine. The tower of Babel story displays a similar reality. There, humankind repeatedly uses language reminiscent of the first creation story—"let us" (Gen 1:26; 11:3, 4; see 3:22). The result of everyone on the earth having "one lip" and "the same words" (11:1) is the ability to erect a boundary-less boundary—a city with a tower touching the sky. Earth touches heaven. Boundaries are crossed. Old anxieties resurface, both on the part of humankind, who fears expulsion or "scattering"; and on the part of Yahweh/the Yahwistic writer/worldview, who fears their limitless capabilities. Like sparks, humankind travels upward; Yahweh and his consort travel downward. Yahweh and his plurality confound their speech, scattering them over the earth. The story works on multiple levels, on the one hand demonstrating a clear anxiety and ambivalence concerning city life and empire building—Cain and his ilk are stopped (see 4:17)—and on the other hand reifying boundaries set between the human and the divine.[5] No casual crossing on the part of the human may be permitted. In the Jacob cycle, there too it is the divine who initiates contact, crossing, both at Bethel and at the Jabbok. Therefore McKay's interpretation of the "intense commitment" on which the Israelites could "rely totally" does not take into account the complexity of that relationship.

Coming Home

While McKay's analysis assumes too easy a relationship to God in the Jabbok story, her reading captures well the theme of displacement. This displacement represents a key reality in the lives of the postexilic community—coming home. In assigning a postexilic date for the composition of the Jabbok encounter, McKay demonstrates the ambivalence felt by those groups returning to Palestine. McKay (1987, 10) states:

> It is possible to see in the Jacob Cycle, and in particular in this story, some of the tensions of the exilic community being worked out. For this story shows an ambivalent approach to the journey from the north to the land of Canaan. It is presented as being difficult, awkward and dangerous, with an eleventh hour hazard of the most tremendous kind which almost stops the patriarch from getting home. And the anxiety about the need to make Israel acceptable to the present inhabitants of the land is expressed in the careful and detailed planning of the gifts sent on ahead to win Esau's favor.

The story of a hero (re)turning home through a journey long and arduous demonstrates the fears of the returnees. McKay's thesis is convincing when considering that the Jacob cycle is largely a story about a displaced

---

5. Other stories outside the Primeval History also function as useful intertexts to discuss the role of divine crossing and the aggressive blocking or punishing of crossing. For the sake of space, I only mention them here: the story of the Akedah (Gen 22), which involves the crossing of God and the angel of the Lord, one of whom sends the child into harm's way, while the other provides a ram which saves his life; and the story of Zipporah and the near murder of Moses at the hand of the deity (Exod 4:24–26).

person transitioning from home and back again. The Jabbok story, as well as the narrative backstory, raises questions about Israel's relationship with God and the land. Is Jacob actually home at the end of the narrative, and if so, is home everything he imagined? Just how much of God did Jacob actually see at the Jabbok, given the darkened space of the encounter? Just how much of God does Israel actually experience in light of its exilic and postexilic history? Just how visible is this God to them? Jacob must grapple with coming home to a place that may no longer feel like home and even live out his latter days in Egypt (Gen 47:27–28), struggle with the reality of family life in the land (34:1–31; 36:6–8; 37:1–8; 38:1–30), and acknowledge an identity that remains *both* Jacob ("heel") *and* Israel ("God-wrestler"; e.g., 35:10; 48:2, 8). Likewise, Israel as a nation faces tension between the returnees and the remainees (Ezra 2:1–67; Jer 16:14–15; 23:7–8)[6] and how best to rebuild land, temple, and relationships in Persian Yehud (e.g., Ezra 9–10; Neh 13; Ruth 1–4, to name a few). For both Jacob and Israel, a rupture exists between the ideal and the real. And for both Jacob and Israel, an aporia exists between the partial fulfillment of a promise and its partial unfulfillment.

Here, the words of Frank (2010, 9–10) provide insight: "Stories do not simply report past events. Stories project possible futures, and those projections affect what comes to be, although this will rarely be the future projected by the story. Stories do not just have plots. Stories work to *emplot* lives; they offer a plot that makes some particular future not only plausible but also compelling." For the exilic and postexilic communities of Judah, violence consistently strained the narrative. Bloodshed rooted their storied lives. Therefore the Jabbok text—and the story it tells of two brothers reconciling, one favored by Yahweh and the other receding into the background—is one peaceable way in which Israel's past is rooted. Once the violence narrated in the wrestling at the Jabbok is complete—and once the violence of the exile is done—some kind of workable present (and future) must be narrated. For a culture whose (hi)story was so deeply rooted in bloodshed, the denouement of the Jabbok proposes a peaceable but cautious reconciliation. The story pictures Idumea and Judah, remainees and returnees, living peaceably but not necessarily together. Ultimately, it not

---

6. Liverani (2005) notes that several places in the patriarchal narratives, by contrast, argue for coexistence between the returnees and the remainees: Gen 12:2; 15:5; 17:6; 20:4; 23:4; 26:3–5, to name a few. See Liverani (250–69) for his discussion of the "invention of the patriarchs."

5. The Crossing

only pictures Jacob/Israel (s)elected by Yahweh to receive material largesse but also narrates a story where Jacob successfully crosses every boundary—physical, human, and divine. Even after these successful crossings, however, what Geller (1996, 19) refers to as the "willed obscurity of the [Jabbok] text" remains. The obscurity of the text is assuredly due, at least in part, to the uncertainty of the exilic and postexilic communities surrounding their relationship not only to God but, equally important, to the land. Foregrounding the theme of sojourn in the Jacob cycle highlights this tension.

In her evaluation of Genesis, Elisabeth Kennedy examines the word cluster of גר/גור/מגור (stranger, sojourner) as a *Leitwort* in the patriarchal narratives. Kennedy believes this word cluster (which she has translated as "sojourn") contributes to the central themes of land and community in Genesis. She follows the definition of Rudolf Bultmann for "sojourn" as a residing place where one did not originally belong (Kennedy 2011, 4–5). Kennedy views Canaan as both home and not-home for the patriarchs. She states, "In a narrative concerned with instituting a strong tie between the ancestors of Israel and their divinely appointed homeland, sojourn sounds a note of discord.... Sojourn seems a jarring and troubling counter-note to the establishment of an ancestral claim in Canaan" (Kennedy 2011, 2). Indeed, throughout the Hebrew Bible a paradox exists in that those who are promised a home never quite receive it. The hope of home can be as elusive as the presence of God. Like God, home too is presence-absence, a kind of docetic reality in the lives of the Hebrew people.

Kennedy notes that the itinerary notice occurs three times in reference to Jacob, allowing for four stages of closure in Jacob's sojourn. First, in Gen 32–33, Jacob returns to Canaan and reunites with his brother; geographically, however, Jacob has not yet come full circle. He has not yet reunited with his father, who had "sent him away" (Gen 28:5) in the opening itinerary notice of the journey to Paddan-aram. Second, in chapter 35, Jacob goes to Bethel, allowing for a second symmetry in his overarching journey (28:20–21; 35:3). This event provides closure to Jacob's extended sojourn circuit. Third, in 35:27, Jacob comes to his father, fully closing the sojourn circuit. Finally, 37:1 repeats the note that Jacob is located in the land where his father had sojourned but with a new verb, וישב ("and he dwelt"), indicating he stayed there continuously. Thus 35:27 records Jacob's arrival in Canaan, and 37:1 describes his ongoing residence there. At the end of his wanderings, Kennedy (2011, 67–68) says, Jacob makes Canaan his permanent home. His movement turns to stasis. The two itinerary notices—

Gen 37:1 and 35:27—do not, however, attribute sojourn to Jacob. The first notice is located at the end of Jacob's sojourn arc in Paddan-aram, thus positioning his arrival in Hebron as a return from sojourn, a homecoming. The second itinerary notice completes the story of Jacob before launching into the Joseph novella. Whereas his father sojourned there, Jacob "settled" in Canaan. Did Jacob belong to Canaan in a way that was different from his fathers? Was Canaan home to Jacob? When God reiterates the promise of land possession (Gen 35:12), it is nevertheless designated as a place of sojourn because it is given by God. The place of belonging, Kennedy (2011, 68–69) maintains, is not the land of origin, which lies in their past, but the land of possession, which lies in their future.

Drawing on Anthony Smith's territorialization of memory, Kennedy notes that the recording of ethnic memory in the land transforms the territory into ethnoscape. She states, "This note underscores Jacob's status in the land as different from the sojourn experience of Abraham and Isaac; it also points to a particular way of seeing the land. It is home, but it is at the same time the place that was not home one or two generations before; it is at once home and not-home" (Kennedy 2011, 72). While sojourn indicates nonbelonging, it is part of the territorialization of memory, which brings about belonging (72). Thus, it appears that Jacob is always to settle in a liminal place—a place that is, for him, at once home and not-home, a place that represents sojourn and belonging. He can plant his feet on its soil, walk heel to toe with the dirt under his feet, and ישב ("dwell") there, but there remains a sense always that his grasp on the land, even on his own life, is tenuous. Jacob's survey of his life as he nears death is as ambiguous as it is poignant: "Jacob said to Pharaoh, 'The years of my earthly sojourn are one hundred thirty; few and hard have been the years of my life. They do not compare with the years of the life of my ancestors during their long sojourn'" (Gen 47:9). As he examines his life, this grand patriarch, the God-wrestler, does not describe his days as blessed or whole or explain how he saw the Face of all faces and lived. Instead, Jacob describes his days as מעט ("few") and רעים ("evil"). His is an acknowledgment that life is fleeting and not always filled to the brim with excess; sometimes life is tenuously and paradoxically filled to the brim with lack. For all his encounters with the Face of all faces, for all his successes in (re)turning home and facing his past, Jacob's words still bespeak unfulfilled desire. Israel still experiences a melancholy longing for home. Life is still fleeting, and his hold on it tenuous. The man Jacob, the nation Israel, and the story Jabbok all expose their liminality. All are, in one sense or another, professing shalom in the face of wounding, exile, and aporia. A new beginning is attempted through the bestowal of a new name for Jacob, yet the old name also remains. For Paul Connerton (1989, 6), new beginnings are fraught with ambiguity: "All beginnings contain an element of recollection. This is particularly so when a social group makes a concerted effort to begin with a wholly new start.... But the absolutely new is inconceivable." Jacob is renamed, yet his life does not change much afterwards. Part of grappling with ambiguity includes construction of a new beginning through commemorative ceremonies and in bodily practices, as Connerton (1989, 7) argues. The commemorative rite established at the Jabbok (Gen 32:32) functions to mark the event of Jacob's crossing. Images of the past and recollected knowledge of the past, Connerton (1989, 4) asserts, are conveyed and sustained by ritual performance. Here, the community's refusal to eat the thigh muscle on the hip socket commemorates Jacob's encounter. The practice becomes communal *habit*, one way in which societies remember (104). Yet this habit, this crossing, does not conclude the story in a neat and tidy way.

After the crossing of the Jabbok and the reconciliation with Esau, it would seem that the loose ends of the narrative would be threaded back together. Crossing the boundary should end the story, but this is not the case. After making it safely across the Jabbok and into the land of Canaan, Jacob's and Esau's stories do not end. The narrative world refuses to close fully the emotional boundary Jacob crosses with Esau (Gen 33:10). They do not travel on together, nor do they arrive in the same place (33:16–17), perhaps a continued symbol of Jacob's mistrust of Esau's intentions and surely a larger symbol of their ancestors' inability to dwell together in peace.[7] The story, like the lives of the people who lived it and composed it, remains open, liminal. This collective memory transmits, in the words of Assmann (2006, 7), a "collective identity." Memories are made here. Assmann (7) states, "It is not a matter of a physical wound that never stops hurting, nor is it a memory trace in the 'archaic inheritance' of the soul. It is a projection on the part of the collective that wishes to remember and of the individual who remembers in order to belong." Nevertheless, there is, in Jacob and his ancestors, a certain belonging achieved precisely through Jacob's limp.

---

7. The scene calls to mind the words of the psalmist—"How very good and pleasant it is when kindred live together in unity!" (Ps 133:1)—as if to convey the rarity of the sentiment and the inevitability of fraternal/familial strife.

Like the community he represents, Jacob's connection to the land, to God, and to proximate others is tenuous and contested. Following the structuralist work of Claude Levi-Strauss, Edmund Leach notes that some anxiety seems to have existed surrounding the people's nonindigenous status. Leach (1969, 31) states,

> The Old Testament as a whole asserts that the Jewish political title to the land of Palestine is a direct gift from God to the descendants of Israel (Jacob). This provides the fundamental basis for Jewish endogamy—the Jews should be a people of pure blood and pure religion, living in isolation in the Promised Land. But interwoven with this theological dogma there is a less idealized form of tradition which represents the population of ancient Palestine as a mixture of many peoples over whom the Jews have asserted political dominance by right of conquest.

The myth of Jacob's limp, then, binds him to the land that his ancestors are to possess. As a lonely exile and wanderer, Jacob's connection to the land is ambiguous. When he is renamed by God, however, he is accorded the status of a "first ancestor with a territorial autochthonous base" (Leach 1969, 18). His lameness, his limp, binds him to the ground he seeks to possess. In (re)telling this story, the community can "remember" that their claim to the land is sacred and binding. In being (re)named, in sustaining a wound, and in crossing the Jabbok, Jacob's encounter legitimizes the community's claim on the land. Consequently, Jacob, Esau, and God are all conduits for meaning making in the (hi)storied lives of postexilic Yehud.

6
Facing the Dark

Throughout this study, I examine the metaphors/images in the Jabbok story: name, face, wound, darkness, and crossing. I argue that these images constitute a fruitful way to discuss how identity is constructed and remembered through this story and its characters. The place to conclude, then, is with the faces of Jacob, his assailant, and the community producing the story. Jacob's displacement, the brutality at the Jabbok, and his ambiguous reconciliation with Esau represent the central story of the Hebrew Bible—the Babylonian exile and the postexilic community's long journey home. The postexilic community's ambiguous relationship to itself, to proximate others such as Edom/Idumea, and to God is embodied and contested in the characters of Jacob and his assailant. The story depicts the ambiguity of these relationships through the polyvalence, multiplicity, and ambiguity of each of the metaphors in the text. This is a community of wounded storytellers who interrupt, correct, and supplement one another's (re)tellings. Consequently, the story is always multiplying meaning through an intersection of theology, ethics, and political strategy. Several concluding comments demonstrate how this is the case, arguing that the Jabbok story is no casual, disinterested recollection of a shared past. Instead, the Jabbok text functions as a hinge between the past, present, and future. The Jabbok is a highly charged textual site where the communal memory of wounded storytellers is recalled.

Theologically speaking, this study has shown that Jacob's antagonist eludes, obfuscates, even apophaticates. His identity is always already deferred, as my examinations of the images of the name, the face, and the darkness suggest. The chapter "The Name" articulates the apophatic nature of Jacob's opponent through the polynomial nature of the Name: both אלהים (God) and איש (Man). Moreover, the larger Jacob cycle reveals/conceals a multiplicity of names for the divine, which include מלאכי אלהים

("messenger/angel of God," 28:12); יהוה (Yahweh, 28:13a, 16, 21); יהוה אלה אברהם אביך ואלהי יצחק ("the Lord, the God of Abraham your father and God of Isaac," 28:13b); and אלהים ("God," 28:20, 21), to name a few. Here it is unclear whether the biblical author is simply unsure how to reference traces of divinity, whether multiple sources and therefore different names underlay these texts, or whether these distinctions are intended to represent Israel's consciousness of gradations of divinity within the heavenly realm. In addition to the multiplicity of names throughout the story, at the Jabbok Jacob's opponent also refuses to say his name (32:29). The narrator's construction of the character of the antagonist demonstrates deep ambivalence about unraveling the mystery of the divine. Something of the Name must be kept, saved. The Name is therefore (un)made, constantly (un)making and elusive, never enclosed by a frame but traced in dotted lines and leaving traces behind. The elusiveness of the Name is a kind of countersignature. To borrow a phrase from Derrida, it is a postscriptum.

The chapter "The Face" also reveals the penchant of the narrator to withhold the identity of Jacob's assailant, or the Face of all faces. The multiplicity of the פנים (Face) presented throughout the Hebrew Bible demonstrates a divine character who hears the cry of the oppressed. On the other hand, the Face also appears more than willing to consider violent course correction. The Face is, to gesture toward Levinas, one who bids Jacob not to kill. Nevertheless, the Face also appears to hold the possibility of killing Jacob. The Face is at once otherworldly and this-worldly, at once monstrous, able to kill, and plaintively beautiful, begging not to be killed. Mystery and multiplicity cohere in the Face. Finally, the chapter "The Dark" argues that Jacob is frequently left in the dark regarding the identity of the divine. The Dark is a chronotope, a time space, where Jacob's experiences with the divine are situated. The dark is also a time space where violence and the concealing of identity takes place. The images in these three chapters—name, face, and dark—each attest to the complexity of the postexilic community's relationship to God and the dark time space of the exile. The same God who claimed to inscribe them on the palms of his hands (Isa 49:16) is the same God who sends the Babylonians, a clear sign of his opposition (Hab 1:1–11). This same God raises up Cyrus to send the exiles home (Isa 45:13). Consequently, it is not difficult to imagine the construction of a divine character at the Jabbok as one who also sends and opposes. For the exilic and postexilic community, this is indeed a God who forms light and creates darkness, who makes weal and creates woe (Isa 45:7). This is indeed a God who hides himself (Isa 45:15). Therefore the name and the face of this divine figure are enshrouded in the darkness of the Jabbok, where he both wounds and blesses Jacob.

The Jabbok also multiplies meaning through a shrewd and ambiguous presentation of ethics. In particular, the chapters "The Face" and "The Dark" raise the question of human and divine agency. The larger Jacob cycle, as well as the Jabbok text itself, demonstrates Jacob's many failures as a moral agent. I foreground the faces not only of Jacob and his opponent but also of those others who are also vulnerable in the story world—the women and the children, even Laban and Esau. Beyond the story's poetics exists the real competition for resources and power, depicted in a text that delights in trickster antics. That Jacob's actions are not censured beyond his temporary exile from home, and appear in some interpretations as being narratively predestined by the character of God (Gen 25:23), raises questions about the ethical mandates now on the table. In Jacob's character, it is not difficult to picture the postexilic community of Yehud doing whatever they could to ensure material blessing, the benevolence of Persian overlords, and ethnic and sexual purity.

The chapters "The Wound" and "The Crossing" articulate the proposition of specific political strategies for the postexilic community. Of primary importance is the community's construction of its identity through cultural memory. That this community envisions itself as both wounded and blessed is critical to their identity. They are enfolded in a multigenerational relationship with a divine character who has promised them land, descendants, and blessing. The community of postexilic Yehud maps its existence through Jacob, who is pursued, wounded, and blessed by this divine character. Consequently, the Jabbok is an example of how wounded storytellers construct a past based on present needs and future anxieties. The past that is remembered is not dead—it is not even past, to borrow a line from William Faulkner. Rather, the past remains alive through continuing to (re)tell and (re)construct rival others as unworthy of the land, even as the story cannot escape the reality of multiple communities laying claim to the land and to the appellation Israel. After Jacob crosses the Jabbok successfully, the reconciliation he makes with Esau is a cautious one, demonstrated, perhaps, by Jacob's refusal to travel together (Gen 33:12–14) and his arrival in Shechem (33:18). While Jacob does not dismiss their reconciliation—they must learn to coexist—he does not display desire to live alongside him. So too returnees and remainees display ambivalence toward one another, vying for the same land and resources. The story's insistence that it is Jacob, not Esau, who is (re)named Israel, demonstrates a decisive word regarding communal politics: the returnees, not the remainees, truly deserve the name Israel. Discussion of more sympathetic depictions of Esau, which are beyond the scope of this study, however, demonstrates the instability of returnees' hold on that identity marker. Nevertheless, the Jabbok story suggests that boundary crossings move life forward through a strained coexistence.

Indeed, that seems to be the point: life must move forward. And if life is to move forward, the darkness must be faced. Perhaps the darkness has been the point all along. When all is said and done, nothing has really been said or done. Darkness remains on the faces of the protagonist and antagonist. In truth, I am uncertain that such labels are even appropriate or helpful descriptors of Jacob and the God-man he encounters. Likewise, darkness remains on the textual face. In its own darkness, the text reifies itself as a Bet Hamidrash—a "home of searching" (Tongue 2014, 199), a textual space where not one meaning but many meanings abound. That is as it should be for any text that self-identifies as living and active (Heb 4:12).

In the end, one question remains: What is to be gained by this particular searching? Admittedly, this study exists somewhere outside what can be traditionally defined as exegetical. This work has been existential and philosophical, even meditative. I began my search because in names and faces, in wounds and places of darkness, and in crossings actual and existential, I saw something of my own experience. At the Jabbok, safe and stable notions about God, selfhood, and the long journey home are displaced and darkened. I strained to see through the darkness of the Jabbok because, while the story resists answers, it does pose profound questions about what it means to be human. The Jabbok encounter is not punctuated with an exclamation point—an emphatic straight line with a dot at the end. Instead, the line bends into the curve of a question mark. Here readers who continue to engage this text share something in common with the unnamed individuals who produced it: the need to live inside questions through story. Frank (2010, 5) states, "Stories always pose that question: what kind of truth is being told? Stories never resolve that question; their work is to remind us that we have to live with complicated truths." The complexity of the Jabbok story, which offers movement yet resists finality, allows for continued unfolding. Such complexity allows for midrash, continued searching and imagination. A story such as this allows for more questions. In that way, the darkness of this text is not without fecundity. As Rabbi Shmuel Sperber attests, "To question is a great religious act; it helps you live great religious truth" (Stern 1998, 240).

A study such as this matters for precisely that reason: this story and its images slip textual boundaries and speak to the heart of human experience. For the wounded storytellers producing the story, the questions raised about identity not only enable them to live religious truth. Indeed, the story enables them to live. In that way, the text continues to unfold through those who wrestle with the complicated truths of their story.

Bibliography

Abramsky, Michael. 2010. "Jacob Wrestles the Angel: A Study in Psychoanalytic Midrash." *IJTS* 29:106–17.
Ahroni, Reuben. 1980. "Why Did Esau Spurn the Birthright?: A Study in Biblical Interpretation." *Judaism* 29:323–31.
Albright, William F. 1927. "The Names 'Israel' and 'Judah' with an Excursus on the Etymology of Tôdâh and Tôrâh." *JBL* 46:151–85.
Alter, Robert. 1996. *Genesis: Translation and Commentary*. New York: Norton.
———. 2008. *The Five Books of Moses: A Translation with Commentary*. New York: Norton.
Althusser, Louis. 2001. *"Lenin and Philosophy" and Other Essays*. Translated by Ben Brewster. New York: Monthly Review Press.
Amichai, Yehuda. *The Selected Poetry of Yehuda Amichai*. Edited and translated by Chana Bloch and Stephen Mitchell. New York: Harper & Row, 1986.
Anderson, John E. 2011. *Jacob and the Divine Trickster: A Theology of Deception and YHWH's Fidelity to the Ancestral Promise in the Jacob Cycle*. Winona Lake, IN: Eisenbrauns.
Assmann, Jan. 1997. *Moses the Egyptian: The Memory of Egypt in Western Monotheism*. Cambridge: Harvard University Press.
———. 2006. *Religion and Cultural Memory: Ten Studies*. Stanford, CA: Stanford University Press.
Auerbach, Erich. 1953. *Mimesis*. Princeton: Princeton University Press.
Bakhtin, Mikhail. 1981. *The Dialogic Imagination: Four Essays*. Austin: University of Texas Press.
———. 1990. *The Dialogic Imagination: Four Essays*. Austin: University of Texas Press.
———. 1993. *Toward a Philosophy of the Act*. Austin: University of Texas Press.

Balentine, Samuel E. 2000. *The Hidden God: The Hiding of the Face of God in the Old Testament*. OTM. Oxford: Oxford University Press.

Barthes, Roland. 1966. *Introduction to the Structural Analysis of the Narrative*. Birmingham: University of Birmingham.

———. 1988. "Wrestling with the Angel: Textual Analysis of Genesis 32:23–33." Pages 246–60 in *The Semiotic Challenge*. Translated by Richard Howard. New York: Hill & Wang.

Bekkum, Wouter Jacques van. 2006. "What's in the Divine Name? Exodus 3 in Biblical and Rabbinic Tradition." Pages 7–16 in *The Revelation of the Name YHWH to Moses: Perspectives from Judaism, the Pagan Graeco-Roman World, and Early Christianity*. Edited by Geurt H. van Kooten. Leiden: Brill.

Bible and Culture Collective, The. 1995. *The Postmodern Bible*. New Haven: Yale University Press.

Brisman, Leslie. 1990. *The Voice of Jacob: On the Composition of Genesis*. Bloomington: Indiana University Press.

Brodie, Thomas L. 2001. *Genesis as Dialogue: A Literary, Historical, and Theological Commentary*. Oxford: Oxford University Press.

Brueggemann, Walter. 2010. *Genesis: Interpretation; A Bible Commentary for Teaching and Preaching*. Louisville: Westminster John Knox.

Buechner, Frederick. 2006. "The Magnificent Defeat." Pages 1–8 in *Secrets in the Dark: A Life in Sermons*. New York: HarperCollins.

Carr, David M. 1996. *Reading the Fractures of Genesis: Historical and Literary Approaches*. Louisville: Westminster John Knox.

Clines, David. 1997. *The Theme of the Pentateuch*. Sheffield: Sheffield Academic.

Connerton, Paul. 1989. *How Societies Remember*. Cambridge: Cambridge University Press.

Derrida, Jacques. 1995a. *The Gift of Death*. Chicago: University of Chicago Press.

———. 1995b. *On the Name*. Stanford, CA: Stanford University Press.

Dickens, Charles. 1986. *A Christmas Carol*. New York: Bantam Books.

Dicou, Bert. 1994. *Edom, Israel's Brother and Antagonist: The Role of Edom in Biblical Prophecy and Story*. JSOTSup 169. Sheffield: JSOT Press.

Dillmann, August. 1897. *Genesis Critically and Exegetically Expounded*. Vol. 2. Edinburgh: T&T Clark.

Docherty, Thomas. 1983. *Reading (Absent) Character: Towards a Theory of Characterization in Fiction*. Oxford: Clarendon.

Driver, S. R. 1915. *The Book of Genesis*. Westminster Commentaries. London: Methuen.

Edelman, Diana V. 1995. *You Shall Not Abhor an Edomite, For He Is Your Brother: Edom and Seir in History and Tradition*. ABS 3. Atlanta: Scholars Press.

———. 2013. "Genesis: A Composition for Construing a Homeland of the Imagination for Elite Scribal Circles or for Educating the Illiterate?" Pages 47–66 in *Writing the Bible: Scribes, Scribalism and Script*. Edited by Philip R. Davies and Thomas Römer. New York: Routledge.

Elliott, Scott. 2011. *Reconfiguring Mark's Jesus: Narrative Criticism after Poststructuralism*. Sheffield: Sheffield Phoenix.

Emmott, Catherine. 2003. "Constructing Social Space: Sociocognitive Factors in the Interpretation of Character Relations." Pages 283–309 in *Narrative Theory and the Cognitive Sciences*. Edited by David Herman. Stanford, CA: CSLI.

Erll, Astrid, and Ansgar Nünning, eds. 2010. *A Companion to Cultural Memory Studies*. Berlin: de Gruyter.

Evans, Dylan. 1996. *An Introductory Dictionary of Lacanian Psychoanalysis*. New York: Routledge.

Fewell, Donna Nolan. 2003. *The Children of Israel: Reading the Bible for the Sake of Our Children*. Nashville: Abingdon.

———. 2015. "Space for Moral Agency in the Book of Ruth." *JSOT* 40:79–96.

———, ed. 2016. *The Oxford Handbook of Biblical Narrative*. Oxford: Oxford University Press.

Fewell, Donna Nolan, and David Gunn. 1993. *Gender, Power, and Promise: The Subject of the Bible's First Story*. Nashville: Abingdon.

Fichtner, Johannes. 1956. "Die etymologische Ätiologie in den Namengebungen der geschichtlichen Bücher des Alten Testaments." *VT* 6:372–96.

Finkelstein, Israel, and Amihai Mazar. 2007. *The Quest for the Historical Israel: Debating Archaeology and the History of Early Israel*. Edited by Brian B. Schmidt. ABS 17. Atlanta: Society of Biblical Literature.

Fishbane, Michael. 1998. *Text and Texture: A Literary Reading of Selected Texts*. Oxford: Oneworld.

Fokkelman, Jan P. 1975. *Narrative Art in Genesis: Specimens of Stylistic and Structural Analysis*. Assen: Van Gorcum.

Frank, Arthur W. 1997. *The Wounded Storyteller: Body, Illness, and Ethics*. Chicago: University of Chicago Press.

———. 2010. *Letting Stories Breathe: A Socio-Narratology*. Chicago: University of Chicago Press.
Friedman, Harry, trans. 1986. *Midrash Rabbah Genesis*. London: Soncino.
Frolov, Serge. 2000. "The Other Side of the Jabbok: Genesis 32 as a Fiasco of Patriarchy." *JSOT* 91:41–59.
Geller, Stephen A. 1982. "The Struggle at the Jabbok: The Uses of Enigma in a Biblical Narrative." *JANESCU* 14:37–60.
———. 1996. *Sacred Enigmas: Literary Religion in the Hebrew Bible*. New York: Routledge.
Gossai, Hemchand. 2010. *Power and Marginality in the Abraham Narrative*. Eugene, OR: Pickwick.
Gunkel, Hermann. 1987. *The Folktale in the Old Testament*. Sheffield: Almond.
———. 1997. *Genesis*. Macon, GA: Mercer University Press.
Gunn, David M., and Danna Nolan Fewell. 1993. *Narrative in the Hebrew Bible*. OBS. Oxford: Oxford University Press.
Hamilton, Victor P. 1994. *Genesis 18–50*. NICOT. Grand Rapids: Eerdmans.
Heard, R. Christopher. 2001. *Dynamics of Diselection: Ambiguity in Genesis 12–36 and Ethnic Boundaries in Post-exilic Judah*. Atlanta: Society of Biblical Literature.
Hendel, Ronald. 1987. *The Epic of the Patriarch: The Jacob Cycle and the Narrative Traditions of Canaan and Israel*. HSM 42. Atlanta: Scholars Press, .
———, ed. 2010. *Reading Genesis: Ten Methods*. Cambridge: Cambridge University Press.
Holladay, William L. 1958. *The Root Šûbh in the Old Testament: With Particular Reference to Its Usages in Covenantal Contexts*. Leiden: Brill.
———, ed. 1972. *A Concise Hebrew and Aramaic Lexicon of the Old Testament*. Grand Rapids: Eerdmans.
Homer, Sean. 2005. *Jacques Lacan*. New York: Routledge.
Humphreys, W. Lee. 2001. *The Character of God in the Book of Genesis: A Narrative Appraisal*. Louisville: Westminster John Knox.
Jacob, Edmond. 1958. *Theology of the Old Testament*. New York: Harper & Row.
Kaiser, Otto, 2000. "Deus Absconditus and Deus Revelatus: Three Difficult Narratives in the Pentateuch." Pages 73–88 in *Shall Not the Judge of All the Earth Do What Is Right? Studies on the Nature of God in Tribute to*

James L. Crenshaw. Edited by David Penchansky and Paul L. Redditt. Winona Lake, IN: Eisenbrauns.

Keller, Catherine. 2003. *Face of the Deep: A Theology of Becoming*. New York: Routledge.

Kennedy, Elisabeth Robertson. 2011. *Seeking a Homeland: Sojourn and Ethnic Identity in the Ancestral Narratives of Genesis*. Leiden: Brill.

Kessler, Rainer. 2008. *The Social History of Ancient Israel*. Minneapolis: Fortress.

Key, Andrew F. 1964. "The Giving of Proper Names in the Old Testament." *JBL* 83:55–59.

Klitsner, Shmuel. 2009. *Wrestling Jacob: Deception, Identity, and Freudian Slips in Genesis*. Teaneck, NJ: Ben Yehuda.

Knight, Henry F. 1992. "Meeting Jacob at the Jabbok: Wrestling with a Text: A Midrash on Genesis 32:22–32." *JES* 29:451–60.

Kunin, Seth Daniel. 1995. *The Logic of Incest: A Structuralist Analysis of Hebrew Mythology*. JSOTSup 185. Sheffield: Sheffield Academic.

Lacan, Jacques. 1977. *Écrits: A Selection*. New York: Norton.

Landy, Francis. 2001. *Beauty and the Enigma: And Other Essays on the Hebrew Bible*. Sheffield: Sheffield Academic.

Lasine, Stuart. 2012. *Weighing Hearts: Character, Judgment, and the Ethics of Reading the Bible*. New York: Bloomsbury.

Leach, Edmund. 1969. *Genesis as Myth and Other Essays*. London: Cape.

Leibowitz, Nehama. 1973. *Studies in Bereshit*. Jerusalem: WZO.

L'Engle, Madeleine. *Walking on the Water: Reflections on Faith and Art*. Colorado Springs: Convergent Books, 1996.

———. *The Rock That Is Higher: Story as the Search for Truth*. Colorado Springs: WaterBrook Press, 2002.

Levinas, Emmanuel. 1985. *Ethics and Infinity: Conversations with Philippe Nemo*. Pittsburgh: Duquesne University Press.

———. 1988. "Useless Suffering." Pages 156–67 in *The Provocation of Levinas: Rethinking the Other*. Edited by Robert Bernasconi and David Wood. London: Routledge.

———. 1989a. "Ethics as First Philosophy." Pages 75–87 in *The Levinas Reader*. Edited by Seán Hand. Cambridge: Blackwell.

———. 1989b. "Martin Buber and the Theory of Knowledge." Pages 59–74 in *The Levinas Reader*. Edited by Seán Hand. Cambridge: Blackwell.

———. 1989c. "There Is: Existence without Existents." Pages 29–36 in *The Levinas Reader*. Edited by Seán Hand. Cambridge: Blackwell.

———. 1989d. "Time and the Other." Pages 37–58 in *The Levinas Reader*. Edited by Seán Hand. Cambridge: Blackwell.

Lewis, C. S. 1956. *Till We Have Faces*. London: Bles.

Lindsay, John. 1999. "Edomite Westward Expansion: The Biblical Evidence." *ANES* 36:48–89.

Liverani, Mario. 2005. *Israel's History and the History of Israel*. Translated by Chiara Peri and Philip R. Davies. Oakville, CT: Equinox.

Locke, John. 2016. *An Essay concerning Human Understanding*. Sydney: Wentworth.

Long, Jesse. 2012. "Wrestling with God to Win: A Literary Reading of the Story of Jacob at Jabbok in Honor of Don Williams." *SCJ* 15:47–62.

Pelikan, Jaroslav, and Hilton C. Oswald. 1970. *Lectures on Genesis: Chapters 31–37*. LW 6. St. Louis: Concordia.

Matt, Daniel C., trans. 2006. *The Zohar*. Vol. 3. Stanford, CA: Stanford University Press.

McKay, Heather A. 1987. "Jacob Makes It across the Jabbok: An Attempt to Solve the Success/Failure Ambivalence in Israel's Self-Consciousness." *JSOT* 38:3–13.

Morson, Gary Saul. 1994. *Narrative and Freedom: The Shadows of Time*. New Haven: Yale University Press.

Moyers, Bill. 1996. *Genesis: A Living Conversation*. Edited by Betty Sue Flowers. New York: Doubleday.

Mullen, E. Theodore. 1993. *Narrative History and Ethnic Boundaries: The Deuteronomistic Historian and the Creation of Israelite National Identity*. Atlanta: Scholars Press.

Nowlan, Alden. *Alden Nowlan Selected Poems (A List)*. Toronto: House of Anasasi Press, 2013.

Parke-Taylor, Geoffrey H. 1975. *Yahweh: The Divine Name in the Bible*. Waterloo, ON: Wilfrid Laurier University Press.

Pocock, David. 1975. *Understanding Social Anthropology*. London: Hodder & Stoughton.

Rad, Gerhard von. 1973. *Genesis: A Commentary*. OTL. Philadelphia: Westminster.

Ramsey, George W. 1989. "Is Name-Giving an Act of Domination in Genesis 2:23 and Elsewhere?" *CBQ* 50:24–35.

Reinhartz, Adele. 1998. *"Why Ask My Name?" Anonymity and Identity in Biblical Narrative*. Oxford: Oxford University Press.

Reulecke, Jürgen. 2010. "Generation/Generationality, Generativity, and Memory." Pages 119–26 in *A Companion to Cultural Memory Studies*. Edited by Astrid Erll and Ansgar Nünning. Berlin: de Gruyter.

Rosenberg, David, ed. 1996. *Genesis, as It Is Written: Contemporary Writers on Our First Stories*. San Francisco: HarperSanFrancisco.

Sanford, John A. 1981. *The Man Who Wrestled with God: Light from the Old Testament on the Psychology of Individuation*. New York: Paulist.

Sarna, Nahum M. 1966. *Understanding Genesis: The World of the Bible in the Light of History*. New York: Schocken Books.

Scarry, Elaine. 1987. *The Body in Pain: The Making and Unmaking of the World*. Oxford: Oxford University Press.

Scherman, Rabbi Nosson, and Rabbi Meir Zlotowitz, eds. 1995. *Bereishis/Genesis*. In *Torah: With Rashi's Commentary Translated, Annotated, and Elucidated*. Brooklyn: Mesorah.

Shinan, Avigdor, ed. 1984. *Midrash Exodus Rabba*. Jerusalem: Dvir.

Skinner, John. 1930. *A Critical and Exegetical Commentary on the Book of Genesis*. 2nd ed. ICC. Edinburgh: T&T Clark.

Speiser, Ephraim A. 1964. *Genesis*. AB. New York: Doubleday.

Stahl, Nanette. 1995. *Law and Liminality in the Bible*. JSOTSup 202. Sheffield: Sheffield Academic.

Stern, Rabbi Chaim. 1998. *Day by Day: Reflections on the Themes of the Torah from Literature, Philosophy, and Religious Thought*. Boston: Beacon.

Stevens, Wallace. 1990. "Phosphor Reading by His Own Light." Page 267 in *The Collected Poems of Wallace Stevens*. New York: Random House.

Stiebert, Johanna. 2016. "The Body and Voice of God in the Hebrew Bible." *JRFM* 2:23–33.

Sutskover, Talia. 2013. *Sight and Insight in Genesis: A Semantic Study*. Sheffield: Sheffield Phoenix.

Syrén, Roger. 1992. *The Forsaken First-Born: A Study of a Recurrent Motif in the Patriarchal Narratives*. JSOTSup 133. Sheffield: JSOT Press.

Tebes, Juan Manuel. 2011. "The Edomite Involvement in the Destruction of the First Temple: A Case of Stab-in-the-Back Tradition?" *JSOT* 36.2:219–55.

Terrien, Samuel. 2000. *The Elusive Presence: Toward a New Biblical Theology*. Eugene, OR: Wipf & Stock.

Theissen, Gerd. 1990. *The Open Door: Variations on Biblical Themes*. Munich: SCM.

Tongue, Samuel. 2014. *Between Biblical Criticism and Poetic Rewriting: Interpretive Struggles over Genesis 32:22–32*. Leiden: Brill.
Trible, Phyllis. 1984. *Texts of Terror: Literary-Feminist Readings of Biblical Narratives*. Philadelphia: Fortress.
Turner, Laurence A. 1990. *Announcements of Plot in Genesis*. JSOTSup 96. Sheffield: JSOT Press.
Vawter, Bruce. 1977. *On Genesis: A New Reading*. Garden City, NY: Doubleday.
Vermeulen, Karolien. 2017. "Hands, Head, and Feet: Body Parts as Poetic Device in Judges 4–5." *JBL* 136:801–19.
Visotzky, Burton L. 1996. *The Genesis of Ethics*. New York: Crown.
Walton, Kevin. 2003. *Thou Traveller Unknown: The Presence and Absence of God in the Jacob Narrative*. Exeter: Paternoster.
Wasserman, Jamie. 2010. *Wrestling the Angel: Poems by Jamie Wasserman*. Self-published.
Wenham, Gordon. 1994. *Genesis 16–50*. WBC. Dallas: Word.
Wessner, Mark D. 2000. "Toward a Literary Understanding of 'Face to Face' in Genesis 32:23–32." *ResQ* 42.3:169–77.
Westermann, Claus. 1985. *Genesis 12–36*. CC. Minneapolis: Augsburg.
Whybray, R. Norman. 1996. "The Immorality of God: Reflections on Some Passages in Genesis, Job, Exodus and Numbers." *JSOT* 72:89–120.
Wilson, Ian Douglas. 2009. "Face to Face with God: Another Look." *ResQ* 51.2:107–14.
Wolde, Ellen van. 1994. *Words Become Worlds: Semantic Studies of Genesis 1–11*. Leiden: Brill.
———. 2009. "Why the Verb ברא Does Not Mean 'To Create' in Genesis 1.1–2.4a." *JSOT* 34:3–23.
Zakovitch, Yair. 2012. *Jacob: Unexpected Patriarch*. New Haven: Yale University Press.
Zornberg, Avivah Gottlieb. 1995. *The Beginning of Desire: Reflections on Genesis*. New York: Schocken Books.
Zucker, David J. 1986. "Jacob in Darkness (and Light): A Study in Contrasts." *Judaism* 35:402–13.

Scripture Index

Hebrew Bible/Old Testament

Genesis
1–11	129, 155
1:1	155
1:4	155
1:6	155
1:7	155
1:18	155
1:26	31, 155–56
2–3	37, 60
2:7	135
2:16–17	155
2:23	148
3:9	45
3:22	31, 37, 82, 155–56
3:22–23	37
3:24	155
4	60
4:10	60
4:17	157
6:1–4	156
6:11–22	60
7:22–23	60
11:1–9	156
11:3–4	156
11:4	82
11:7	31, 37
11:7–9	60
12:1–3	56, 80, 126, 143
12:2	22, 158
12:16	148
12:20	148
13:1–6	148
13:14–15	114
14:21–24	148
15:1–5	80
15:1–21	126
15:2–3	81
15:3–5	60
15:5	158
15:7	35
15:12–16	5
16:1	14
16:1–21	8
16:2	45
16:3	46
16:4	46
16:5–6	45
16:6	46–47
16:7	45
16:7–13	43
16:8	45, 48
16:9	46–47, 60
16:11	46
16:12	47, 138
16:13	5, 11, 44–45
16:15–16	49
17:1–8	80
17:1–16	126
17:5	22
17:6	158
17:9–14	22
18	60, 129
18:22–23	60
19:1–26	60
19:18–22	60
19:26	60
20:4	158
20:14–16	148

Genesis (cont.)

Reference	Pages
21	49
21:1–2	77
21:3	11
21:9–21	8
21:12–13	47, 60
21:14	46
21:15–22	143
21:17	47
21:17–21	60
21:19	47
21:20	46
21:31	110
21:33	110
22	157
22:1–19	125
22:9	116
22:19	110
23:4	158
24:1–67	52, 77
24:2-9	89, 100
25	133
25:8–10	73
25:19–26	9
25:21	8, 63, 77
25:21–26	9, 63
25:22	75, 78
25:23	4, 11, 63, 80, 87, 94, 104, 112, 133, 141, 165
25:23–26	20
25:23–33:20	138
25:24	104
25:24–26	13
25:25	13, 107
25:26	13
25:27	107
25:28	16, 78, 110
25:29	79
25:29–34	5, 108
25:30	24, 79, 135
25:30–34	63
25:31	142
25:31–33	65
25:32	79
25:34	136, 141
26:3–5	158
26:20–21	14
26:23	110
26:23–24	80
26:25	110
26:26–33	110
26:33	110
26:34	19
26:34–29:30	89
26:34–35	17, 51, 78, 137
27	133, 139
27:1	16, 41, 109
27:1–29	5, 9, 103
27:1–40	63
27:7	110
27:10	81
27:11	17
27:11–12	81
27:12	18–19
27:13	78
27:18–19	65
27:18–19, 24	110
27:18–25	12
27:19	19
27:19	83
27:20	17, 113–14, 143
27:21	18
27:21–25	41
27:21–31	5
27:22	18
27:24	110
27:25	18
27:26	18
27:26–29	18
27:26–38	127
27:28–29	113
27:29	21
27:30–40	143
27:36	4, 18, 20
27:39–40	137
27:41	52, 122
27:42	141
27:42–45	19, 111, 122
27:46	78, 137
27:46–28:6	51, 111

28:4	149	30:22	128
28:5	159	30:22–24	77
28:10	5, 110, 113, 120	30:25–43	63, 127
28:10–22	9	30:26	148–49
28:11	111, 113	30:29	148
28:12	31, 164	30:30	149
28:13	31, 149, 164	31:1–3	55
28:13–15	23, 80, 83, 114, 128	31:1–9	19
28:13–22	127	31:2	117
28:14	114	31:3	126, 149
28:15	87, 126	31:3	128
28:16	31, 113, 123, 164	31:5	55, 117, 150
28:16–17	83	31:6	148
28:17	19, 113	31:7	57, 143, 148
28:18	103	31:9	143, 150
28:19	40, 113	31:10–13	19, 55
28:20	87	31:11	32
28:20–21	31, 65–66, 115, 159, 164	31:13	32
28:20–22	5, 19, 63, 84, 138, 151	31:14–16	56, 138
28:21	31, 85, 164	31:16	148, 150
29:1	52	31:17–18	56
29:1–30	89	31:20	117
29:7	116	31:21	21, 56, 117
29:10	148	31:22	21
29:13–14	148	31:24	127–28
29:15	148–49	31:24	57, 117, 138
29:17	53	31:25	89
29:18–20	59, 148	31:26	56
29:21–30	103	31:27	21
29:23	117	31:27–28	57
29:25	148	31:29	57, 117, 138
29:27	148	31:31–32	89
29:30	52, 148	31:32–33	148
29:31	128	31:38–42	150
29:31–32	53	31:41	148
29:31–35	13, 32	31:42	17, 143
29:33	14	31:43	57
30:1–24	13	31:44	58
30:2	54–55, 68	31:50	57
30:6	14	31:52	57
30:6	54	31:53	17
30:8	68	31:53–54	150
30:9	68	32:1	32, 57
30:16	68	32:4	135
30:17–24	32, 54	32:5	57

Genesis (cont.)

32:7	122
32:7	121
32:8	19, 57
32:9	66
32:9–12	63, 87
32:10	93, 126
32:10–13	5, 19, 126
32:11	57, 141
32:12	57, 59, 66, 118
32:14	57
32:14–22	19, 58
32:21	58, 66
32:21–22	151
32:22–32	5, 9, 125
32:22	41
32:23–24	9, 151
32:24	31, 41, 57, 60, 119, 128
32:24–31	60
32:25	88, 121, 151, 155
32:25–26	8
32:26	37, 62–63, 65, 90, 119
32:26	38
32:27	13, 37–38, 69, 75
32:27	13
32:28	5, 21–22, 68, 121
32:29	5, 13, 24, 29–30, 61, 87, 121–22, 164
32:30	31, 60, 69, 123
32:31	8, 40, 31, 43–44, 61, 91, 123
32:32	71, 74, 89, 98–99, 111, 128, 154, 161
32:33	71
33	133
33:1–2	58, 128
33:3	128
33:4	123
33:5–6	58
33:8	58, 94
33:8–11	96
33:9	58, 142
33:10	41, 44, 68, 71, 94, 116, 161
33:11	59, 64–65, 70, 94, 143
33:12–13	59
33:12–14	165
33:12–18	19
33:12–20	94
33:14	59
33:15–20	67
33:16–17	161
33:18	165
34:1–7	59
34:1–31	158
35:1–15	29
35:3	159
35:7	40
35:8	78
35:9–15	28
35:10	158
35:12	160
35:15	40
35:16–20	54
35:16–21	59
35:27	159–60
35:28–29	73
36	142
36:1–5	17
36:6–8	158
36:17	135
37:1	159–60
37:1–8	158
38:1–30	158
38:27–30	135
41	148
41:45	14
43:11	151
46:1	110
46:5–27	59
46:26	100
47:9	29, 73, 160
47:27–28	158
47:28	73
47:29	100
48	139
48:2	158
48:8	158
48:33	73
49:3	79
49:29–32	73
49:31	59

Scripture Index

Exodus		22:22–35	90
1:5	100	23:10	23
2:10	11	32:31–42	14
2:15–22	52		
2:23–25	45, 53, 60	**Deuteronomy**	
3	34, 44	7:1–6	51
3:1–17	7	14:3–21	100
3:2	35	15:13–14	150
3:4	35	16:3	54
3:5	34, 37, 60	21:17	65, 79
3:6	35, 39, 60, 127	22:6–7	57
3:7	35	26:19	24
3:15	35	28:1	24
3:16	35	31:17–18	127
3:20–21	150	32:15	23, 92
4:22	24, 79	32:20	127
4:24	60	32:48–52	27
4:24–26	90, 123, 125, 157	33:5	23, 92
6:2–3	35	33:26	23, 92
19:7–23	34	34	27
19:10–13	60	34:10	5, 43
19:21–25	37		
20:15–18	34	**Joshua**	
20:18–21	60	5:9	14
21:3–6	149	5:13–16	90
32	129	13:1	27
33	44	19:47	14
33:11	43		
33:17–23	33	**Judges**	
33:20	5, 43, 60, 65, 90, 116, 121	27	
33:20–23	37, 60	1:22	28
34:29–35	34, 60	3:15	151
		4:9	47
Leviticus		6:22	43–44
11	100	8:30	100
25:35–36	149	13:17–23	33
		13:22	44, 60
Numbers		20:18	113
11	60, 129	20:26	113
14	60, 129	21:2	113
16	60		
20:14	141	**Ruth**	
20:17	141–42	1–4	158
20:18–19	142	4:11	58
20:14–21	9	4:13–14	77

Ruth (cont.)		Job	
4:16–17	11, 16	1–2	129
		1:6	31
1 Samuel		2:1	31
1–2	48	2:2	45
1:19–20	77	13:24	127
4:21	14	34:29	127
7:16	113	36:15	53
7:23	24	36:21–22	53
8	23, 60		
8:4–8	34	Psalms	
22:2	57	10:11	127
25:13	57	13:2	127
30:10	57	20:1	5
		22:25	127
2 Samuel		24:6	5
2:4	25	27:9	127
5:2–3	25	30:8	127
5:6–9	14	34:18	101
15:7	35	44:25	127
		46:7	5
1 Kings		51:11	127
11:1–8	51	69:18	127
		75:9	5
2 Kings		88:15	127
23:15	113	99:2	35
23:34	14	102:3	127
24:17	14	104:28	127
25	144	133:1	161
25:29	27	137	9
		137:7	139, 145
1 Chronicles		143:7	127
1:37	135	147:3	101
2 Chronicles		Isaiah	
36:16	18	1:5–6	101
		1:9	23
Ezra		1:18	135
2:1–67	158	3:1	23
9–10	158	6	44
9:1–2	51	6:3	23
		6:13	51
Nehemiah		8:3–4	11
13	158	8:17	127
13:23–27	51	10:5	5

Scripture Index

27:9	5	12:2–6	4
43	115	12:4	32, 60
44:2	23		
45:7	164	Amos	
45:13	164	5:5	113
45:15	127, 164	7:10–13	113
48:1	4, 24		
49:16	74, 164	Obadiah	9, 140, 145
50:6	127		
53:3	127	Micah	
54:8	127	2:7	4, 24
59:2	127	3:4	127
61:1	101	4:4	23
64:6	127		
		Nahum	
Jeremiah		2:14	23
3	51	3:5	23
9:4	21		
10:15	18	Habakkuk	
16:14–15	158	1:1–11	5, 164
23:7–8	158		
24:1–10	51	Zechariah	
30:18	5	1:14–17	23
33:5	127	8:1–23	23
39:1	144		
40	144	Malachi	
49:15	140	1:2–4	9
51:18	18	1:3	88
52:4	144	1:4	140

Deuterocanonical Books

Lamentations			
1–5	27		
4:21–22	9, 140, 145	Sirach	
		13:25	64
Ezekiel			
44		1 Esdras	
16	51	4:43–45	145
20:35	43		
24:1	144		

New Testament

39:23–24	127		
39:29	127	Luke	
		7:34	105
Hosea		9:51	56
1–3	51		
10:5	113		

John
   20:17   37

Romans
   9:13   88

1 Corinthians
   13:12   12

Philippians
   2:9   31

Hebrews
   4:12   166

Revelation
   22:20   86

Modern Authors Index

Abramsky, Michael 95–96
Ahroni, Reuben 79
Albright, William F. 23, 92
Alter, Robert 12, 104, 113, 115, 136
Althusser, Louis 7, 15
Amichai, Yehuda 6
Anderson, John E. 105, 108, 114
Assmann, Jan 134, 146, 161
Auerbach, Erich 22
Bakhtin, Mikhail 9, 42, 103–4, 106–8, 110–12, 120
Balentine, Samuel E. 63, 126–27
Barthes, Roland 6, 88, 153–55
Bekkum, Wouter Jacques van 35–36
Brisman, Leslie 136
Brodie, Thomas L. 56–57, 65, 89, 92, 142, 151
Brueggemann, Walter 26–27, 36–37, 105
Buechner, Frederick 88, 91, 123
Carr, David M. 26–27, 138–39, 154
Clines, David 27
Connerton, Paul 161
Derrida, Jacques 1–2, 4, 6–7, 9, 29, 34, 36–39, 70, 87, 115–16, 121–23, 164
Dickens, Charles 121
Dicou, Bert 104
Dillmann, August 104
Docherty, Thomas 30–31
Driver, S.R. 104
Edelman, Diana 144–45, 148
Elliott, Scott 132
Emmott, Catherine 38
Erll, Astrid 143, 147
Evans, Dylan 76, 83–84, 89, 97

Fewell, Danna Nolan 3–4, 6, 12, 17, 42, 48–49, 52–56, 58, 67–68, 104, 109, 131
Fichtner, Johannes 14
Finkelstein, Israel 144, 148, 150
Fishbane, Michael 71, 93
Fokkelman, Jan P. 27, 28, 38, 66, 114, 129
Frank, Arthur W. 6, 8, 15–16, 20–21, 74–75, 97–99, 101, 132, 134, 147, 158, 166
Frolov, Serge 8, 50–51
Geller, Stephen A. 24, 92, 159
Gossai, Hemchand 48–49
Gunkel, Hermann 37, 90, 104, 129
Gunn, David 3–4, 6, 12, 17, 42, 52–56, 58, 67–68, 104
Hamilton, Victor P. 104
Heard, Christopher R. 47, 104, 133–34, 136–37
Hendel, Ronald 32, 104
Holladay, William L. 65–66
Homer, Sean 76, 78, 82, 84–85
Humphreys, W. Lee 45, 55–56, 86, 128
Kaiser, Otto 125–26
Keller, Catherine 9, 119
Kennedy, Elisabeth Robertson 159–60
Kessler, Rainer 24–26
Key, Andrew 13
Klitsner, Shmuel 19–22, 28, 75, 77, 82–84
Knight, Henry F. 28, 36, 37, 93
Kunin, Seth Daniel 104
Lacan, Jacques 2, 8, 74–78, 80–87, 89–90, 97

Landy, Francis 4, 6, 64, 87
Lasine, Stuart 43
Leach, Edmund 162
Leibowitz, Nehama 82
L'Engle, Madeleine 2–3
Levinas, Emmanuel 2–3, 8, 42, 48, 51, 59–63, 65, 67, 69–70, 74–75, 105, 164
Lewis, C. S. 116
Lindsay, John 145
Liverani, Mario 146, 158
Locke, John 147
Long, Jesse 93–95
Mazar, Amihai 144, 148, 150
McKay, Heather 9, 152–53, 157
Morson, Gary Saul 103–6, 108, 110, 112, 114, 120
Moyers, Bill 62, 91, 112, 116
Mullen, E. Theodore 23
Nowlan, Alden 14
Nünning, Ansgar 143, 147
Oswald, Hilton C. 125
Pelikan, Jaroslav 125
Parke-Taylor, Geoffrey 35
Pocock, David 152
Rad, Gerhard von 6, 14, 32, 37, 90, 104
Ramsey, George W. 14, 16, 39
Reinhartz, Adele 11, 15, 30–32, 39
Reulecke, Jürgen 134–35
Rosenberg, David 92–93, 120
Sanford, John A. 97
Sarna, Nahum M. 79, 80, 106, 108–9
Scarry, Elaine 98
Schmidt, Brian B. 144, 148, 150
Skinner, John 104, 129, 136
Speiser, Ephraim A. 104, 107, 136
Stahl, Nanette 71, 100
Stern, Rabbi Chaim 166
Stevens, Wallace 130
Stiebert, Johanna 44
Sutskover, Talia 55
Syrén, Roger 104
Tebes, Juan Manuel 144–46
Terrien, Samuel 7, 33–34, 126–27
Theissen, Gerd 48
Tongue, Samuel 1, 6, 123–25, 166
Trible, Phyllis 14, 47–49
Turner, Lawrence A. 104
Vawter, Bruce 39, 51, 113, 135, 137–38, 151–52
Vermeulen, Karolien 47
Visotzky, Burton L. 68, 69
Walton, Kevin 39, 110
Wasserman, Jamie 6
Wenham, Gordon 17, 21, 23, 88, 90, 92, 104, 110, 136, 148–51
Wessner, Mark D. 43, 125
Westermann, Claus 17, 90, 104
Whybray, R. Norman 125, 129
Wilson, Ian Douglas 43–44, 125
Wolde, Ellen van 4, 155–56
Zakovitch, Yair 19, 23–24, 57, 134–35, 140–42
Zornberg, Avivah Gottlieb 13, 18, 20, 54, 62, 69, 88, 92, 107, 111–12, 115, 117, 130
Zucker, David J. 107, 117

www.ingramcontent.com/pod-product-compliance
Lightning Source LLC
Chambersburg PA
CBHW031834230426
43669CB00009B/1344